OUR HISTORY OUR VOICE

The Mexican American History Project of Greeley

Lorretta Chávez

Juli Sarris

Andrés Gonzales Guerrero, Jr.

Poudre Heritage Alliance

Windsor, CO

Our History
Our Voice
The Mexican American History Project of Greeley
Copyright 2025 by Poudre Heritage Alliance

Second Edition: Printed in the U.S. of America.
Publisher: Poudre Heritage Alliance 130 North 5th Street Windsor Colorado 80550
www.poudreheritage.org | admin@poudreheritage.org

ISBN paperback: 979-8-9994217-0-8
ISBN eBook: 979-8-9994217-1-5

KEYWORDS:
1.Mexican American history 2. Greeley, Colorado history 3. Greeley migration 4. Greeley immigration 5. Greeley Mexican American education 6. Greeley Mexican American culture 7. Greeley Mexican American community 8. Spanish families

Cover Design: Robert W. Pacheco

Cover Images: Top—Rodarte Community Center, Greeley, CO, Mural by artist Armando Silva; Right— Greeley History Museum, Mural, "Laying the Foundation" by artist Mario Echevarria, 2005; Left—Photo: Al Frente de la Lucha stakeholders by permission; Our Lady of Peace Catholic Church, 1948, at dedication.

This project was made possible in partnership with the Cache la Poudre River National Heritage Area. Views and opinions expressed in this book are the those of the individuals interviewed and source texts and do not necessarily reflect the views or positions of the publisher or project partners.

This book is dedicated in loving memory of

Dr. Genevieve Canales,

whose passion for storytelling and commitment

to preserving history continue to inspire us.

Although her time with us was far too short,

her vision and spirit motivated us to carry forward

the message of this book.

It stands as a tribute to her enduring legacy.

Project Committee

Front row, left to right: Katie Ross, Emma Peña McCleave, Adriana Trujillo, Andrés Gonzales Guerrero, Jr.

Back row, left to right: Clarence Lopez, Juanita Martinez Rocha, Yvette Flores, Maria Sanchez, and Lorretta Chávez.

Committee members not pictured: Daniel Reyez, Caleb Flores, Madeline Milian, Nancy Wendirad, Beth Bullard, Juli Sarris, and Jay Trask.

Committee

In appreciation of the Mexican American History Project of Greeley, for their years of dedication to this project (2021–2025).

Project Leadership

    Emma Peña-McCleave, B.A., B.S. – Project Coordinator

    Maria Sanchez, Ph.D. – Project Co-Coordinator & Chair, Grants

    Juanita Martinez Rocha, M.A. – Treasurer

Project Committees

    Yvette Flores, B.A. – Chair, Communications & Co-Chair, Grants

    Clarence Lopez, B.A., B.S. – Chair, Publications

    Daniel Reyez – Chair, Oral History

    Jay Trask, M.A. – Liaison, UNC, James A. Michener Library

    Adriana Trujillo, M.A. – Chair, Translations

Project Cache la Poudre River National Heritage Area
Grant Project Manager & Technical Assistance

    Beth Bullard, M.S. – Liason, Cache la Poudre River National Heritage Area

Chapter Authors

    Lorretta Chávez, Ph.D. – Lead Writer

    Juli Sarris, Ph.D.

    Andrés Gonzales Guerrero, Jr., Th.D.

Narrative Writers

    Beth Bullard, M.S.

    Caleb Flores, M.A.

    Yvette Flores, B.A.

    Madeline Milian, Ed.D.

    Maria Sanchez, Ph.D.

    Adriana Trujillo, M.A.

Spanish Language Translation & Editing

Nancy Wendirad, M.A. – Translator

Madeline Milian, Ed.D. – Editor

Past MAHPG Members

Genevieve Canales, Ph.D. – Writer (in Memoriam)

Mil Hart, B.A. – Chair, Membership

Katie Ross, M.S. – Liaison & Researcher, Greeley History Museum

Table of Contents

CHAPTER 3

Education

CHAPTER 4

Civic Engagement in Greeley

CHAPTER 5

Social Justice Issues in Greeley

CHAPTER 6

Conclusion

Preface

The possibility of writing a book about our Greeley Mexican American community grew from simple yet powerful conversations, fueled by concern and the need to share who we truly are by telling our story. Too often, our presence is overlooked or misunderstood, and we seek to fill that gap, not with statistics or assumptions but with our voices, our lived experiences, and the integrity of our heritage. This project isn't only about documenting history; it's about celebrating our families, our contributions, and our rightful place in the fabric of Greeley.

When the Mexican American History Project of Greeley Committee learned about the idea of creating a book about Greeley Mexican Americans, there was no hesitation—just a strong belief that our stories needed to be told, heard, and preserved. The committee's commitment has been unwavering, and even in the face of numerous challenges, seven founding members saw this project through publication. They also welcomed seven new members, who served as writers, Spanish translators, and editors. Every member contributed immeasurably to the success and completion of this book project.

In Greeley, Mexican Americans range from recent immigrants to those who lived here before this land became part of the U.S. There is a saying: "We didn't cross the border; the border crossed us." We have called Greeley home for generations and proudly embrace each new generation.

Our ancestors were here long before us, cultivating the land, building our neighborhoods, nourishing our families, and driving the industries that shaped Greeley into the thriving community it is today. From agriculture to meatpacking to construction to oil and gas, our labor has been the foundation of Greeley's prosperity for generations, a vital truth that has too often gone unrecognized.

This book is a collaborative effort created with the participation of Greeley Mexican Americans through their oral histories. Their stories have been recorded on video, carefully transcribed, and written into narratives to preserve the details of their journey.

We share these stories with the hope that they will educate and inspire our present community, future Mexican American generations, and the broader public. We welcome opportunities to present our work and spark further conversation about who we are and our role in Greeley's past, present, and future. Together, we celebrate our legacy, uplift one another, and continue to share the rich tapestry of our culture

EMMA PEÑA -MCCLEAVE,
Project Coordinator

Author's Note

For clarity and explanations, we refer to the individuals interviewed for this book as "historians." We use this label because that is precisely what they are; they have shared their history living in the Greeley area and *La Colonia* (the Spanish Colony). We honor the oral histories they have shared with us, just as other historians have shared their history and those of others. Therefore, their words are prominently featured throughout this book.

Again, for clarity, flow, and reader's ease, the authors' original writing, which augments the interviews, has been edited to be accessible to a broad audience.

LORRETTA CHÁVEZ, PH.D.

Introduction

In the heart of Greeley, Colorado, a rich tapestry of stories woven by the threads of Mexican American culture lies; its contributions stand out as a vital part of the community's history. This vibrant group often remains unrecognized, overshadowed by more prominent historical narratives of the White community. The Mexican American History Project of Greeley aims to fill a gap in the community's history by documenting and celebrating the contributions of Mexican Americans and their ancestors in publishing the book *Our History Our Voice: The Mexican American History Project of Greeley*. The project represents a significant milestone, as it is the first for the Mexican, Mexican American, and *Latino* Greeley communities.

As the authors document the history of this population beginning in the 1920s, the terms "Mexican" and "Mexican American" are used. These two descriptors accurately identify where the early settlers came from as they made their journey to Greeley and its surrounding area. As history is told throughout the decades of the twentieth century, the term "*Latino*" is then used in the text. This perspective reflects the evolving conversation around identity within the Mexican American community and its broader implications in American society. Initially, the focus may be on the specific experiences of Mexicans and Mexican Americans, emphasizing their unique cultural heritage and history. However, in the writing process, *Latino* is introduced to encompass a broader spectrum of identities within the context of America and Latin America.

The historical themes in this book encompass areas such as immigration, employment, culture, religion, education, civic engagement in local government, and social justice issues. Each chapter and conclusion are carefully organized to guide the reader through these significant topics. This book also presents oral histories from forty-four historians from the Greeley community. Their voices and perspectives are noted, recounting experiences from the post-World War I era to Generation Y. In addition, the book sheds light on *Latinos'* influential role in Greeley's cultural and economic landscape through research of Mexican Americans' rich heritage and substantial impact. It includes first-hand historical accounts and research detailing the presence of Mexican Americans in Greeley, tracing their roots back to the 1920s. This journey was one of resilience and determination, as they navigated challenges while fostering a strong sense of identity and belonging.

The book is organized into six distinct chapters, each addressing a key aspect of the topics covered. It starts with "Immigration and Employment," which explores the relationship between immigration trends and job opportunities. Chapter 2, "Culture and Religion," delves into the community's diverse cultural and religious practices. Chapter 3, "Education," focuses on the educational landscape and its impact on immigrants to the Greeley community. Chapter 4 highlights "Community and Greeley Government Participation," examining the historical past and current civic engagement and local governance of Greeley's immigrant families. In Chapter 5, many of our historians share their familial narratives, highlighting experiences of discrimination and struggles for social justice as they established their homes in Greeley. Some families faced the segregation of their children, who were transferred to the Gipson School, separate from their White peers, while others were not allowed to sit in the center pews at St. Peter Catholic Church during Sunday services. Finally, the book concludes with a summary that ties together the insights from the previous chapters, providing a comprehensive overview of the discussed themes.

Our History Our Voice. The Mexican American History Project of Greeley is essential for younger generations of Mexican Americans and *Latinos*, as it helps them acknowledge their ancestors' contributions and encourages incorporating these stories into local school curricula. One of the most important goals of this book is to foster ethnic pride and strengthen connections to an often-overlooked heritage. Moreover, the book highlights the crucial role of Mexican Americans in agriculture. This labor-intensive sector has not only supported families but has also been a foundational structure to Greeley's economic development. By acknowledging these contributions, the historical events detailed in this book aim to foster a dialogue within the community that values diversity, identity, and promotes inclusivity.

The book is designed to be accessible to all readers, especially those in eighth grade through high school. It is a rare resource translated from English to Spanish, showcasing the contributions of Mexican Americans and *Latinos* in Greeley. This book will be distributed in English and Spanish to every school in Weld County and to museums, community centers, and libraries.

Dr. Maria Sanchez

CHAPTER 1

Immigration, Migration, and Employment

This chapter will discuss and document Mexican and Mexican American's immigration and migration to the U.S. and Greeley. For this chapter, and ultimately this book, Mexicans are defined as people who have come to the U.S. from Mexico. Immigration is defined as coming to the United States from another country, and migration is defined as moving to another place within the United States.

Mexican and Mexican American immigration and migration to the Greeley area began in the 1900s and continue to this day. We will begin in 1924, as that is when the Great Western Sugar Company (GWSC) created *La Colonia* (the Spanish Colony) (Donato, 2007). Both names for this community are used throughout this book and in referenced materials.

There were several waves of immigration and migration to the Greeley area from Mexico, New Mexico, Southern Colorado, Texas, and other Southwest states. These waves were often connected to job opportunities, such as farming and meatpacking. Immigration and migration started around 1900 and have continued until today. Before 1910, the U.S. Congress made it difficult for people from certain countries, like Ireland and China, to immigrate. However, there were no strict limits for people from the Western hemisphere, which encouraged people from Mexico, Central America, and South America to come. By 1900, about 12,816 immigrants from Mexico had moved to Colorado and joined the large Mexican, Native American, and Mexican American communities already living there (History Colorado, 2020).

The first major wave of immigration began in 1910 and lasted for many years. Mexican Americans moved to Greeley to work in the sugar beet fields managed by GWSC. Mexicans affected by the Mexican Revolution also came to the area and other parts of the U.S. (Steinhouser, 2015). Many of these immigrants worked in Greeley during the summer and moved to warmer places in the winter (Donato, 2007). Some men left their families in southern places, like Florida, and returned there during Greeley's winters (Cache la Poudre, 2024).

To save money and have more skilled workers, GWSC created *colonias* (small adobe hometowns) for workers near the sugar beet fields. These *colonias* appeared in many parts of Northern Colorado. By 1916, GWSC employed 2,836 *Latinos* in Greeley. Although many moved back and forth between Greeley and northern New Mexico, more workers began staying in Greeley all year after GWSC offered better housing (Lopez et al., 2007).

1920s

Greeley's Spanish Colony (La Colonia) began in 1924, with forty homes paid for by GWSC (Cache la Poudre, 2024; Lopez et al., 2007). The Spanish Colony is

This is a replica of the adobe style house that was built in the Spanish Colony. This house is found in Centennial Village. Photo courtesy of the Gabriel and Jody Lopez Collection. Date unknown.

still located in the northwest part of Greeley at O Street and 25th Avenue. The families, showing their strength and determination, made homes for themselves with help from GWSC. These houses were two-room adobe homes without electricity or indoor plumbing. The Mexicans and Mexican Americans built these homes using materials given to them by GWSC. The new homeowners paid back the cost of the materials over five years (Donato, 2007). While living in *La Colonia*, the new homeowners created a close community with community halls, a baseball field, barbershops, and events. *La Colonia* also had its own set of rules, and everyone who lived there had to follow them (Cache la Poudre, 2024; Lopez et al., 2007).

What Was Life Like in *La Colonia*?

One of the historians we interviewed, Andrés Gonzales Guerrero, Jr., grew up in a *colonia* in East Texas. The area was similar to the Spanish Colony, and like the families there, Gonzales Guerrero was part of a big Mexican American family. He shared his experiences.

The kindergarten through fifth-grade boys would play close to home with other boys their age. They played hide-and-seek games and marbles, and they loved to run up and down the gravel streets in front of their homes until sundown. The K-5 girls would play hopscotch, hide and seek, and with their dolls. The older boys in middle school would ride their bikes, play ball, go to the river to fish, swim with older boys around to watch them, and walk the streets. The middle school girls played hopscotch, hide-and-seek, and with their dolls, and they jumped rope and worked closely with their moms.

The older high school boys would borrow Papá's 22-caliber rifle and hunt for rabbits, squirrels, or birds. If the boys were lucky, they took home what the family would eat for supper that night. This meat "trophy" would be covered with flour and cornmeal and then fried. The older boys also went fishing in the Poudre River, their paradise. Up and down the river, they would fish until sundown. The river was always a happy refuge, as it was so close to La Colonia. *Once chores were done at home, it was off to the river. Vegetation was abundant there, so there were places called "hide-outs" where the boys talked and dreamed about their futures. Of course, they would also talk about the girls they liked and who they would like to marry someday. Many boys were cousins or close friends, so if you got into trouble while swimming in the river and were flailing, they would jump in to save you. That is how strong their bonds were and how much they cared for one another.*

In the 1920s, children worked in the sugar beet fields along with their families. www.greeleyhistory.org.

These boys were also an example for the younger boys and helped their dads and moms in the fields, thinning, hoeing, and preparing the sugar beets for the harvest. Once the sugar beet harvest started, there was no time for pleasure or recreation, as exhaustion would take over. These boys just wanted to eat and sleep because the next day would bring another long, grueling, and arduous day. They worked with their parents from sunrise to sunset.

Mamá and the older girls often worked the hardest because they had to wake up earlier and prepare the lunches for the day. Usually, the lunches were burritos or tacos with beans and eggs, potatoes with eggs, or—if you were lucky that day—added bacon, ham, or ground beef.

Some older girls loved to listen to music, and some had beautiful voices. However, they were too shy to sing for an audience when asked. They helped Mamá around the house, from cooking to cleaning to child-rearing. In most cases, the older girls were like second mamás to the younger children. Mamá and the children often joined Papá in the fields to make ends meet. Therefore, many older children did not attend, or sporadically attended, school during the harvest season.

For Papá, one of his jobs was maintaining repairs to his home's adobe walls so they would not fall apart. Adobe is made of mud and grass, and these earthly materials were used to make the walls of a home in the Spanish Colony. Thus, Papá had to keep his home operational, or he would hear from Mamá! Usually, Mamá was in charge of the inside, and Papá was in charge of the outside. That meant that he oversaw the garden, the flower beds, etc., to make the home look attractive and clean on the outside. Of course, he also worked long hours in the field to bring in income. These long hours and, many times, maltreatment from the growers gave Mamá another job: being the family's peacemaker. She would step in when disagreements or domestic discipline were too harsh. This harshness was often due to the mistreatment that Papá experienced as he worked in the sugar beet fields (Gonzales Guerrero, Jr., 2024).

Life in La Colonia was all about survival, so everyone had to work. During the harvest season, children were taken out of school to help their families. About one-third of the field workers were children and teenagers aged five to fourteen. Working in the sugar beet fields included hoeing and thinning the sugar beets to load them into two- and three-ton trucks. These trucks carried the sugar beets to the factory on First Avenue and 16th Street in Greeley, where the beets were turned into white sugar. Train tracks were built to move the sugar to GWSC warehouses for storage, and from there, it was shipped around the world. GWSC made a lot of money because of the hard work of the men, women, and children of La Colonia (Donato, 2007).

As more people moved into *La Colonia*, tensions grew. Donato (2008) notes that in September 1924, Greeley saw one of the largest Ku Klux Klan (KKK) rallies in the state. Jenny and Abraham Garcia said:

> *Alvin (Abraham's father and her father-in-law) remembers the Ku Klux Klan. I didn't know anything about that. I just remember what I saw in the paper: a Ku Klux Klan parade was in town … Alvin told me that the parade was across the street from his little grocery store at the Spanish Colony, burning crosses.*

Jenny and Abraham Garcia remember:

> *Yeah, my dad thought they were priests because they had the white gowns. This happened when Alvin was little (A. and J. Garcia, 2023).*

Susana (Susie) Taes Grimm also remembered the KKK.

> *You know, I've lived here my whole life, and it's always been a racist town. When my family was growing up, they always had the Ku Klux Klan over in the Spanish Colony, and when I was going to school, you could tell that they didn't like us (Taes Grimm, 2023).*

The children from *La Colonia* were kept separate from other students in different classrooms or even in separate schools. The Gipson Mexican School was opened in 1929, as many people in Greeley did not want the children from "The Colony" to attend school with their children. Despite these problems, migration and immigration continued. By 1930, almost sixty thousand Mexicans and Mexican Americans lived in Colorado (Donato, 2007).

1940s–1950s

During World War II (WWII), many young men joined the military or worked in defense jobs to help with the war. This created a labor shortage, so the U.S.

government, with help from the Mexican government, started a program to find more workers. The *Bracero* Program began in 1942 and ended in 1964. The program brought workers from Mexico as "guest workers" to work in various fields (Calavita, 2010). The word "*bracero*" means a person who works using their arms or a manual laborer (History Colorado, 2021). Almost five million *braceros* came to the U.S. through this program (Library of Congress, n.d.), and many came to Greeley. Although the program gave jobs to Mexican and Mexican American workers, it also involved unfair treatment.

The *braceros* and other workers faced very low pay, exposure to dangerous chemicals, charges for room and board, and harsh working conditions from the White growers who managed the fields. They worked long hours doing hard physical work. Some were far from their families, who had stayed in Mexico (National Archives, 2023).

In addition, some Coloradan Mexican American servicemen who returned from the war moved their families from rural areas in the south to bigger cities like Pueblo, Denver, Greeley, and Fort Collins. In these cities, they enjoyed city life and activities (History Colorado, 2021).

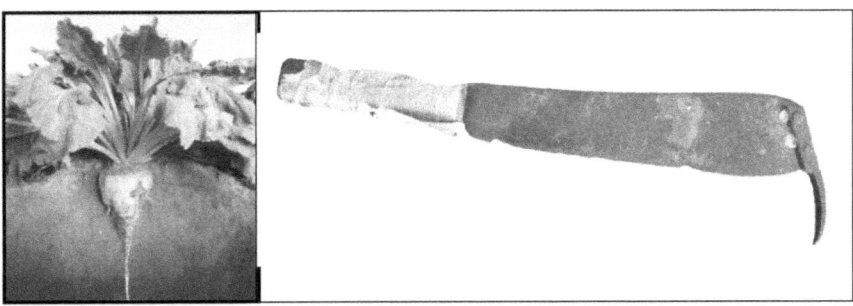

The sugar beet knife was used by the stoop laborer to "top" the sugar beet at the end of the season. The knife was about seventeen inches long, and the hook was used to poke the beet off the ground and bring it up to the other hand. Then workers would cut the top of the beet off. The leaves also had to be cut off so the beets would not damage the machinery when making sugar. Photo from the Gabriel and Jody Lopez Collection.

1960s

In the 1960s, a new wave of immigration to Greeley started because of the meatpacking industry. In 1960, the Monfort Company bought the Capitol Pack Inc. Meatpacking Plant and expanded it to include more processing. At that time, there were big changes in the industry in both equipment and work processes. Before the changes, meat was sent from slaughterhouses to butchers in towns where it was cut and processed. The Monfort Company added the processing stage to their plant, which saved on shipping and labor costs. This was made possible by refrigerated train cars and the interstate highway system.

However, this change brought hard, dangerous, and repetitive work to the plant, leading to high worker turnover (Cooper, 2007; Marsh, 2016). Because of this, Monfort needed to find more workers (Marsh, 2016), so they started recruiting workers from Mexico. Mexico is relatively close to Greeley geographically, and workers from Europe were not available due to Europe's postwar rebuilding. Therefore, Europeans had fewer reasons to leave their homes, and the strict Soviet Union laws made immigration from Eastern Europe impossible (History Colorado, 2021). This led to more immigration from Mexico, Central America, and South America.

Although some workers from Mexico, Central America, and South America were on temporary work visas, others were undocumented. "Undocumented" is defined as not having the proper paperwork, a work visa, or citizenship. Due to this, they weren't in the country legally. Having undocumented workers meant it was easier for the companies to exploit them with low wages and poor working conditions. Also, safety was not strictly enforced. This situation continued for decades, as the demand for low-wage workers continued into the twenty-first century (History Colorado, 2021). This bolstered immigration to the Greeley area.

Maria Sanchez's family used this harvest belt for stoop labor in La Salle, CO. It wrapped around their waist as they stooped to fill the burlap bags with potatoes. As the bags became full, they set them aside and reached to the belt for another bag. This harvest belt belonged to Maria's father, Gabino Lara, Sr. Photo courtesy of the Maria Sanchez Collection.

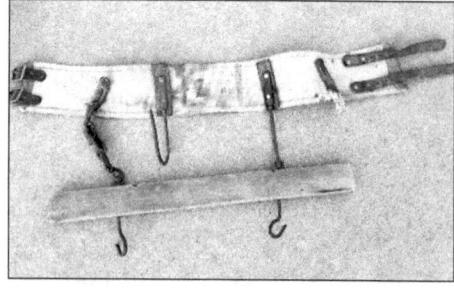

1980s–2000s

In the 1980s and 1990s, meatpacking plants and the farming industry kept bringing *Latino* migrants from other parts of the U.S. to Greeley. We use the term *"Latino"* here, as it is more inclusive to workers from Mexico, Central and South America, and Mexican Americans from the U.S.

Many Mexican and Mexican Americans were recruited to work at the Monfort Meatpacking Plant, which later became part of ConAgras & Co. (a.k.a. JB Swift.) During this time, the Swift plant continued to "automate and downgrade much of the workforce to less-skilled, lower-paid positions. The local plant became a magnet for Mexican and Central American migrants" (Cooper, 2007, para. 23).

This immigration to Greeley largely stopped on December 12, 2006, when Immigration and Customs Enforcement (ICE) raided the JB Swift plant to find undocumented workers. ICE took 265 workers into custody, and nearly "Two hundred children in Greeley came home that day to find one or both parents gone" (History Colorado, n.d.).

After this raid, the Swift Company began hiring refugees, many from Somalia and Burma/Myanmar. This reduced the number of *Latinos* working at the plant, which also reduced immigration from Mexico, Central America, and South America.

Immigration, Migration, and Employment of Historians

Immigration, migration, and employment are closely intertwined. Many of our historians' families immigrated or migrated to the Greeley area because of the economic opportunities the area provided.

Although the reasons for historians coming to Greeley are varied, there are many commonalities. Some of our historians' parents or grandparents came here because of the *Bracero* Program: Teresa Rodriguez-McNeill, Nancy Wendirad, Angelina Bustillos, Patricia Garcia-Nelson, Tomasa (Cynthia) Duran Silva, Yolanda Mendoza, Ana and Adriana Trujillo, and Ben (Mitch) Gonzales.

Bustillos explained her dad's experience with the *Bracero* Program, which he began at the age of twenty-one.

My dad had stories of both experiences. Sometimes the farm owner was very respectful to them and treated them well. Then there were others that weren't so much and, at times, didn't pay them fully, worked them longer than they were supposed to, or didn't give them the living quarters that they had been promised. If you were to ask my dad, overall, he would say that he was very proud and enjoyed being a bracero, *and ultimately, it gave him the path to become legal in this country and to have his family be born and raised here. He was very grateful to the program, and he would say that despite all the bad, the good overshadowed what he experienced (Bustillos, 2023).*

Duran Silva's family also came to Greeley as part of the *Bracero* Program in the 1940s. Her father coordinated caravans of immigrants and migrants traveling here in his capacity as a *bracero* (foreman). In that role, he also cared for the immigrants by paying them and providing snacks and water as they toiled in the fields. He also took them to the movies and the grocery store. Duran Silva remembers being a bit jealous of the workers he cared for in his foreman capacity.

Mendoza's grandpa also participated in the *Bracero* Program. She explained:

My grandpa used to tell us that when he was a bracero, *they would go to Arizona. That was the only place that I knew he went. He would tell us about how hot it would get. They would drop some eggs and try to cook them on the floor without any fire! The eggs would start cooking, just from being exposed there in the sun! He would tell us some of those stories, and then he always encouraged us to educate ourselves, to go to school, because that was going to change for us, for future generations (Mendoza, 2023).*

Cleto Robles Vázquez was born in Zacatecas, Mexico, and immigrated to work in the fields in the U.S. He received his citizenship from the 1986 Amnesty Program and moved to Greeley.

Susie Velasquez's family has been in the Greeley area for many generations. Her grandparents were sheepherders and farm workers, and her mom worked at the Greeley potato docks. In their youth, Velasquez and her siblings worked picking beans and cherries.

Another one of our historians is Polly Baca, who is a retired Colorado legislator and longtime activist. Although her parents were not directly part of the *Bracero* Program, she was involved as an activist in the early 1960s.

I was very supportive of the Bracero Program. No, let me take that back. I was not supportive of the Bracero Program later on because of what we learned when I was in college, when I became aware that the braceros *were being treated badly, that they had bad housing, working, and living conditions. Then I no longer supported it. The Bracero Program was bringing in farmworkers, but they were not providing them with good living, working, and housing conditions.*

… because they didn't have appropriate food or housing, we tried hard to get the program to be more humanitarian for the workers. Because they didn't meet the standard, we did not support the reauthorization of the Bracero Program in 1964. And so, when Cesar (Chavez) was trying to organize the farm workers, the Asian Americans and Filipinos were also trying to organize. They couldn't organize because every time they went out on strike, the farmers would bring in (other) braceros. As a consequence, to help them and to organize for better farmworker conditions, we opposed the reauthorization of the 1964 Bracero Program, and it wasn't reauthorized (Baca, 2023).

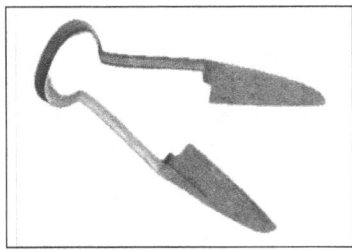

From the 1960s to the early 1970s, Maria Sanchez's family used these onion shears or "onion toppers" to trim onions. This labor-intensive process involved bending over to grasp the onions, clipping the tops of the mature onion bulbs, and then throwing them into large plastic buckets. Photo courtesy of the Maria Sanchez Collection.

Overall, whether they were immigrants or migrants, whether the agricultural work was done by their families or by our historians themselves, this work was an economic mainstay all those years ago.

Rhonda Solis' grandmother and Vivian Watson's grandparents were agricultural workers. Maria Sanchez's parents worked in agriculture, thinning beets in Colorado each spring and returning to Texas in mid-July to harvest cotton. Josie Duran's parents worked the sugar beet and cabbage fields in Ault. Kathleen (Romero) Horning's family came to this area from New Mexico and Southern Colorado to work in the fields. Her maternal side came in the 1920s, and the paternal side came in the 1940s. Vicente Vega Ruiz's mother and grandparents also worked in the fields.

Similarly, both sets of grandparents and Garcia-Nelson's mother were agricultural workers.

My parents were farm workers. Generations of my family worked in the fields here in Greeley. My mom did farm work, mostly in the fields. They would do the planting, the harvesting, and the picking (Garcia-Nelson, 2022).

Gabriel Lopez's family also came to the Greeley area to work the fields in the 1920s. His parents came in 1924 and moved into La Colonia. Taes Grimm, Deborah Suniga, and Theresa Solis's families all lived there and were farm laborers. Pauline Montalvo's parents and siblings all worked together in the fields.

A young Pauline Montalvo working in the fields, harvesting potatoes alongside her family of migrant farmworkers. Photo courtesy of the Pauline Montalvo Collection.

We became migrant workers when I was eight, and we traveled with a troca *(truck), which had a canvas (covering) that had holes. When it rained, we'd all get wet. In Ohio, there's one picture of me picking potatoes. We ended up in Ohio in a big house, and every family had one room, and we all slept there. The kitchen was there, and everything was there. The bathrooms were outside, but we were always together (Montalvo, 2023).*

Like Montalvo and Rodriguez-McNeill, Ray Romero worked in the fields from the time he was four years old. Francisco Cortez worked in the fields beginning at age nine. Cortez was still harvesting fruits in high school to pay for sports, his high school ring, and yearbook. The rest of his money was for his family.

Pres Montoya's father, Press, was originally from Dixon, New Mexico. His family moved to Alamosa, Colorado, when he was fifteen. They later moved to Fort Lupton, where his father worked in the fields and the canning factory in Brighton. Joe Perez, Theresa Solis, Eddie Treviño, and Polly Baca's parents and grandparents were all migrant workers who planted, harvested, and packed crops in the Greeley area. Jacob and Josie Duran's family were migrants who worked in the sugar beet factory in Fort Collins and the sugar beet fields here in Greeley.

Stacy Suniga's great-grandfather bought a farm between La Salle and Gilcrest in the 1940s, and her family migrated to the Greeley area.

As a legislator, Baca worked to improve the lives of agricultural workers in Colorado. She explained:

I was also active in the early years to help pass legislation for migrant workers. As a matter of fact, I carried legislation in the Colorado State Legislature to provide emergency assistance for farm workers. I was involved in the passage of a lot of that legislation (Baca, 2023).

Some of our historians were born in the U.S., and their families were not involved in agriculture. Fabian Garcia Martinez's parents came from Mexico and worked in restaurant kitchens. They cleaned hotels and homes. Abraham Garcia has been here for many years, growing up in the Spanish Colony. His dad, Alvin Garcia, ran the local grocery store there and was a community leader. Jenny Garcia, his wife, grew up in Gilcrest, and her family has lived in this area for many generations. Penny Gonzales-Soto's family has been here for many generations.

In 1943, Romero's family came to the Brighton area, following his grandparents from New Mexico. He first came to Greeley in the 1960s to attend the University of Northern Colorado (UNC). After leaving for employment in other states, he eventually returned in the 1970s. At that time, UNC President Dick Bond hired him to be his assistant. Clarence Lopez's family came to Greeley from Chama, Colorado, looking for work and better opportunities in the early 1950s. During that same decade, Nickie Archibeque and Brittni Laura Hernandez' family came to this area, and her grandfather worked for the railroad.

Damion Córdova's parents, Roberto and Betty Córdova, came here in the 1970s. Roberto was hired as a professor in the Hispanic Studies Department at UNC. Gonzales Guerrero, Jr. came to Greeley because he was recruited by Dr. Alfonso Rodriguez to teach Hispanic studies at UNC. Attending UNC was also the catalyst for Lori Gama's arrival in 1980 as well.

Alicia Johnson's family came to Greeley after her aunt met a U.S. soldier in the Dominican Republic. They fell in love, and he moved her aunt to Colorado. The aunt was instrumental in helping the rest of her family immigrate to Colorado. Johnson was born in Greeley after that immigration.

Ben (Mitch) Gonzales' mother, Filda, and father, Ben, started a business in 1969 called Ben's Furniture. The family has been in business for over fifty-four years.

I'm very proud of our family. We've built ourselves up, educated ourselves, and become community leaders. I've got a lot of really good role models to thank (B.M. Gonzales, 2023).

Juanita Martinez Rocha followed her sister Filda to Greeley in 1967. After spending some time in Wyoming, Martinez Rocha returned to Greeley in 1991. Henry Lee Martinez, Martinez Rocha and Filda's brother, came here seeking employment after his military service in Vietnam, in 1969. Like Martinez, Perez moved to Greeley after returning from the Vietnam War for job opportunities. The same goes for Cortez. He was born in Texas and came to Greeley in 1972 after his tour of duty in Vietnam. Brandi L. Nieto came to Greeley in 2005 because she was dating a young man who lived here, and she was able to land a job working in the prosecutor's office in Greeley.

The stories of how our historians immigrated or migrated to Greeley are colorful and varied. For many, the economic opportunity brought by agricultural work runs deeply in their family's generational DNA. UNC was also a catalyst for bringing some of the historians here. As is the case for most cities, some came to Greeley for specific reasons.

Current Employment of Historians

As we explored the historians' employment histories, we found that many went into jobs where they could advocate for other *Latinos*. Here, we define Latinos as people with family ties to Latin America, consisting of Mexico, Central America, and South America.

Gonzales-Soto is an attorney and works as the director of Student Legal Services at Colorado State University (CSU) in Fort Collins. She has been there since 2019. She previously worked at Catholic Charities for a program called Supporting Immigrant and Refugee Families after graduating from law school in 2002. Gonzales-Soto practiced there as an immigration attorney for nineteen years until she took a job at CSU. She continues to interact and advocate for the immigrant community in Greeley by attending legal clinics and offering legal advice.

Velasquez is a retired lawyer. After high school, she worked as a legal secretary at a law firm, and she feels that her boss somewhat influenced her to eventually get her law degree. Velasquez was the first *Latina* public trustee appointed by Governor Ritter, reappointed by Governor Hickenlooper, and reappointed again by Governor Polis. Later, she worked for the Colorado Civil Rights Commission, where she investigated discrimination complaints. She also served as the director of action there. She was responsible for investigating discrimination complaints from students, faculty, and staff at UNC.

In addition to her bachelor of arts in sociology, Nieto earned her juris doctorate (J.D.) and has been a Greeley municipal judge and lawyer. She became a prosecutor after her internship at the public defender's office. Afterward, she went into private practice and served as an alternative defense counsel for the Greeley Municipal Court. Later, she became the City of Greeley's first *Latina* municipal court judge. At the time of the interview, she contracted with the state to represent and advocate for childrens' best interests in juvenile delinquency, domestic relations, truancy, dependency, and neglect cases. She also works part-time as a judge in four other jurisdictions.

Gonzales Guerrero, Jr. taught English as a second language, Mexican American studies, and citizenship classes at Aims. He also taught in the Hispanic Studies Department at UNC for three years. A retired bilingual elementary teacher, Martinez Rocha worked for many years at Billie Martinez Elementary School in Greeley. Likewise, (Romero) Horning taught for twelve years in local Greeley schools. She was also a human resources coordinator in Greeley's School District 6 and finished her thirty-five-year career as a school principal.

Watson was a longtime kindergarten teacher in School District 6. She is now retired. Currently working at the high school level, Ana Trujillo teaches students much like herself, who are second language learners. Romero has had a long, storied history of being an educator. He is retired now, but his many jobs included being a public school teacher in Fort Lupton, director of the Migrant Program of Northern Colorado (which also included Grand Junction, Colorado, Kansas, and Nebraska), and as an education consultant for the Washington, D.C. Department of Health, Education, and Welfare.

Duran Silva received her degree in education as well. She has worked in various situations, including social work, and taught English as a second language (ESL) at Aims Community College. She was also a drug and alcohol counselor and a Head Start teacher, and she worked for the Colorado Immigrant Rights Coalition. There she taught about civil rights and social justice. She has taught classes on strengthening *Latino* families and parental leadership.

An army veteran of twenty-eight years, Damion Córdova is now a part-time economics instructor at Aims. His father, Roberto Córdova, taught at UNC for twenty-seven years in the Hispanic Studies Department. Betty Córdova (Brito), his mother, was a long-time high school counselor at Greeley Central High School. Clarence Lopez has been a realtor in the Greeley area for thirty-eight years, using his Spanish and other skills to service the *Latino* population here in Greeley. Montoya has also been a realtor since the 1980s. Leading his own real estate team, Vega Ruiz is also a realtor.

Garcia-Nelson is employed in accounting for Green Latinos, an advocacy group that works to uplift Latino voices and prioritizes Latino rights when it comes to climate change and environmental justice. She is currently working on an accounting degree. Johnson is employed by the Department of Human Services as a housing specialist, helping the community stay "house secure." This includes homeless prevention (to ensure homeowners are caught up on utilities, etc.). Mendoza is a lead investigator with the public defender's office. Montalvo

The Bella Romero Education Fiesta, —established in 1996.
Left to right: Unknown, Jose Calderon, Cortez. Photo courtesy of the Francisco Cortez Collection.

worked with migrant workers at East Memorial Elementary School. After that, she worked for the phone company and retired there. Montalvo later earned her college degree in social work while working full-time and attending night school. She has also worked for Catholic Charities as a caseworker after earning her degree and for the Weld County Food Bank doing food stamp outreach and helping the elderly with life skills. Bustillos is currently a child protection social worker in Greeley.

Cortez, now retired, began working as a fireman when he was eighteen. After that, he joined the military and fought in Vietnam. Upon his return to Greeley, he worked in construction. However, he was homeless at one point due to the low wages paid in construction at that time. In the 1980s, he became involved with the Statewide Parent Coalition, where he and Bella Romero, a longtime Greeley educator, worked to involve more parents in their childrens' education. He was also instrumental in creating the Educational Fiesta at Sunrise Park.

Because we believe that every child deserves a better sunrise. Now, it's at Archibeque Park, but in any case, we started in 1996. At the Fiesta, school supplies and backpacks were given to underserved students in District 6 (Cortez, 2023).

Rodriguez-McNeill worked at the Bayly Jean Manufacturing Company when she was seventeen. After an abusive relationship, she attended nursing school as a single mother of four children. While in nursing school, she worked from eight a.m.–five p.m. at Bayly's and six p.m.–two a.m. at a diner in Eaton. She had no car, so she got a ride home from the owner. Rodriguez-McNeill has taught ballet *folklorico* dancing in Greeley for many years. She taught dance at UNC and at many Greeley elementary schools. Today, Rodriguez-McNeill and her daughter America still teach *folklorico* dance and perform in and around Greeley.

Sanchez began her journey becoming a registered nurse in 1972, and her nursing career has spanned over forty-two years. She furthered her education and received her master's degree in public health and then a doctorate in education. In the past, Sanchez developed a family literacy program at the Monfort Meat Company (now JB Swift Company) and Greeley Central High School.

At Monfort, her literacy program was offered on-site to support the employees in learning English and receiving a GED. At Greeley Central, Sanchez's program helped at-risk youth's parents to read and write in English. It also taught them the ins and outs of keeping up with their childrens' education, for example, accessing their childs' grades.

Rhonda Solis has worked for dentists in town for many years now. She is currently the office manager at a dental office. She also served for eight years on the Greeley School Board and, at the time of the interview, was serving on the Colorado State Board of Education.

Theresa Solis (deceased, 2023) began working at UNC in 1974. She worked there for thirty-four years. She was also active in advocating for agricultural workers and homeowners. As a member of Greeley's Women's International League for Peace and Freedom, she worked with an attorney to support farm workers living in harsh conditions without necessities such as electricity, water, food, or proper shelter. She helped organize media coverage, and the farmer committing the abuse was forced to provide better living conditions and was fined.

Finding out that her neighbors were paying massive fines to the neighborhood homeowner association (HOA) spurred Theresa to research what an HOA can legally implement regarding fining homeowners. She discovered that this HOA was not even a valid and could not fine homeowners in the way it had. For example, many of her Spanish-speaking neighbors were being charged thousands of dollars for ridiculous violations, such as parking an inch over the curb. Filing a complaint with the attorney general in Denver was successful, and the HOA was forced to reimburse some of the people who were fined.

At the time of the interview, Stacy Suniga worked for the State of Colorado in the Department of Public Health and Equity. This department coordinated the vaccine bus and the locations where it provided vaccines to the community.

Deborah Suniga, Stacy's spouse, has had many jobs, from sales and marketing to paramedic work to car sales. At the time of the interview, Deborah was actively involved with the Democrats of Weld County.

For many years, Taes Grimm worked at UNC in multiple positions. She began as an attendance clerk in UNC's laboratory school. After multiple other positions, she retired as a financial aid officer. After retirement, she worked at the Greeley Medical Clinic for ten more years.

Like Taes Grimm, Adriana Trujillo works at the UNC Library in the Archives and Special Collections Department. Nickie Archibeque also works for UNC as the director of the Colorado Opportunity Scholarship Initiative (COSI) program. This state-funded grant program offers tuition assistance and wrap-around services to support students through graduation.

Pictured is Cesar Chavez, director of United Farm Workers Organizing Committee (AFL-CIO). With him is Polly Baca, public information officer with the Inter-Agency Committee on Mexican Affairs, which was set up by President Johnson. Baca formerly served as the secretary of the Colorado Young Democrats. Photo courtesy of the Polly Baca Collection.

Hernandez, Nickie Archibeque's daughter, has worked for the University of Colorado at Boulder. There, she directed of a program called "A Queer Endeavor." Her program supported educators, administrators, and school districts in creating safer, more equitable schools and classrooms. Currently, she works at Brentwood Middle School in Greeley.

Garcia Martinez works with students at Aims Community College to ensure they have access to all the services offered by both Aims and the broader community. Specifically, he connects the students to resources that help minimize the barriers they may face while attending college. These resources include financial support, transportation, proper housing, and food, among others.

Baca has a very long, storied employment record. Working with Cesar Chavez, the Farmworkers Union Leader of the 1960s, Baca was asked by him to help organize the grape boycott in Washington, D.C. She was also the co-chair of the Wilder Committee in Washington, D.C., in 1965, 1966, and 1967.

In those years, I also worked for the labor movement. I worked for the International Brotherhood of Pulp, Sulphite, and Paper Mill Workers. The second was the Brotherhood of Railway and Airline Clerks (Baca, 2022).

Later, in 1967, she went to work at the White House, where she was the first *Latina* to oversee public relations dealings with Mexican American issues. This included working with the White House Press Corps.

From 1969 to 1972, Baca was an original staff member of what was to become the National Council of La Raza, an organization looking out for the civil rights and better treatment of *Latinos*. After that, Baca worked for the Democratic National Committee and helped organize the very first meeting of delegates at the Hispanic (*Latino*) Heritage meeting of the National Democratic Party Convention. During this time, she vice-chaired the Democratic National Committee and served as a Colorado state senator.

Traveling the country and giving speeches was part of her political duties at the time. Her tenure at the Colorado Legislature included chairing the Democratic Caucus of the Colorado House of Representatives (1976–1978). She was the first woman and *Latina* to hold that office and the first *Latina* to be elected to the Colorado State Senate (in 1978). She served in the Colorado State Legislature for twelve years. Currently, she's the president and CEO of Baca, Barragan & Perez Associates. This consulting firm specializes in multicultural leadership, political campaigns, motivational presentations, and diversity training.

Many of our historians are proud to be role models and "visible" to the community in their employment endeavors. Ben (Mitch) Gonzales' father came to Greeley because of a transfer to a Gambles store, and then he began his own furniture store. Ben (Mitch) now owns Ben's Furniture, and it has been in operation for over fifty-four years. Jenny's Malt Shop has been owned by Jenny Garcia and her husband, Abraham Garcia, for thirty-eight years. Before working for the shop, Abraham worked at the Greeley Welfare Department and Monfort Beef, and he retired from the Eastman Kodak Company.

In 1995, Gama started her career as a web designer. She now owns her own digital marketing business, the DaGama Web Studio & Digital Marketing Agency. She is a *Latina* pioneer in this type of marketing company. Jacob Duran began Duran Excavating/CG & S Company in 1978. His multimillion-dollar company provides construction services, specializing in concrete. His wife, Josie Duran, worked at the Bayly Jean Manufacturing Company and as a waitress, and she assisted a tax accountant for eleven years. Gabriel A. Lopez began as a journeyman electrician in 1966 and continued until 1990. He became a welder in 1995 and later became disabled. He is now retired.

Before coming to the Greeley area in 1986, Robles Vázquez was an agricultural worker in Texas, Florida, and Colorado. After his agrarian work, Robles Vázquez worked at a sheepskin leather plant. At the plant, he specialized in classifying wool types. After that, he worked as a carpenter making furniture, and he also worked at JB Swift Company.

Henry Lee Martinez came to Greeley after serving in Vietnam and worked for Hensel Phelps, and then the Greeley meat company. He retired from Kodak. Perez also moved to Greeley after fighting in Vietnam, seeking gainful employment. He has worked in community action programs and the migrant program in Nebraska. He has also worked for the City of Greeley.

Treviño also worked for the city, employed as an industrial pretreatment technician, utilizing his zoology degree from CSU. He did this job for twelve years. In this capacity, Treviño would visit the schools and give presentations about clean water and anything related to the sewer system. Eddie explained:

> *I've been around. Most of that was due to my mom's connections in the school district because she was with the school district for almost thirty years. She would introduce me to different teachers in different schools, and she would let me know where she felt that teaching them would be most beneficial. She had me go to Billie Martinez and any of the predominantly Latino schools. She would make sure that I got to them to show them that if I could make it as a scientist, they could make it as*

a scientist. That was the message I always pushed: you could be like me; you don't have to work at the Monfort (now JB Swift) or anything like that. You can go to school (Treviño, 2023).

Our historians have contributed their energy and advocacy to the community, as did their great-grandparents, grandparents, and parents before them. These historians have worked *hard* not only for themselves but for other *Latinos* as well.

Some have worked as educators, business owners, and authors to document Greeley's history of the Spanish Colony or the Greeley Grays baseball team. Others support and advocate for neglected and abused children or work in the political system as legislators to change laws that better the lives of *Latinos*. Some historians work to ensure museum and library displays and programming represent Brown folk everywhere. Our historians also support those who want to attend and graduate from college.

With this strong work ethic and the strong collectivist culture passed down for generations, our historians not only want to make it better for themselves and their immediate families—but also for their fellow *Latina* sisters and *Latino* brothers.

Abraham and Jenny Garcia

I'm comfortable living in Greeley. We were brought up here. I've never felt that different from anybody else because I treat everybody the same as I would like to be treated. —Jenny Garcia

Abraham and Jenny Garcia's family.
Left to right: Tess, Abraham, Polly, Troy, and Jenny.
Photo courtesy of the Abraham and Jenny Garcia Collection.

For decades, Jenny and Abraham Garcia have been at the heart of Greeley, building a legacy rooted in family, entrepreneurship, and giving back.

Abraham was born in 1941 in Greeley's Spanish Colony, where only four families were Mexican. His family came from New Mexico in search of opportunity. It was a tight-knit place where neighbors looked out for each other, kids played in the streets, and families built a life amid cultural hardships. Baseball was central to Abraham's childhood. His father, Alvin Garcia, coached teams in the Colony, and Abraham played and later helped coach as well.

My dad was a baseball man. That was the main thing in the Colony. Everybody played baseball.

His father also helped bring in water and sewer services, making life better for the families who lived in the Colony.

Jenny, born in 1944 in Gilcrest, Colorado, grew up in a similarly close-knit community. She valued hard work early on.

My mom was influential for me because she had a little grocery store. She was an entrepreneur, and I think I took after her.

Jenny left school at sixteen to work, but she always had a dream—to open a 1950s-style malt shop like one she loved and would visit as a kid. In 1988, that dream came true when she opened Jenny's Malt Shop in Downtown Greeley. More than thirty-six years later, as described by *The Greeley Tribune:*

Jenny's Malt Shop is one of those places that can provide a reality break. It may be that it swooshes you back to a time when life was simpler and slower.

As Jenny grew the business, Abraham worked behind the scenes to support it, spending twenty-five years at Kodak before retiring—only to continue working alongside his wife at the malt shop. He joked:

I told her I'd work for a year, and I retired twenty years ago ... I'm still there.

Beyond their business, the Garcias have remained deeply involved in the community. They sponsor the NAKs, a *Latino* fraternity at UNC, supporting their events, including a carnival for children. They have also organized Christmas drives, donating gifts and food to families in need.

Through their business, their dedication to community, and their love for their culture, Jenny and Abraham Garcia have created a legacy that will last for generations. Their story is proof that when you stay true to your roots, work hard, and give back, you can build something that stands the test of time.

—Caleb Flores

Pauline Montalvo

I think we need to step up. We need to fight more. We can't just take hand-me-downs—we need to get out there and do it. We have fought for years to be respected, to be acknowledged as Mexicanos, hard workers. —Montalvo

Pauline Montalvo's life is defined by resilience, determination, and commitment to her community. Born in Morton, Texas, she was raised in a migrant family traveled across the country for farm work. By eight, she was working in the fields alongside her parents and siblings, enduring long days and harsh conditions. Despite the hardships, her family remained close, always working together to survive.

In 1960, after her grandfather's passing, Montalvo's family moved to Greeley to support her grandmother. School became more stable, but discrimination was ever-present.

When I was in eighth grade, I was doing so well they moved me to the tenth. But when I asked for help, the teachers would say, "Pay more attention and read your book."

They didn't care about the Mexicanos. They were just passing us along.

Frustrated and unsupported, she dropped out in the tenth grade and entered the workforce.

Montalvo worked various jobs before enrolling in Job Corps, where she completed her education. She worked as a waitress, in a migrant school, and for a phone company—the latter providing an opportunity that changed her life. While working full-time, she attended night school at New Rochelle College, earning a degree in social work. She reflected:

My dad was the most influential person in my life because he always pushed us to go to school.

Joe Montalvo, Pauline's father, and her brother Samuel, one of her eleven siblings, working together in the fields. Photo courtesy of the Pauline Montalvo Collection.

With her education and life experience, Montalvo dedicated herself to helping others. She worked for Catholic Charities as a caseworker and later joined the Greeley Food Bank, helping families access resources. She also assisted elderly residents with life skills and became active in Hispanic Women of Weld County, using her voice to uplift Latinas in the community.

Montalvo has witnessed discrimination throughout her life and believes it has worsened, especially in schools. She is frustrated by what she sees as performative inclusivity in Greeley, feeling efforts are financially motivated rather than genuine. She said:

I think we need to step up. We need to fight more.

Montalvo has built a legacy of service and advocacy. Her story is a testament to the strength of Mexican-American families who have fought for a better future, ensuring the next generation has the opportunities she and so many others had to fight for.

—Yvette Flores

35

Dr. Maria Sanchez

I believe my decision to become a nurse has been one of the best things in my life; education has opened many doors of opportunities for myself and my family. —Sanchez, Ph.D.

Dr. Maria Sanchez's family's journey exemplifies resilience, hard work, and dedication. Her father, Gabino Lara, Sr., crossed the border without documentation at seventeen in search of a better life. After marrying Lucia, the family was hired by GWSC as seasonal farm workers and traveled from Texas to Colorado each spring to harvest beets. They faced numerous challenges, including grueling drives between Texas and Colorado, housing without plumbing, and long days in the fields.

My father valued hard work and would regularly share, "In the U.S., the money's on the floor. All you have to do is sweep it up with a broom." Meaning, it's waiting for you. You just have to earn it.

Throughout the 1950s, her family worked as seasonal migrant farm laborers doing difficult stoop work using short hoes to thin beets, pick potatoes,

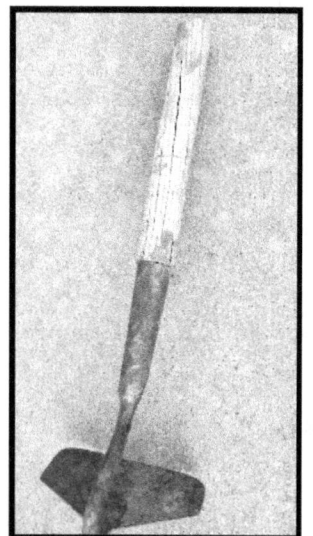

and top onions. Sanchez's mother was born with a congenital defect of only one hand and used a short hoe for stoop labor in thinning beets. She recalls her parents' admiration for John Strohau-

Maria Sanchez's mother, Lucia Lara, used this hoe in the early 1960s as a migrant farmworker for the Great Western Sugar Beet Company. It was used to thin beets in the fields of LaSalle, Colorado.

At that time, farmworkers, particularly those involved in sugar beet labor, used a short-handled hoe, known as *el cortito*. These hoes forced them to stoop for long hours, leading to chronic back pain and other health issues.

It's use was so brutal on the body, it was also called *el brazo del diablo* (the arm of the devil.) This sparked a movement to ban use of the short hoe in Colorado.

Photo courtesy of the Maria Sanchez Collection.

er, a farmer, who lent her mother a long-handled hoe. The simple act of kindness alleviated her mother's discomfort while working, which filled her family with gratitude.

In 1969, the family moved to Colorado permanently, and her father secured a full-time job at a local meat-packing plant, transforming their lives. The constantly moving farmworker lifestyle had impacted school attendance and academic performance, resulting in Sanchez dropping out of school in the eighth grade. With this permanent move, her five younger brothers could attend school family purchased their first home.

Motivated by her family's hardships, Sanchez chose to pursue a different path, ensuring a better future for herself by becoming a first-generation college graduate. After earning her GED from Aims Community College, she earned a nursing degree and eventually obtained a Ph.D. in education and human resource studies from CSU. She attributes her success in education to the support of her mentors, with her mother and grandmother being the most significant influences.

Sanchez went on to develop a family literacy program for the Monfort Meat Company and Greeley Central High School. Her on-site literacy program allowed employees to learn English and earn their GED. At Greeley Central, her program taught at-risk youths' parents to read and write in English and how to oversee their children's education.

—Beth Bullard

Cleto Vázquez Robles and Fabian Garcia Martinez

The poverty my parents lived in didn't allow me to continue school. I felt a bit angry and powerless because I had to leave school to work at the age of eleven or twelve to help at home. I didn't have much education, and what I learned, I learned later in life. I went to Aims to learn English, but it's not the same because you arrived tired and could only learn for two or three hours. It wasn't as easy anymore. But I had the intention to improve myself a bit. I knew where I stood and what I needed, so I had to find a way. —Robles Vázquez

They (my parents and my in-laws) minimize all their experiences, but if you really think about it, the sacrifices they made are significant. Leaving behind their culture, their language, everything they knew, to live in a completely different place and succeed there—I'm not sure how they did it, but they did. For me, it left me in a state of deep appreciation for everything they have done. —Garcia Martínez

Cleto Vázquez Robles' experiences illustrate the humble beginnings that many of our Mexican immigrants share and the reasons why they left their communities back home. In contrast, Fabian Garcia Martínez's (Robles Vázquez's son-in-law) life validates how those sacrifices can positively alter the trajectory of their children's and grandchildren's futures.

Born in Zacatecas, Mexico, Robles Vázquez has spent most of his life as an agricultural worker in the U.S. He received his residency through the 1986 Amnesty Program when he moved to Greeley. He is now retired and often reflects on his frequent moves around the U.S. doing different jobs to earn a living and support his family. He has three daughters, two sons, and eleven grandchildren.

Cleto Robles Vázquez overlooks lands near his hometown of Cicacalco, Zacatecas, Mexico, in the summer of 2024. Photo courtesy of the Vázquez Collection.

Garcia Martínez was born in Glenwood Springs, Colorado, to immigrant parents and grandparents from Mexico. His parents moved permanently to the Vail Valley, where they worked in the service industry. Later, they relocated to Colorado Springs, and finally, Garcia Martínez moved to Greeley, where he completed college at UNC. There, he met Vázquez's daughter Maria, who was also a UNC student. They are now married and have one son. Both Garcia Martínez and Maria earned graduate degrees, and Maria is in the process of completing her Ph.D. in modern and contemporary Latin American literature at the University of Colorado-Boulder.

Factors such as education, English proficiency, and experiences growing up in two different countries influenced Vázquez and Garcia Martínez's opinions on areas such as integration into the community, cultural identity, and views on the *Chicano* Movement. Overall, Vázquez now enjoys the results of his early sacrifices through the successes of his children, while Garcia Martínez recognizes and appreciates the enormous sacrifices his grandparents, parents, and father-in-law made so that he and his family could achieve a comfortable and productive life in Colorado.

—DR. MADELINE MILIAN

CHAPTER 2

Culture and Religion

T he word "culture" connects to a persons' identity and includes both visible part (things you can see) and deeper parts that you can't see. Visible parts of culture are the heroes, holidays, and the Four Ds: diet, dress, dance, and deity (food, dress/clothing, folk dance, and religion). Visible parts of culture are also sometimes called "surface culture." These parts of culture are easy to see, but they can create stereotypes and present a simplified view of a people. If we focus only on these visible parts, we miss other important aspects of culture, such as beliefs, values, attitudes, ways of communicating, and relationships with others. This chapter will explore the culture of our historians, both the visible, surface culture and the deeper parts.

When many Mexicans and Mexican Americans began immigrating and migrating to Greeley in the 1920s, they brought their culture and religion with them, as immigrants have done throughout American history. They found people already living in Greeley who were part of mainstream American culture, mostly White, Anglo-Saxon, Protestant, and English-speaking (WASPE). The Mexicans and Mexican Americans were very different: Brown, Mexican, Catholic, and Spanish-speaking. As this chapter will explain, these visible differences naturally led to racism, conflict, and stress that were dealt with in different ways.

Religion

In Greeley's *La Colonia*, religion played a large part in bringing families together to pray and socialize. At that time, the Catholic Church had the largest population of Mexicans and Mexican Americans, followed by the Pentecostal Church. In the winter months, White women from the different churches would come to help the Mexican and Mexican American families in *La Colonia*.

They would bring food, clothes, toiletries, furniture, and other things people needed. Food in the winter months was scarce because the field work done by the men was lacking. They would take whatever job they could find. The women also found work cleaning, ironing, and babysitting outside *La Colonia*. Wages were at the mercy of their employers at the time.

Churches knew by this time that if the mother or grandmother could be converted to their religion, the family would follow. In Mexican and Mexican American culture, mothers and women lead the spiritual life of the family. Mexican and Mexican American fathers' faith was not as influential in the culture. *Mamá's* religious influences dominated. Mothers have always been a great influence in the moral and religious development of their children in Mexican and Mexican American culture. The reason for this religious influence is because, up until modern times, the mothers and grandmothers spent most of their time with their children. Most mothers in the community, as in *La Colonia*, kept strict tabs on everything their children did. Many mothers in those early days took their families to St. Peter's Catholic Church.

Built in Greeley in 1909, St. Peter's served the growing Catholic population as they immigrated to Greeley and the surrounding areas. The church's website states that "Neither the State nor the Church anticipated or was prepared to cope with the situation" of more Mexican and Mexican American Catholics attending the church (St. Peter's, n.d.). *Latinos* were led to seats on the sides of the church or the balcony, while Anglos sat in the middle. Further, it was a problem for Spanish speakers to receive religious support from English-speaking priests (Our Lady of Peace, n.d.). As a result, many Mexicans and Mexican Americans did not feel welcome at St. Peter's (Brooks, 2013). One of our historians, Baca, directly experienced this type of situation as a three-year-old.

> *... there was a lot of bigotry, and my earliest memory at three years of age was going to church. I wanted to sit in the center aisles because I saw that all the little White girls in white dresses would be paraded around the church. I wanted to see them go around the church, so I wanted to*

sit in the center aisles. You know how three-year-olds can be; I insisted. And so, we—the family—sat in the center aisle. And, of course, the usher came and told us we had to move because the church was segregated (Baca, 2023).

As a result of this segregation and an un-welcoming environment, a new Catholic church was built in 1947–48 to serve Mexicans and Mexican Americans. Our Lady of Peace Catholic Church has served the religious needs of Latinos since that time. Construction began in December of 1947; its dedication was celebrated on July 8, 1948 (Our Lady of Peace, n.d.). This church was built with many fundraising activities and dona-tions from private individuals in the community. This effort to build the church showed *La Colonia* community's commitment to their religion and

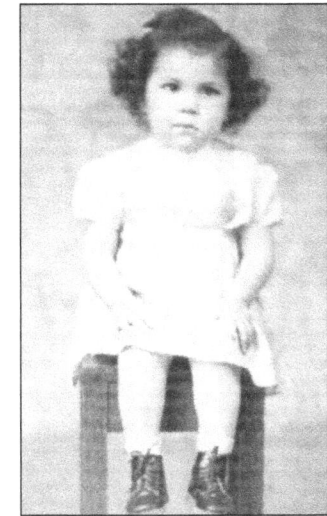

Polly Baca at age three.
Photo courtesy of the Polly Baca Collection.

culture. Today, Our Lady of Peace Church offers daily mass throughout the week in Spanish, with only one mass in English on Sundays (Our Lady of Peace, n.d.). Some of our historians' parents and grandparents helped raise money to build Our Lady of Peace Church. Stacy and Deborah Sunigas' grandparents and Theresa Solis' parents said in their interviews that their family had donated to building a church where *Latinos* felt welcome. Deborah Suniga stated:

The reason our families helped build the church, Our Lady of Peace, is that, as Mexican Americans, we weren't allowed to go to St. Peter's—or we could go, but we weren't allowed to sit in the pews. We weren't allowed to. The Mexican Americans were seated alongside the walls or in the basement. Even in the winter, they were outside. Therefore, six families decided to get together and, with the help of Father Dominic, built Our Lady of Peace in 1947–1948 (D. Suniga, 2023).

Over the years, many Mexicans and Mexican Americans have left the Catholic Church for other churches and other Christian faiths "because they were welcomed and treated better in the Protestant churches" (Lopez et al., 2007, p. 78). A Pentecostal Church opened in *La Colonia* in 1930 and still holds services as the Bethel Spanish Assembly of God. Currently, many Protestant and non-denominational churches in Greeley offer services in Spanish.

Dedication of Our Lady of Peace Catholic Church. Construction began in 1947, and it was dedicated in July 8, 1948. The name reflected the desire for peace after WWII. Funding came solely from community donations. Photo from church records. Used with permission.

Thus, the tensions between Mexican and Mexican American Catholics and the Catholic Church began long ago. The church's negligence and unwelcoming environment were seen in its lack of training and education for Mexican American priests and decision-making leaders (Guerrero, 1987). Perhaps this negligence was also because they did not know how to relate, connect, or identify with the colonized Mexican and Mexican American communities (Gonzales Guerrero, Jr., 2024).

When Protestants and other denominations converted others to their religion, they got them from the Catholic community. This was due, again, to the lack of support from St. Peter's. Many denominations or other churches in Greeley at that time were on a fast pace toward assimilating their minority (or Mexican and Mexican American) church members. This assimilation process is similar to what many immigrant communities experience as they come in contact with the dominant American religious culture (Guerrero, 1987; Vasconcelos, 1997).

Out of forty-four historians, thirty-one reported growing up in the Catholic religion. Many Mexicans and Mexican Americans brought their Catholic faith with them when they came to this area long ago, which was an important part of their everyday lives. Watson reports that her maternal grandparents thought that her dad, Carlos Leal, was not "good enough" to marry her mom, Alice, because he was not Catholic. Carlos did indeed marry Alice, and Watson was raised in the Catholic Church. Others who reported that they grew up going to mass regularly were: Nickie Archibeque, Polly Baca, Angelina Bustillos, Damion and Betty Córdova, Jenny Garcia, Ben (Mitch) Gonzales, Susie Tellez Grimm, Henry Lee Martinez, Juanita, Martinez Rocha, Brandi L. Nieto, Ray Romero, Maria, Sanchez, Duran Tomasa (Cynthia) Silva, Rhonda Solis, Eddie Treviño, and Nancy Wendirad. Some historians reported receiving Catholic sacraments, such as baptism, First Holy Communion, Reconciliation, etc., and going to Catechism (Catholic religious class) while growing up.

Martinez recalled growing up Catholic.

Well, you know, we were brought up strictly Catholic, and I went through grade school in the Catholic school. We were pretty, I would say, holy, I guess (H.L. Martinez, 2023).

However, many reported that Catholicism is not a huge part of their everyday lives today. Many reported that although they may not attend church regularly, they are still "spiritual."

Sister Tomasa (Cynthia) Duran Silva (1963).
Photo courtesy of the Tomasa (Cynthia) Silva Collection.

Garcia-Nelson and Damion Córdova discussed their Catholic upbringing in this way.

I think religion definitely has had an impact on my family, just because my mom is very, very religious. My grandmother was as well. And, so, I feel like, the religious influence for us has definitely been upholding the importance of family and always trying to honor and respect your family. So I think, for us, that's been the biggest influence. I know the newer generations of our family aren't as religious as previous generations (Garcia-Nelson, 2023).

Damion Córdova concurred with Garcia-Nelson.

Yes, it has; it's (being) born and raised Catholic, practicing Catholics, some Catholics are more devout than others. But, you know, it's the idea of being good to one another and taking care of each other (Córdova, 2023).

As mentioned in the first part of this chapter, religion is considered a "visible" and integral part of culture. For many *Latinos*, the Catholic faith has provided a foundation and guided how they live their everyday lives.

Collectivist vs. Individualistic Society

Another source of conflict and challenge for the *Latino* community in Greeley was their strongly collectivist views. In collectivist societies, the community is much more important than the individual. This differs from the individualistic view of American culture, which values independence and self-reliance. The collectivist view was part of the deep culture of Mexicans and Mexican Americans back in the 1920s, and it still is for many today.

Although every culture values family, Mexicans and Mexican Americans who immigrated to Greeley held a very strong collectivist view. This view puts the well-being of their families as most important, along with the well-being of their community. The GWSC, in establishing *La Colonia*, realized that men would not be willing to stay there without their families. The "idea of settling families became more appealing than the relocation of single men" (Bilotte, 2020, p. 112). Therefore, the GWSC focused its recruiting efforts on both Mexican and Mexican American men and women.

GWSC "acknowledged the strength of Mexican and Mexican American family ties and understood the importance of the family to Mexican workers" (Bilotte, 2020, p. 123), although they did so in a racist and derogatory manner. Bilotte, a researcher (2020), cites GWSC recruiting materials calling Mexican women "either corpulent (chubby) as a medieval friar or stringy and lean, without any claim to good looks, and surrounded by a numerous brood of offspring" (p. 123).

Family is still central to the Greeley *Latino* community in modern times. Households with many generations—grandparents, parents, and children all living together—are common rather than unusual.

The people who lived in *La Colonia* built a community gathering place in 1924 called the *Salón*. The *Salón* became the social center for the community to meet and celebrate holidays and special events, such as lunches, music, dances,

Greeley Spanish Colony *Salón* (community house) in 2002. Jose Marquez owned the Colony's *Salón*, and it was used for dances, box socials, beauty pageants, boxing matches, wedding receptions, and plays, such as the Christmastime play *Pastores*. Photo courtesy of the Gabriel and Jody Lopez Collection.

and wedding receptions (Lopez et al., 2007).

> *When they arrived at the* Salón, *the festivities began! Everyone in the*
> *Colony participated (Lopez et al., 2007, p. 127).*

Fundraisers for the community were also held at the *Salón*. In addition, a
health clinic operated out of the *Salón* until the early 1940s. This gathering place
was active until 1987, when it became the Guadalupe Center for the Homeless
(Lopez et al., 2007).

In 2011, Catholic Charities built a new facility—the current home of the
Catholic Charities Guadalupe Community Center. This emergency shelter serves
men, women, and families. It offers meals, showers, and job referrals. The shelter
also advocates for its residents when they need support.

In thinking about the Mexican and Mexican American collectivist views,
valuing community more than the individual, one of our older historians,
Abraham Garcia, remembered:

> *… it seemed like most of the people came from New Mexico to the*
> *Colony, so they knew each other; it was like a big family. I remember*
> *they used to have a pump in the middle of the Colony. Everybody was a*
> *community. Water used to be drawn from the pump (and whoever was*
> *there) would pump water for everyone! And they used to have "commis-*
> *sioners." They'd have a cleanup crew go through the whole Colony every*
> *Friday or Saturday. La Colonia was pretty much immaculate. One of*
> *my aunts would sweep her dirt yard like it was the inside of her house.*
> *I thought it was perfect back then; everything was clean, not what it is*
> *today (A. Garcia, 2023).*

Abraham's father, Alvin Garcia, was a very important leader in *La Colonia*.
He owned a grocery store there for many years, helped bring water and sewer
to the homes, and assisted in building the baseball field. Alvin owned and ran
his store in the Spanish Colony for close to sixty years (A. Garcia 2023).

Nickie Archibeque described her father, Charles Archibeque, as a typical

Mexican American who had the same values and ideals as Alvin.

Another value, now that I'm thinking of Dad: he was always so humble. I remember a story of him telling us that his city council peers would (say), "Chuck, you still live on the east side?"

And he (would say) "Well, where else would I go?"

We laughed because he knew his humble beginnings, and he always kept them. My mom would fight and fight with him every time he'd go to a council meeting because he'd want to wear his old jeans and his dirty shoes from the garden! You know, he was a humble man. He did not care what he was wearing. He would've probably gone from the garden to the meeting if he could! That has been instilled in me. And so, to us, it was all about helping; he was always so humble (Archibeque, 2023).

Charles Archibeque was also a community leader for many years. He was one of the first Mexican American city councilmen to serve on the City Council, and he did so for sixteen years. He was also instrumental in getting a low-income housing unit, the *Milagro del Sol*, and a homeless shelter, the Guadalupe Homeless Shelter, built. There is a park now named for him and his wife on the northeast side of Greeley—Charlie and Laura Archibeque Park.

González Guerrero, Jr. reflected on values.

Thinking about the Mexican and Mexican American values that Charles and Alvin lived every single day of their lives, the concept of vergüenza *(shame) was very strong and continues in our culture today. No Mexican or Mexican American wants to be a* malcriado *(a person who was not raised well or brings shame to themselves or their family).* Tener mucho corazón y orgullo de ser Mexicana/o *(to have a great deal of heart and pride is to be Mexican) is also a deep cultural tenet in Mexican and Mexican American culture (González Guerrero, Jr., 2024).*

People like Charles and Alvin and their community involvement were key to keeping the village/*La Colonia* alive and happy. Respect for families, community, and leaders was not questioned in those days. Promoting the value of developing human relationships was of key importance, as we see in the lives that Charles and Alvin led. Mexican and Mexican American culture respects the rights of others, and this promotes peace in the community (González Guerrero, Jr., 2024).

However, acts of racism perpetrated by the White residents in Greeley were something of an everyday occurrence in *La Colonia*. One facet of this racism was the creation of the stereotype of Mexicans and Mexican Americans being dirty and lazy. The culture of the U.S. was/is White, Anglo-Saxon, Protestant, and English-speaking (WASPE). The Mexican and Mexican American culture was Brown, New Mexican or Mexican, Catholic, and Spanish-speaking. Thus, assimilation was a big problem for this population. However, most of these WASPE immigrants easily let go of their native cultures and assimilated into the U.S.'s WASPE culture. They were White and not going back home anytime soon (Vasconcelos, 1997).

La Colonia residents challenged the racism experienced in their community in many ways, including planting vegetable gardens and flowers to beautify their homes (Bilotte, 2020). As mentioned earlier, Charles Archibeque had a large garden, and Theresa Solis remembered:

My grandmother was a stay-at-home mom, but she did a lot of gardening. She had one of the biggest herbal gardens here in Greeley, and she would use a lot of the herbs for remedies and healing. And we always had to take them. If we had any kind of problem or something—if we didn't feel well—she always knew what type of herb to give us. She took care of a lot of the farm animals too (T. Solis, 2023).

Adriana Trujillo recalled the importance of growing their own food and working the land, taught to her by her grandfather, Jose:

But going back to my grandpa, I remember when I was growing up, he would encourage his kids and grandkids to go work in the field with him. He wanted to teach us how to work. He wanted to teach us how to use the land in a way that we can survive off the food. I remember one time going to the fields, and I told my mom, "I want a hat like Grandpa's."

I wanted to be just like him. ... he would have a hat that would cover the back of his neck. Usually, he would have a handkerchief on the back of his neck, so I got a hat to look like him. And then he would teach me how to pick and prune onions. ...

And he told me, "Okay, put them in this bag, and just go down this row."

And I looked down this long row, and I said, "This, all the way?" ... He said, "Yes!"

And I remember just trying to pull the bag of onions, the sack of onions, and I was smaller, younger. I was tiny, and I told him, "I can't carry this, Grandpa!"

And he said, "You have to. You have to."

And that's when I learned how hard it is to work in the field! And I looked up to him even more. I looked up to all the family members who did that work (Adriana Trujillo, 2023).

"Creating 'respectability' was a common strategy for marginalized communities to push back against racist discourses" (Bilotte, 2020, p. 133), and the residents of *La Colonia* used that strategy in many ways. From the very start, residents took great strides to maintain cleanliness and decorum. Though race relations between ethnic Mexicans and White Greeley residents were strained, the Colony endeavored to demonstrate residents' sense of civil responsibility. In September of 1935, for example, *The Greeley Daily Tribune* reported that the Colony's very first telephone had been installed. The reason for this technological advance was to "facilitate quick calls to Sheriff Gus Anderson when there is trouble." The article also noted Sheriff Anderson's assurance that there had "been no particular trouble at the Colony lately." Phone access connected the Colony to the greater Greeley community (Bilotte, 2020, p. 135–6).

The people of *La Colonia* wrote and enacted a community constitution in 1927 (Bilotte, 2020, p. 135–6). In keeping with the collectivist view, this constitution focused on the residents working together to benefit the community. It included everything from community cleanliness to the need to send children to school, to curfews for children, to a speed limit of fifteen m.p.h., which disallowed any behavior from boys "that may bring trouble to them and to the parents" (Lopez et al., 2007).

Family Values

Many of our historians spoke about the same values shared by Lopez et al., (2007). Hernandez stated:

> *And so, that's really a value. We saw our parents involved with the youth; we saw them involved with the council. We saw Grandma feeding anybody, welcoming anybody. We saw the way that they were at the restaurant. (Charles and Laura owned the Mirasol Restaurant in the late 1980s in Greeley). To us, it was all about helping your community and giving back. And that is instilled in all of us. It's not something that you do for accolades or for leadership roles; you*

A tile portrait honoring Alvin Garcia located on the side of the Greeley History Museum. Echevarria, M. (2005). "Laying the Foundation" (ceramic tile).
Photo courtesy of Greeley History Museum.

52

do it because that's what we do. We support one another, and we help our community. It was a big value that was instilled in the grandchildren (Hernandez, 2023).

Many families of our historians valued having a strong work ethic as well. Gama remembered:

I remember when I got my first job at seventeen. My grandmother and my mom told me, "If somebody doesn't show up to work and they call you in, go in and just work extra hard and always do your best."

And that's just been ingrained in me. I always do the right thing and always tell the truth (Gama, 2023).

Wendirad had similar memories.

Honesty, always say the truth. Hard work ethic. Be respectful and responsible. Even when we get together now, my siblings, cousins, and I, we say, "Remember when Grandma used to say this or Grandma would say that?"

Something that is part of our culture is what we call, in Spanish, refranes (proverbs). When I refer to "grandparents," I mean my maternal grandparents because that's who I grew up with. Both of my grandparents had so many dichos (sayings). To this day, I saved them, and I have passed them on to my daughter, and I can totally see them being passed on to my granddaughter because we use them a lot. For example, a very common one: "En boca cerrada, no entran moscas" (keep your mouth closed, and if you remain quiet, sometimes it's better). The English equivalent idiom would be "silence is golden" (Wendirad, 2023).

Vega Ruiz shared that his family also valued working hard and, ultimately, that it will give one a better life.

Well, thinking about values, it's more like hard work, responsibility, integrity, and that really comes down from seeing my parents do every-

thing and anything they could to provide for us, from having a roof over our heads to having food on the table, and it was always doing as much as they could the right way. There were never any shortcuts or any ideas of shortcuts. It was always, "We're here to work hard and get beyond" (Vega, 2023).

Cortez, Velasquez, and Garcia-Nelson all share the collectivist versus individualist value that puts the family first.

We always believed that the family was first, always, and courtesy. Always be courteous to people unless they show you otherwise. Always offer somebody in your home a beverage or invite them to dinner or whatever the situation may be. If you're about to sit down to eat and they show up, invite them; put an extra plate out because it doesn't take that much more (Cortez, 2023).

Velasquez clarified passing on personal values.

I think some of the most important values were the ones of family, and I think, you know, just how important family and spending time with them is. And on weekends, we used to go to Milliken to my mother's (and she) would cook for us. And that's something that I've done a lot, with my kids, is I would cook on Sundays (Velasquez, 2023).

Garcia-Nelson analyzed the continuing values.

Now that my grandpa has passed, I'm not really worried that things will change for our family. We don't really have a tradition, but we do get together almost every weekend, and there's so many of us that it's always like a party. I think that just the closeness that we have, even with our extended family; it's something really special. And it's not something that a lot of families do. I can call my aunt or my cousin and then just say, "Hey, let's go get breakfast," on the spot (Garcia-Nelson, 2023).

(Romero) Horning and Sanchez remembered the importance of education and a good work ethic in their families.

They expected us to behave, and when we didn't, we heard from it both at the school and at home. I think that's true of lots of families at the time. We were encouraged to set our sights beyond high school and to go to college. Neither of my parents graduated from high school, so that was very important to them. Church—we spent a lot of time there. What Mom and Dad modeled during that time, though, was a commitment to service to others. Both of them were volunteers in the church settings, and early on, we learned that that was important not to just go and be a bench warmer but to be involved—to be helpful. Hard work was another ethic. We were expected to contribute in some way, shape, or form. If you weren't inclined to go out to the field to help pull weeds or shovel cuts or whatever else needed to be done. You were expected to help clean the house, take care of the yard, and be educated (K. (Romero) Horning, 2023).

Sanchez added:

My mom instilled our Catholic faith in us. We always had to go to Catechism, make sure that we went to church every Sunday, and we did our readings for church. That was a big thing on my mother's side of the family. On my father's side of the family was hard work, learning how to work hard and be appreciative of what we had (Sanchez, 2023).

Gonzales Guerrero, Jr.'s father strongly believed that getting good grades was very important.

If I made a B he would say, he knew Bs and Cs, of course. He couldn't read, but he knew what it said.
    "Tell your mother to sign that shit!"
    So, I had to make all As! Yeah! (Gonzales Guerrero, Jr., 2023)

Many of our historians' parents had little education, and because of this, they wanted their children to graduate from high school and go to college. They knew that education was a way out of the back-breaking work of the fields.

Gender Roles

In many societies, gender roles reflect cultural values. Many Mexicans and Mexican Americans have, in the past, followed a very traditional family structure. Researchers (Lam et al., 2012) write that in traditional Mexican and Mexican American families, men were the leaders of the household, and women were mothers and homemakers. This was the situation even as women worked outside the home and earned money for the family. Women had to obey their husbands and care for their homes and children (Knapp et al, 2009). However, over time and with contact with other cultures in the U.S., gender roles changed in these families. Over several decades of contact with American culture, Mexican Americans from younger generations are now more open to different gender roles than those from older generations (Su et al., 2010). Today, *Latina* women in Greeley attend and graduate from college, own and manage businesses, and hold political office.

These gender roles of a traditional Mexican or Mexican American family were reflected in *La Colonia*. Women worked in the fields and as domestic servants. They earned money for the family. However, they also had to care of the home and children. Women planted and tended vegetable gardens and raised goats and chickens to feed their families. They were active in their church and community. They took care of the community in the early 1920s and 1930s (Bilotte, 2019). *La Colonia's* community constitution set a curfew and ways for boys to behave but not for girls to behave (Lopez et al., 2007).

To understand our historians' experience with gender roles growing up, this question was asked of them: "When you were a child, were males and females treated differently?" Many women reported that their roles were in the house and the field. They said that their brothers had much more freedom than they did. Fathers were more strict with the girls; fathers monitored where girls could go and when they were supposed to be home. Duran Silva, eighty-three years old, shared in her interview:

Oh, yes, we were not allowed to go anywhere. There were four of us. I was the youngest of the four growing up. And my father would ask us where we wanted to go, and one of my sisters, my older sister, Tina, she always wanted to go dancing … On weekends, we went dancing, but my father would be right there to take us and drop us off in front of the dance club. And he would be right there to pick us up at about eleven-thirty. He didn't want us to stay until the end.

I remember my sisters, Tina and Mary Ellen, used to say, "Don't look through the door. Don't look through the door, towards the door, because it's time for Dad to come pick us up!"

And so, we were always trying to hide from him because he'd be right there, Johnny on the spot! If we went to the theater, the theater was on the same block where we lived, he still had to go take us and drop us off in front and pick us up when the movie was over. That's how protected we were as girls. But the boys, my brothers, they—they could go anywhere they wanted to. They didn't even have a curfew for them. That's what I didn't like (Duran Silva, 2023).

Clarence Lopez (sixty-eight) agreed with Duran Silva.

Boys could stay out longer, stay out as late as they wanted, not the girls. They cleaned, did dishes, and did chores, and Mom paid them. Boys did not do any of those chores (C. Lopez, 2023).

Watson shares that her parents had different limitations for the girls and boys. The girls had to go to UNC and live at home or close to home, while her brother went to CU and lived in the dorms.

Seventy-three-year old Taes Grimm shared similar experiences in her family growing up.

Yeah, my brothers … were treated like royalty, like kings. They were the kings of the house. Whenever we would cook or my mother would have supper, they would be served first, and then we would eat after them or be served after they did. And to this day, we still do that (Grimm, 2023).

Montalvo, seventy-one, agreed with Taes Grimm.

… the women had to do the cooking and go and help work out in the field. I think that was different. You know, women had more work (Montalvo, 2023).

Bustillos, forty-one, who is much younger than the historians mentioned earlier, discussed the gender roles in her family.

We were raised in a very traditional Mexican family, and Mexican female and males rules were followed. The women were kept at home. They were the child caretakers; they were the homemakers. They're the ones who prepared the food. The man is the one who would go out and earn the money and be responsible for finances. And … women were asked to keep their opinions to themselves. My mom remembers the first time that she returned back to Mexico and she was wearing jeans. How upset my grandmother was!

"Why are you wearing pants? Women don't wear pants!"

And my mom said, "But in the U.S., they do."

And my grandma said, "Well, you're in Mexico right now, so go change!" Even with dressing, the women usually would have to ask their spouses if their attire was appropriate, whether it wasn't too short, too tight, or too revealing.

That also followed into the children. There were specific traditional childrens' roles that we had to take as well. I remember that when my dad would ask for something to drink, we would bring him a glass of water, and then we would have to cross our hands and wait for him to be done. That was the expectation of all the children. Then, when you said hello to someone who was older than you, who you respected, you would kiss their hand. And those were a few of the things I remember doing as a child (Bustillos, 2024).

Like Bustillos, Johnson was born in the early 1980s and remembered:

The gender roles: women are in the kitchen, women do this; males go out and work, provide for the family" (Johnson, 2023).

Garcia-Nelson was thirty-one at the time of the interview and had similar experiences growing up as Susana Taes Grimm, Clarence Lopez., Pauline Montalvo, Angelina Bustillos, and Alicia Johnson.

… the males, you know, it was a lot more casual and relaxed for them, whereas the women were always in the kitchen getting everything ready, taking care of the kids, and things like that" (Garcia-Nelson, 2023).

Theresa Solis (seventy-three) was a little more indignant as she shared:

Yes, they were. Yeah, when we, the women, of course, always did all the cooking and preparing. When it was time to serve our meal, the men would sit down first, and then we would make sure that once they were all seated and ready to eat. Then we would sit. We would sit down with them, but they always started the meal first. And I always wondered why we always had to wait on them. I mean, there were times when they were two hours late, and we had to wait! We couldn't eat, and we were so hungry. And I would ask my mom, "Why do we have to do this all the time?" (T. Solis, 2023).

Ana Trujillo (fifty-five) had similar memories of how she was treated differently from the men and boys in her family.

Definitely, when I was a child, we were treated differently, except when it came to field work. Everybody did that.
*   That's what I thought, "Well, this is not fair."*

As one of the oldest, I was expected to clean and take care of my younger siblings, and especially as a woman, you had to be in the kitchen, cleaning and cooking most of the time (Ana Trujillo, 2023).

When asked about gender roles, Rhonda Solis (fifty-three) brought up a very interesting point.

I think so. I think there was still that struggle of what women could do, what they couldn't do. I was never held back from anything, but I wasn't necessarily encouraged either. I was one of those kids who was very quiet when I was growing up (R. Solis, 2023).

However, it was different for some. Gama (sixty-two), when asked about gender roles, answered:

In America, yes, but in my home, that wasn't the message I kept hearing. … I wasn't encouraged to grow up and be a housewife. I was encouraged to do whatever I could to have a better life than they did (Gama, 2023).

Other historians who had experiences like Gama were Jenny Garcia (eighty), Francisco Cortez (seventy-six), Damion Córdova (fifty-three), Gabriel A. Lopez (sixty-eight), and Kathleen (Romero) Horning (sixty-nine). Jenny shared:

… and with chores, we all had something to do because, like I said, there were eight of us in our family, and it was up to the girls to iron for the two boys. I used to do the ironing for Mom while she worked. We all had something to do (J. Garcia, 2024).

It was also different for Hernandez, who was thirty-four at the time of the interview:

And growing up with you (Nickie Archibeque is her mother) as my mom, you know, she grew up in the 1970s and 1980s. To me, that's like hip hop;

that's women's empowerment. That's, like, a different wave of feminism. And she grew up with that. You can do whatever you want, you can be independent, and you don't need a man. She really instilled in us what it means to be a strong, independent woman. And so we still saw the differences, of course, with our cousins and who was babied and who wasn't (Hernandez, 2023).

However, Nickie Archibeque (fifty-four) remembered:

And the funny thing is, my dad raised six strong women, and we're all opinionated. We're strong, we're independent, we're intelligent. He'd always ask my brother for his opinion before. It's funny because he raised six strong women, but he would always refer back to my brother. We laugh, we get a joke out of it. My brother has passed on now, but we … It was a struggle for me being the youngest, being heard. I'm doing the same thing. But I get it now that I'm older (Archibeque, 2023).

Many things have changed with gender roles and the expectations for men and women through the years. However, it is clear that many people from Gen X and later are working to change those strict gender expectations from traditional *Latino* culture and values. The role of the man, often the father and main breadwinner, is still very important in many of the historians' lives. However, it was the strong leadership of women in the home: the mother, the grandmother, and the aunties who helped both the home and the community thrive. Their strength and determination were examples for their children every day, helping them grow into more educated and financially stable adults.

Identity

Identity is also part of a persons' culture. For the *Latino*, there are several ways in which one can identify. This can come from different times and spaces in their lives. Some identify as Mexican, Mexican American, *Mexicana*, *Mestiza*, *Chicana/o*, *Latino*, American, or *Latinx*. Historians shared parts of their identity and some explained them in the following ways. Nickie Archibeque stated:

That's a good question for me because I'm from all these different eras. And you know, first, the government labeled us as Hispanic, and then, you're … are you Latina? Because you're not really from a Latin country. (She was born here in the U.S.). And then, if you don't speak Spanish, you can't be Hispanic. To be honest, I was confused a lot. It's like that from the Selena movie, you're not Mexican enough for the Mexicans, and you're not American enough for the Americans. Growing up, I probably had an identity crisis. Like, wait, who am I? What am I? I don't speak Spanish. I kind of speak Spanish. I understand it. Now, I'm pretty firm in what my identity is in Southern Colorado, Northern New Mexico. When I'm feeling radical, I could be called a Chicana. *I consider myself a* Latina *(Archibeque, 2023).*

Gonzales-Soto had similar views about her identity.

That has evolved over time. It's funny, I spoke to some students at CSU recently about my history, and I said, "There was a time that I was Mexican American. Right? There was a time that I sort of delved into Hispanic until I realized where the hell the term "Hispanic" came from, and it wasn't real. There was a time in college when I was "Chicana." There was a time that it was … Right, now I come from the "Latinx" community.

Right? Learning to be more inclusive, realizing that Mexican American encompasses a huge number of identities, and how do you actually define that? Right? So today, I'm from the "Latinx community" (Gonzales-Soto, 2023).

Deborah Suniga, who is related to another of our historians, Baca, explained her evolving identity in this way.

I think we've evolved because I've had this conversation with Polly (Baca). I know when I was growing up in school, I was Mexican American, then it was Hispanic, and now Latina, and I'm with Stacy. I don't get the whole

Latinx thing because you can't change Spanish from Latino *to* Latina *with the O and the A. Right now, I go by* Latina. *I don't know. Ask me in a couple years. It may change, but right now, I'm a* Latina *(Suniga, 2023).*

Baca explained her identity's evolution over the years.

First Spanish American, then Spanish Mexican, then Mexican American, until 1972, Chicana, *Hispanic until 1980,* Latina *now. I identify with all of them" (Baca, 2023).*

Others also explained an evolving identity. Romero said:

Hispanic or Latino, *but I've been a Mexican, I've been a Mexican American, I've been a* Chicano. *I've been all of those names that as time have changed, right? (R. Romero, 2023).*

Duran Silva said:

I tend to like being called Latina *because to me that includes all the different (words),* "Chicana," "Latina," "Hispanic." *I'm a* Latina *(Silva, 2023).*

Some, like Martinez, have multiple identities at the same time.

Mexican, Latino, *Hispanic, Indian American, Mexican American, and Mexican Indian.*

Garcia Martinez explained his identification as *Hispano* or Mexican American.

I think, like my father-in-law, I identify as Mexican American as well. He has the experience of being born in Mexico, growing up in Mexico, and having a deep connection to the culture. My only connection is through my family and the limited experiences I've had traveling and staying there Mexico for certain periods. Although I would like to always consider myself fully Mexican, I am not because I don't have the broader context of the culture. The same thing happens to me here in the U.S. I live here and work with people from here, but I've never really fully immersed myself in this community. Just like over there, you could say my cultural identification is more based on family ties. That's how I define my culture the most (F. Martinez, 2023).

These quotes explain how, especially for *Latinos*, there are many "labels" or identities that define a part of who we are. For many, identity changes as we age, evolve, and grow. For some of the historians, identity stayed the same, or they just said one identity and did not say if it had ever changed. Wendirad and Montalvo are *Mexicanas;* Vega Ruiz, Perez, and Treviño are *Latinos;* Robles Vázquez is a *Hispano,* Ana Trujillo, Bustillos, and Nieto are Mexicans; Rhonda Solis, Taes Grimm, and Johnson are *Latinas;* Sanchez is Mexican American; and Montoya and Gonzales Guerrero, Jr. are *Chicanos.* Jacob Duran is "American, that's what I am, (the) American Spanish race" (Jacob Duran, 2023).

Baseball

The year after *La Colonia* was established in 1924, the residents of the Colony started a baseball team. The "Spanish Colony of Greeley team" began playing other teams in other towns nearby (Brooks, 2013; Gonzalez, 2016a). The players "gathered a ball made of socks and rubber, gloves made of rags, splintered bats held together by nails, and bases made of dirt-filled gunnysacks" to play (Greeley Grays Baseball, n.d.). In 1938, the team changed its name to the Greeley Grays.

In interviews with Channel 9 news, many Greeley residents spoke of the importance of the Greeley Grays to the community. One resident said that he fell in love with the Grays in the 1940s, noting that there were many *Latino* teams in the area (Garcia, 2018).

In 1938, the Grays were an integrated team, with Blacks, *Latinos,* and Whites playing together. This was nearly nine *years* before Jackie Robinson broke the racial barrier in the major leagues!

From my perspective, that's what the Grays were all about (A. Garcia, 2018).

The 1937 Spanish Colony team that was renamed the Greeley Grays in 1938. It became competitive in the 1940s—and the team to beat in the 1950s and 1960s.
Back row, left to right: Alvin Garcia (Abraham Garcia's father and Gabriel Lopez's uncle), Lalo "Pancho" Villa, Fred Salazar, Mario Lopez, Dave Lopez, Unknown, Augustine "Gus" Lopez (Gabriel Lopez's father), Frank Lopez (many of the Lopezes are Gabriel Lopez's uncles).
Front row, left to right: Unknown, Unknown, George Villa, Jess Gonzales.
Photo courtesy of Robert Duran/Gabriel and Jody Lopez Collections and from Gabriel and Jody Lopez's book *From Sugar to Diamonds: Spanish/Mexican Baseball 1925-1969: Stories of the Greeley Grays and the Teams That Dared to Challenge Them.*

Baseball games back then became community events, with many families eagerly spending their Sunday afternoons at the ballpark (Albaladejo, 2024). Lopez and Lopez (2009) wrote a great deal about the Sunday afternoon games that became so important to the Spanish Colony community. They shared that everyone in *La Colonia* would attend the games, bring picnics, honk their car horns when the team made a home run or a good play, and that young children would chase foul balls. The entire community gave money to build the ball field. In 1942, the team joined the Rocky Mountain League, which also had teams from several towns throughout Northern Colorado (Ault, Laramie, Fort Collins, Loveland, and Cheyenne). The team is still known today as the Greeley Grays. They have several young men's and women's teams and play other local teams.

The role of baseball in the *Latino* community should not be underestimated. The game itself is a quintessentially American game invented and played in the U.S. Yet, *Latinos* in Northern Colorado created their own teams, leagues, and spaces where they could move between their own culture and American culture. Furthermore, players could use baseball to fight against the discrimination they felt in the community.

> *When the Greeley Grays defeated White teams, they not only won on the field but also challenged the notion of racial inferiority, all while adapting to American culture (Flórez, 2024).*

An interview with community leader and author Gabriel A. Lopez appeared on Channel 9 News in 2016. He discussed the importance of baseball in the *Latino* community back then (Gonzalez, 2016b). He also said the following in his interview:

> *All those little* colonias *that were around there would play. But when the families and the* colonias *get together, they would surround the ballpark with cars, and then, once they parked, the trunks would open up. Talk about aroma! You had every piece of food in there, and the kids would go catch foul balls, collect the foul balls. If you wanted to go visit someone from Brighton, you'd go over there and sit and eat and visit. At the end of the game, the players would meet together and eat, which brought the communities together (G. A. Lopez, 2023).*

Some of the information shared here about the Greeley Grays comes from a book Gabriel and Jody Lopez wrote about baseball in the Greeley area. It is called *From Sugar to Diamonds: Spanish/Mexican Baseball 1925–1969: Stories of the Greeley Grays and the Teams that Dared to Challenge Them.*

Abraham Garcia also shared his fond memories of growing up around baseball.

> *But I guess what I liked the most was coming to Greeley and watching my dad play for the Greeley Grays. We packed up the car, and the three kids would sit in the seat, and I would sit in the back window ... talk about*

safety! Huh? We'd drive to Greeley on Friday night and stay until Sunday evening and then go back. Dad had to work the next day. We'd stay with my grandmother, who lived here (the Spanish Colony) until she died in 1995. … but mostly all through summer, starting from April and ending in September (A. Garcia, 2023).

The Smithsonian Institution has recognized the important baseball history of Greeley. They worked with the National Museum of American History to build a traveling exhibit entitled *¡Pleibol! In the Barrios and the Big Leagues/ En los Barrios y Las Grandes Ligas.* This bilingual exhibit traveled the U.S., including Greeley, in 2024. It highlighted "how the game can bring people together regardless of race, class, or gender" while at the same time showing

Greeley Grays 1955

Back Row L To R: Richard Villa, Nudy Lopez, Dave Lopez, Jesse Gonzales, Marion Gonzales, and Manager Alvin Garcia. Front Row L to R: Gus Lopez, Dave Madrid, Dave Martinez, George Villa, Mario Lopez.

Photo courtesy of the Greeley Tribune September 1, 1955, the Gabriel and Jody Collections, and from Gabriel and Jody Lopez's book "From Sugar to Diamonds: Spanish/Mexican Baseball 1925-1969: Stories of the Greeley Grays and the Teams That Dared to Challenge Them."

"how baseball has provided an important platform from which to celebrate and challenge what it means to be American" (Smithsonian Institution, 2021; see also SISP, n.d.).

The exhibit included objects, interviews with the players, and a detailed study of the importance of baseball to the Latino community. One such object is a sugar beet knife, similar to a machete, donated by Gabriel and Jody Lopez (NMAH, n.d. a); (See photo on Page 2.) In addition to objects from Greeley, objects from other Latino teams appear in the collection, including a jersey from the Kansas City Aztecas baseball team (NMAH, n.d. b). These and many more items are in the permanent Smithsonian Collection. In addition, the Greeley Grays were inducted into the National Baseball Hall of Fame archives in Cooperstown, New York, on June 30, 2013 (Front Range League, n.d.). They will celebrate their one hundredth anniversary in 2025.

Holidays and Festivals

Holidays and festivals were widely celebrated in *La Colonia*. In 1929, newspapers wrote about the community renting the Greeley Amusement Park to celebrate their annual festival and Mexican Independence Day. The celebration included firecrackers and a four-block-long parade of over fifty cars (Greeley Daily Tribune, 1929). This Mexican Independence Day celebration continues today. In 2024, the celebration closed Greeley's Friday Fest Concert Series and was even promoted by Greeley's local Irish Pub (Patricks, 2024).

Many other holidays and celebrations are celebrated in the Greeley area. Despite *Cinco de Mayo* (May fifth) not being widely celebrated in Mexico, Greeley celebrates the holiday with a "family-friendly and community-focused event" featuring a variety of activities. These activities include an "array of vendors and food trucks selling unique goods, a car show, live musical and dance performances" (Downtown Greeley, n.d.). Several local organizations hold *Día de los Muertos* (Day of the Dead) celebrations throughout Greeley in October and November. These include *ofrendas* (altars) viewing, arts, face painting, food, music, and dancing (Greeley Creative District, n.d.). Many places are now available for *quinceañeras* (a celebration when a girl turns fifteen), and dress shops have grown over the past decades to serve the *Latino* community.

Fiestas

When asked what holidays, *fiestas* (parties or celebrations), and traditions they celebrated, Gama, remembered the following as if it were yesterday.

> *When I was a little girl, my aunt and uncle were getting married, and so my parents threw them a party in the backyard. They got a sheep and a goat and slaughtered them in the garage. My father didn't want us to watch, so we didn't watch, which I'm glad! And then they just all celebrated and had a great celebration in the backyard while roasting those animals. There was Mexican music and mariachi music. It was an interesting memory. We have many traditions. We have Easter, birthdays, Christmas, Lent. Lent is big for us (Gama, 2023).*

The topic that surfaced many times about how the holidays were celebrated was that they were a "hybrid" of American and Mexican cultures. Adriana Trujillo explained:

> *Thanksgiving. We've adopted a lot of Euro-American traditions, of course. I think when I was thinking about that question, it brought this urge to learn more about our ancestral, traditional culture and celebrations. I want to start celebrating* Día de los Muertos. *We didn't grow up celebrating that, and that's part of our culture. And so, in learning about decolonization and our indigenous history, I want to be closer to our culture through other traditions and other celebrations (Adriana Trujillo, 2023).*

Ana Trujillo continued:

> *And even though, like I was telling Adriana, obviously we didn't celebrate Thanksgiving in Mexico because we don't do that, when we came here, we incorporated Thanksgiving. It turned into one of our celebrations. We*

would still make tamales *for Thanksgiving. And slowly we lost that, and now it's just turkey and ham (Ana Trujillo, 2023).*

Bustillos shared a delightful story about when her father celebrated Easter with an egg hunt in his old Mexican village.

We were raised rather poor, but my dad always made it a point to make every holiday special. And when he first came out of the Bracero *Program, he learned about the Easter bunny and the Easter egg hunts. And he just thought that was just so cool because that's not a Mexican tradition. The Easter Bunny is a very American tradition.*

As he learned about it, he thought, "Okay, I'm going to share this with my village."

The following year when he returned to his village, he did an Easter egg hunt in the cornfields, and he invited the entire village's children to attend. And to this day, I will have people tell me that is their best child-hood memory! And that was just an example about my dad.

He just loved to learn things and share with others and make them feel special and enjoy every holiday! That picture of where all my cousins are, that's the day of Easter. My dad also taught us to be very proud of our culture. But he also taught us to appreciate this country and all the opportunities it would give us. He really wanted us to participate in both holidays, the traditional Mexican holidays but also the American ones (Bustillos, 2023).

Treviño declared:

Oh, we (Treviños's family) celebrate Cinco de Mayo. *We celebrate all the holidays. Our holidays, though, are a mixture of White and* Latino. *For Thanksgiving, we may have a turkey, but we also have our green chile, our* tamales, *our rice, our beans. And just like I said, the turkey will be the only thing that we have that is traditional American. Everything else is a layout, and it is a good spread (Treviño, 2023).*

Just like the combination of celebrating American and Mexican holidays, so it is the same with foods at the holidays. Perez shared one of those family stories.

> *We traditionally celebrate American culture, and I enjoy the* Latino *culture as well. We celebrate Fourth of July, Christmas,* Cinco de Mayo, *and the sixteenth of September. I like listening to and playing* Latino *music. With a flavor or a blending of* Latino *and American cultures. I love my Mexican food,* tamales *for Christmas.* Enchiladas, tacos, frijoles *(pinto beans), and* papas *(fried potatoes). We celebrate birthdays and showers, anything to do with the family. We celebrate, we make* tamales, *and I make* buñuelos *(fried cinnamon and sugar tortillas) and all that (Perez, 2023).*

Oral Traditions

As evidenced in the historians' memories about their childhood, the *Latino* oral tradition of passing stories down from generation to generation was noted. Vega Ruiz shared one of those family stories.

> *But in a very close-knit community, my family from my mom's side, her family was known as* los buzos, *like the divers, right? The reason that came about, apparently my grandpa really loved to go snorkeling, but really, it was just swimming in the river and the lakes that were nearby! And he also really enjoyed smoking cigarettes, and they would say that he was smoking cigarettes underneath the water! Something that is something that gets told when the joke comes out, when their family gatherings are on my mom's side of the family being called, you know,* los buzos *or the divers! (Vega Ruiz, 2023).*

The story of money on the floor of the U.S. was alive and well in Sanchez's family.

The story that my father would always share with us or a saying was that in the U.S., "The money's on the floor! All you have to do is pick it up!"

In other words, "Pick it up; it's there! It's for you to, you have to earn it, but it is there, and it's easy to do."

My father, being from Mexico, valued the hard work of having a job in the U.S. (Sanchez, 2023).

A memory from Wendirad repeated the value of a strong work ethic, getting an education, and storytelling.

My grandparents' house had a courtyard. You would be in the center, and that's where all the trees and flowers were. And we would sit there with my grandpa, and he would share stories. And one that always sticks in my mind is that his father died when he was about ten years old. So when my grandpa was only in the fourth grade, he had to quit his school to work for a rich farmer to help raise the family.

He always instilled in us the work ethic, but he (also) said, "I did not have the opportunity to study. I want you to study."

That is a childhood memory that always sticks with me. You know, you're sitting together after dinner and talking about different stories (Wendirad, 2023).

Language

Language is a very important part of culture because we use language to think and communicate our thoughts, feelings, and love. Language is how we transmit our culture from one generation to the next.

One of the interview questions was about which language was spoken when growing up. Nineteen historians grew up speaking Spanish, seventeen grew up speaking English, and eight grew up bilingually speaking both English and Spanish.

It was interesting that this point was brought up with many who spoke only English or mostly English growing up.

I'm sad to say that the Spanish language in my family actually ends with my generation. When I was younger, it just really wasn't talked about. My grandparents spoke it, my mom spoke it, but they almost used it as a time to talk about adult things without us kids knowing what they were talking about.

My mom also comes from that generation where kids were punished in school. There were lots of things that happened in their lifetime that really made it seem as if passing on the Spanish language wasn't a good thing, which I'm really sad because my daughter really wishes that she spoke Spanish (R. Solis, 2023).

Martinez Rocha, who is twenty years older than Rhonda Solis, had the same experience with English.

We spoke mostly English. We spoke very little Spanish because my parents were part of that generation that got punished for speaking Spanish in school. They didn't want us to endure those same punishments and those same biases. They spoke mostly English to us, but then they spoke Spanish to each other and to everybody else. But we kind of understood; we had a little bit of a foundation in it, we could understand. We didn't speak very much. We knew just a few words, like simple commands and statements, but not fluent, not any fluency (Martinez Rocha, 2023).

Like Rhonda Solis and Martinez Rocha, Ben (Mitch) Gonzales shared:

Spanish was the language that was spoken about us, not spoken to us. Back then, it wasn't good if you were a Spanish speaker because they treated you quite a bit different (B. M. Gonzales, 2023).

Gabriel A. Lopez grew up speaking English.

English. Dad would not let us speak Spanish. Which I wish at this point in time (that) we did, but we didn't. We learned a few words, not the kind words or the good words because that's what they would use when they were scolding us! But we learned a few words. And the difference between my dad and my mom was my dad was from New Mexico and had the New Mexico dialect. My mom was from San Luis Valley, Conejos area, and she had the slang version of it. The family had to learn both languages in order to understand what they were screaming at us when we were getting in trouble! Usually, it was the broom though. That was pretty bilingual; you got smacked the same way! We didn't have the chancla (sandal); we had a broom!

Because my mom was small, she would chase us. She knew she wasn't gonna hurt us, so she'd grab the broom. But usually, it was my dog that created the problem, and then he'd take off and hide underneath the full-size bed. Mom couldn't reach him, so then she'd turn around and smack me instead of the dog! And Whitey would come out and look at me and wag his tail. And how are you going to get mad at that? Huh? (G. Lopez, 2023).

To end this chapter, Hernandez eloquently shared her family's experience with the land and a chile pepper. Her words show parts of the deep culture of collectivism and the incredible work ethic of *Latinos*, who worked the land to make a living in a society that often saw them as less than equal, an attitude that many still hold today. She reminds us that *Latinos* have been brilliantly and defiantly resilient in the face of a long history of racism and oppression. Thus, both the deep and surface culture have helped *Latinos* in their ability to survive and thrive in an often hostile White-dominated environment that saw them only as dirty field workers who were "allowed" to live on the outskirts of their town.

My great-grandfather, my mom's grandfather, brought the mirasol *chile seed with him when he came to the Greeley area. When they followed the railroad and came to work the fields, he must have already had a relationship with the land and the chile and had been growing it. The* mirasol *chile pepper and the seeds, which ended up becoming the* Pueblo *chile pepper! And so, many of our community migrated, bringing with them things from New Mexico. He brought seeds here to Pierce and grew it. And then Grandpa grew it. And to us, to me, that has continued to be a symbol of our resilience.*

"Mirasol" *means to look up to the sun ... to look toward the light and to look toward the sun when we need to do that. And so, it's become this symbol for us. The chile peppers also could be red chile or green chile, depending on how long you let them grow. And so then, it's this symbol of being able to adapt. I would see my great-grandfather coming up from New Mexico, bringing the seed with him and continuing to grow it. And now we continue to grow it from that same seed. And so it's just this story of resilience, adaptation, and culture to us (Hernandez, 2023).*

NARRATIVES FOR CHAPTER 2

Patricia Garcia-Nelson

"We have like a small community, and it's a very strong community, but as far as representation, at different levels of government, I don't feel like we are reflected in that yet." —Patrica Garcia-Nelson

Patricia Garcia-Nelson's parents lived near her grandparents' home off 9th Avenue. This picture was taken in the late 1980s.
Photo courtesy of Patricia Garcia-Nelson Collection.

Patricia Garcia-Nelson, a Greeley native, comes from a lineage of strong, influential women. Her grandmother, Agustina, born in 1906 in Mexico, was a memorable figure. Even at an older age, she'd walk around smoking cigarettes with a machete on her hip. Nobody ever messed with her! Garcia-Nelson's devout Catholic mother taught her children acceptance and to help others without expecting anything in return. The importance of family and the preservation of their culture were important ideals.

We weren't allowed to speak English at home. We didn't even watch American TV. And at the time, all of the kids, we were really grumbling about it, but now, as an adult, I appreciate that because I'm a very strong Spanish speaker, and I really do have strong ties to my culture as well.

Garcia-Nelson, who learned about Mexican Americans and the *Chicano* Movement in school, is grateful to the Hispanic Women of Weld County for hosting community events, bringing inspirational people to speak, and being role models.

It was crazy to see this person (Dolores Huerta, an American farm labor leader and civil rights activist) that I admire so much, sitting two seats down from me. That was a really special moment for me. And now, being part of the organization myself, I just hope that we're able to impact young women in our community like I was impacted.

Active in community service, Garcia-Nelson became a board member of the Hispanic Women of Weld County, president of the Young Democrats of Weld County, treasurer of the Democratic County Party, and a volunteer coordinator for the Guadalupe Shelter. She currently works as a policy advocate for Green *Latinos*, an advocacy group that works to uplift *Latino* voices and *Latino* priorities when it comes to climate change and environmental justice.

Garcia-Nelson felt that historically, downtown property owners and businesses have primarily catered to an older White demographic, but with the next generation of *Latinos* assuming leadership roles and starting businesses, she sensed a shift coming.

I feel like the tide is changing, and I really hope that downtown will be a hub for everybody. We saw last year, the first time we celebrated Mexican Independence Day for Friday Fest, and you know, the streets were full of people.

Garcia-Nelson hopes Mexican Independence Day in downtown Greeley becomes an annual tradition.

—BETH BULLARD

Dr. Andrés Gonzalez Guerrero, Jr.

I was told this by a professor. "Well, Andrés, if we educate all the Mexicans, who's going to do the work?"

My response was, "Hell, we can all do the work, but we've got to get educated primero (first), so we can have a choice of what we want to do." —*González Guerrero, Jr.*

When Dr. Andrés González Guerrero, Jr. began his educational journey, he hoped to become a Catholic priest, earning two theology degrees from Harvard University. During his studies, a professor named Father Sullivan asked him, "What do you think?" encouraging Gonzales Guerrero to offer his cultural viewpoint as a Mexican man.

The question bewildered him because:

The way we were brought up, we were not supposed to think; we were just supposed to do.

That influential moment shaped his perspective and informed his path.

Gonzales Guerrero spent seven years

Family of Andrés Gonzales Guerrero Jr., Th.D. (1984).
Back row: Andrés Gonzales Guerrero Jr., Th.D., Andrés H. Guerrero III.
Middle row: Juanita Hernandez de Guerrero (wife), Miguel H. Guerrero.
Front row: Raquel H. Guerrero and Gabriel H. Guerrero.
Photo courtesy of Andrés Gonzales Guerrero Jr. Collection.

in the seminary, but despite his achievements, persistent questions remained, leaving him disillusioned. He was working in a rectory as a gardener when Dr. Alfonso Rodriguez, the chair of Hispanic Studies at the University of Northern Colorado, offered him a teaching position.

Well, that's my living, that's what I do. That's my life. The community's my life. I love them.

Education, ministry, and leadership development became his mission. Gonzales Guerrero taught Hispanic studies at UNC and English and citizenship classes at Aims Community College.

That's one of my key things, I want every Chicano to get a Ph.D. in whatever area they want to. My thing is that the potential is there but not the support. Universities and schools are not supporting our students. They don't encourage them, motivate them. They fail their spirits.

Gonzales Guerrero, a pioneer and champion of bilingual education, feels that representation and education are closely related.

I don't think it's represented at all. We're an invisible people here, people in captivity. If you don't change the educational system, you're not going to change anything. Everybody wants to be monolingual, monocultural, and mono-thinking. We are bicultural and bilingual. We need that reflected, not only in the institution of education but also in the church.

He feels churches focus on Anglo-Saxon thinking and assimilation.

I think the concept of love is not understood if we don't understand culture and we don't understand our history. We don't even understand the that key to love is this: you have to love yourself first. You have to love others like God loves you, and with God, there are no exceptions. He loves you unconditionally. That's the way we have to love: unconditionally.

He hopes that'll create more room for freedom and justice in our community.

—BETH BULLARD

Gabriel A. and Jody L. Lopez

I love the history of the Spanish Colony and the Greeley Grays;
it's just an amazing history. —Gabriel A. Lopez

This narrative revolves around a two-time author whose profound passion for baseball was influenced by the love and support of family and friends. Gabriel's admiration for the sport is rooted in his childhood, when his father's love for baseball inspired him. His father, Augustine (Gus), played for the Greeley Grays for twenty-five years, a team that initially bore the name the "Spanish Colony of Greeley" from 1925 to 1938. Following the name change to the Greeley Grays, Gabriel's father contributed to the team until 1959.

Gabriel's paternal grandparents established themselves in Hurley, New Mexico. In 1919, the GWSC contracted them to join the sugar beet industry, leading them to Greeley, Colorado, where they found their home in the Spanish Colony. Gabriel's father, Gus, served in World War II from 1941 to 1945 and returned to the Spanish Colony upon his discharge in 1945. In 1948, the family relocated to Cheyenne, Wyoming, where his father secured a position with Union Pacific. Following his father's retirement in 1982, the family returned to Greeley, Colorado.

My father instilled in me a strong work ethic and a passion for baseball,
making him one of the most influential figures in my life.

Gabriel fondly recalls his childhood summers driving from Cheyenne, Wyoming, to Greeley, Colorado, to support his father during games with the Greeley Grays. His parents sat in the front seat while his three siblings were in the back seat, and Gabriel would lie down in the back window during the drive.

In 1995, Lopez was injured in a gas explosion at work, which led him to explore the history of the Greeley Grays and the Spanish Colony. Inspired, he and his wife, Jody, authored two books chronicling the narratives of the Greeley Grays and the Spanish Colony. The stories featured in the publication re-

80

Gabriel and Jody at their 50th Wedding anniversary.
Photo from the Gabriel and Jody Lopez Collection.

flect the experiences of individuals from the Spanish Colony, particularly those from earlier generations. Lopez remarked that he and Jody serve merely as spokespersons for the stories of the families in their books, sharing their heritage and life experiences. The books inspired their first museum exhibit: the Greeley Grays's Story of Rocky Mountain League's baseball history. It began their

traveling exhibit in 2006. In 2012, their research material on the Spanish Colony baseball team (the Greeley Grays) was inducted into the National Baseball Hall of Fame archives at Cooperstown, New York. The Greeley Grays are also celebrated in an exhibit at the Smithsonian's National Museum of American History in Washington, D.C.

Five-year-old Gabriel Lopez in his baseball cap, watches his father play baseball with the Greeley Grays at Island Grove Park. His Uncle Alvin Garcia stands behind him. Photo from the Gabriel and Jody Lopez Collections.

Gabriel and Jody Lopez reside in Greeley, Colorado, and their two books are titled: *White Gold Labors: The Story of Greeley's Spanish Colony* and *From Sugar to Diamonds: Spanish Mexican Baseball 1925–1969: Stories of the Greeley Grays and the Teams That Dared to Challenge Them.*

—DR. MARIA SANCHEZ

Yolanda Mendoza

This is a country of immigrants, and we all have something to share from our own experience. It helps others.—Mendoza

Mendoza's grandparents. On the left is Aurora Gonzales, known as Mamá Bora, and on the right is Honorio Arroyo, called Papá Noyo (1980s). Photo courtesy of the Mendoza Collection.

Yolanda Mendoza was born in Tendeparacua, Michoacan, Mexico.

For the first thirteen years of my life, my siblings and my mom lived in Mexico. My dad (who was working in the U.S.) would send money and visit one week each year.

In time, her family moved to Platteville, Colorado, and in 2006, Mendoza relocated to Greeley to attend the University of Northern Colorado. Her Grandmother Aurora was an influential figure in her life.

My daughter's name is Aurora, and that's in her honor because she had thirteen kids, and she never gave up. She was always looking forward, had a positive outlook, even though she had her challenges.

Her parents and grandparents taught their children the importance of faith, family, integrity, education, and honor. When her mother was about to marry, her father said to her, "*Vas a mandar, no a que te manden* (you are going to command, not be commanded)." That meaningful statement was a pivotal moment for her mother and an influential story that molded Mendoza's life.

As a teen, Mendoza developed an interest in law enforcement and crime investigation and followed that path after high school. She earned an associate's degree in criminal justice from Aims Community College and a bachelor's degree from UNC. She went to work in the public defender's office, where she is currently a lead investigator.

I feel like I fit right in because I share a lot of the same values that the office has.

While bilingual, Mendoza's primary language is Spanish, and she refers to herself as *Mestiza*, a person of mixed blood.

For me, that my children speak Spanish is important. At home, we speak Spanish to them.

Her children attend *Salida Del Sol* Academy, the only school-wide dual language and AVID education program in Weld County. Mendoza was on the founding Board of *Salida del Sol* Academy. She is a Hispanic Women of Weld County board member and volunteers at the Community Grief Center.

I would really love for our kids to have a better understanding of our history because this is what's going to send us forward to have a better policing system, better rules, more representation in government, making those decisions that really impact our communities as a whole and bring us together.

—BETH BULLARD

Teresa Rodriguez-McNeill

We're all the same. We all bleed the same. We all cry the same. We all want the same things, and we strive to be better. —Rodriguez-McNeill

The Rodriguez children in farmland in Eaton, CO.
Left to right: San Juana Rodriguez, Juan Rodriguez, Santiago Rodriguez, and Rosa Rodriguez.
Photo courtesy of the Teresa Rodriguez-McNeill Collection.

At the age of ten, Teresa Rodriguez-McNeill went to work in the fields of Natalia, Texas. She joined her father and siblings after school and on weekends. At home, the girls in her family had chores such as cooking and cleaning while the boys sat at the table and were served.

We didn't feel discriminated against because that was how we were raised. It was accepted.

In 1956, the family joined the *Bracero* program, traveling in trucks to Colorado. Rodriguez-McNeill, fourteen at the time, worked alongside her parents and older siblings despite not being old enough. She would hide in the ditches when the supervisor came by so he wouldn't send her home.

She entered school not knowing English. Her teachers would hit her on the back of her hand or palm when she spoke Spanish. Rodriguez-McNeill was rebellious and proud of her language.

My dad didn't speak English; my mom didn't know very much English. My whole family didn't know English, so we spoke it anyway.

Her parents taught them to respect their elders. Each time they left or returned home, they were expected to kiss each parent on the forehead and hands. Family celebrations were centered around religious holidays. On Easter, they would perform the Stations of the Cross, have an egg hunt and meal. At Christmas, the *Posadas* (a nine-day celebration of the Christmas story) was held. Rodriguez-McNeill fondly remembers performing during the September 16 Mexican Independence Day celebrations.

Rodriguez-McNeill credits her knowledge of Mexican culture to her aunt, Teresa Ramirez.

We were brought up with a lot of joy and with a lot of music.

Her aunt played the guitar and loved dancing, and she instilled in Rodriguez-McNeill a love of dance that she has shared with countless students over the years.

(In 1992) *I went to Mexico to find out where I came from, where I was raised. Because we were not White; we were not Black. "What were we?"*
I always had that in my mind. What?
"What am I, and why don't they like us?"

During her time in Mexico, Rodriguez-McNeill studied Indigenous medicine and spirituality, embracing her Native American heritage. She runs sweat lodges, performs healings, and teaches others about Native American ways. Rodriguez-McNeill hopes for greater unity in Greeley.

We all have the same needs, but we come from different cultures, and I think whoever runs the city needs to acknowledge that.

—BETH BULLARD

Tomasa (Cynthia) Duran Silva

Oh, I have so many people that have influenced my life, but I think most of all, number one, my grandparents, my Grandpa Mucio, taught me my faith. —Duran Silva

Tomasa (Cynthia) Duran Silva's grandmother, Dominga Zavala, Johnny Duran (brother) and Tomasa (Cynthia) taken at her parents' fiftieth Anniversary in 1978.
Photo from the Tomasa Silva Collection.

In the late 1940s, Tomasa (Cynthia) Duran Silva's family left their small town in Texas every summer to work in the fields. Her father, a foreman in the *Braceros* Program, coordinated caravans of immigrant farm laborers. He counted the sacks of produce, provided food and water to his laborers, and handed out pay each week. He also took them to the movies and the grocery store. Whatever they needed, he took care of it.

Duran Silva recalls feeling jealous of her father's dedication.

He was like a shepherd caring for the workers. He spent more time with them than us.

Culture, faith, and tradition grounded her family. Good manners, respect for elders, saying the rosary, and attending church were expected. Easters were spent at the town park, and her father made sure they had new clothes for Christmas mass.

In the evenings after work, her aunt and uncle told Mexican folklore stories. A favorite was *La Llorona* (the weeping woman). *La Llorona* is said to roam near bodies of water, mourning her children, whom she drowned in a jealous rage after discovering her husband was unfaithful. The story is meant to warn children not to stray far from home, encouraging them to stay in at night and away from water, for if they did not, *La Llorona* may come for them!

Traveling in the caravan was fun, but as Duran Silva got older, her desire to be in school became more important. Her mother didn't value education and needed help with her siblings, so after missing a placement test, Duran Silva reluctantly dropped out of school. Despite that decision, she prayed daily for the opportunity to return to school, and the sisters of Mount St. Benedict Convent answered her prayers.

Duran Silva spent twelve years at the convent, strengthening her faith and completing her education. The nuns changed her first name to Cynthia. She became fluent in English, graduated from high school and junior college, and earned a degree in social work. She earned many certifications and spent her career educating children and strengthening *Latino* families through the Parent Leadership Group Program and the Colorado Immigrant Rights Coalition.

My higher power gave me the education I always wanted. God has blessed me.

Duran Silva believes Mexican Americans are talented, kind, and loving people who are undervalued by their communities. She encourages leaders to pay attention, interact, and learn from everyone.

All lives matter. Together, we can do a lot.

—BETH BULLARD

Jessie Theresa Solis

I saw that the farm workers feed the world, and I thought, "Gee, they're mistreated." —Solis

Jessie Theresa Solis, born in Greeley in 1949, grew up in the Spanish Colony. Her parents had moved to Greeley via the *Bracero* Program, and the GWSC wanted year-round workers, so they offered her parents the opportunity to build a home in a small, segregated neighborhood outside of town.

We lived way on the north side of Greeley on D Street, and we lived in a house called el chante *(the shanty). It was just like a two-room little cabin type thing, but it didn't have running water or electricity, so everything that we had to do—it took a lot of work.*

Solis recalls spending afternoons with her grandmother, teaching her English and helping her study for the citizenship test. Her grandmother was a skilled herbalist.

Theresa Solis at Cesar Chavez Day – Theme of the Celebration: "Social Justice – Our Responsibility." Photo courtesy of Teresa Solis.

They had one of the biggest herbal gardens here in Greeley, and she would use a lot of the herbs for remedies and for healing. If we had any kind of problem or if we didn't feel well, she always knew what type of herb to give us.

Solis's family valued religion and service to others. Her mother lit candles on their altar for Our Lady of Guadalupe, her father's patron saint. They helped build Our Lady of Peace Church—a grassroots endeavor due to the prejudice they faced while attending mass in town.

When I started working at the university, I always doubted myself. It was difficult at times, and I felt like I was balancing two cultures 'cause I had to be one way at work, and then I'd go home, and I could be myself.

A coworker introduced Solis to *Al Frente de Lucha*, an anti-colonial organization dedicated to the struggle for the self-determination and liberation of all oppressed people.

It was then that I had an opportunity to learn that it's okay to question authority. It's okay to express yourself.

She learned about the grape boycotts, Cesar Chavez, and the United Farm Workers. Solis joined the Women's International League for Peace and Freedom, where she advocated for voting rights, fought against discrimination, and supported farm worker rights.

She also worked with attorney Kimmy Jackson, supporting farm workers living in harsh conditions and not being paid correctly. Despite the threat of being shot by the farmer, they visited the workers at night, finding them without electricity, water, food, or proper shelter. They organized a protest with media coverage that exposed the injustices.

—BETH BULLARD

CHAPTER 3
Education

The schooling of Mexican children in Greeley in the 1920s and 1930s was directly tied to the GWSC, whose managers and growers frequently sat on local school boards (Donato, 2007). Mexican children often missed school to work in the fields. "Educators knew that cheap labor in general, and child labor in particular, was central to the economic prosperity of sugar beet towns" (Donato, 2003).

According to Donato (2008), "Circumventing compulsory school laws was part of local culture, an accepted practice, and how things were generally done in these towns" (p. 66). Adding to this abuse of cheap child labor was the sense of community in Mexican families. This meant that the needs of the family were more important than the needs of the individual (Chávez, 2007). Lopez et. al., (2007) write that "parents relied on even very young children to meet the financial needs of the family" (p. 138). GWSC abused this sense of community, leading to children as young as six years old working eight to ten hours a day in the beet fields (p. iii). The parents also had little opportunity for schooling, and many could not read or write (Maddux, 1932).

Because of this lack of schooling, many schools began summer school programs. These summer schools tried to improve the problem of children missing school during the beet harvest. By the late 1920s, up to 134 schools in Colorado offered summer classes for Mexican children. However, there were still problems, especially the lack of language help. Most teachers were not well-trained to teach English, and schools were more focused on making Mexican children and adults adopt the White culture (Maddux, 1932).

The Gipson School in Greeley

In Colorado during this time, Mexican children faced differing educational experiences. Some went to schools with White children; these were called *integrated* schools. However, others went to separate schools for Mexican children only; these were called *segregated* schools. In Greeley, the school district created the segregated Gipson Mexican School near *La Colonia* (Donato, 2003, p. 79). The Gipson School started in 1924 in an abandoned building and was a one-room school.

1949 image of Gipson School.
Photo courtesy of the Gabriel and Jody Lopez Collection.

The school was later separated into two rooms for different levels, from one through eighth grade. This was done to keep the Mexican children at Gipson rather than integrate Greeley's other schools (Donato, 2007). Lopez et. al., (2007) write that Greeley "did not want the Hispanic children in the Spanish Colony interacting with the Anglo children" (p. 141). The Gipson School focused on vocational education, handiwork, hygiene, and civics. Lessons were taught in English (Chávez, 2007; Lopez et al., 2007; Maddux, 1932; Ruiz, 2001). This was the same in segregated schools for Mexican children throughout the Southwest. Ruiz (2001) added, "Many teachers and administrators believed that their students possessed few aspirations and fewer abilities beyond farm and domestic work" (p. 24).

Originally built two miles from La Colonia, in 1933, the community convinced the school district to move the building within two blocks of the Colony (Cache la Poudre, 2024). This allowed more children to go to school (*Greeley Daily Tribune*, 1934). However, although the school was moved closer, it still did not have many resources. Gipson did not receive electricity until 1947 and *never* received running water (Lopez et al., 2007). The school closed in 1949 because of low enrollment, and students were bused to Lincoln Elementary. There is little data to pinpoint how many students graduated from Gipson because the emphasis was not on graduation but sugar beets. Most students were taken out of school in October to harvest the sugar beets, and then in April, they were taken out of school to thin and hoe the beets. Out of nine months, these children only went to school for five to six months. After a while,

Gipson School classroom, 1949.
Photo courtesy of the Gabriel and Jody Lopez Collection.

the children just left school because it was difficult for them to finish a grade, and they were getting too old to stay in the same one. At the whim of the farmer and their parents, they had to work one-third of the school time, so they left because they would get so far behind. Many did not even learn how to read or write. All they learned was how to work and help their families survive.

Lopez et al., (2007) interviewed many adults who were bused to integrated schools as children. These adults said that they felt they had better opportunities to finish their education at these non-segregated schools rather than a segregated school like Gipson. The Gipson School building was demolished in 1963.

However, even the integrated schools had problems. One of our historians, Romero, experienced a different kind of segregation in the Brighton School District in the 1950s. Apparently, there were four tracks, A-D.

> *All of the Mexican kids went into the D (track) immediately, and then the C (track) was probably 90 to 95 percent Mexican also. And then, the B had a sprinkling of Mexicans, and the A had no Mexicans. I started out in the D. Then the second, well, I flunked the first grade. In the second grade, they put me into the C. In the third grade, they put me into the B. Then, in the fourth grade, the middle of the fourth grade, they put me into the A.*
>
> *I was the only* Latino. *They were all (Anglos), and they were kids of the wealthier people, the mayor and the doctors. I hated it because, you know, I was just not used to that. But I stayed there all the way through school (Romero, 2023).*

Segregation and Racist Attitudes Toward Students

The lack of school success for *Latina* and *Latino* students came, in part, from segregated schools in terrible conditions. There were also racist attitudes toward *Latinos* in general and their children in particular. Maddux (1932) writes in her master's degree thesis that the Mexican worker in Greeley "finds himself in a constant state of poverty. He is further unable to better his economic condition because of his strange ways, his inability to understand English, and his passive acceptance of his fate" (p. 11).

As we see, in 1932, authors such as Maddux were extremely racist and had many negative things to say about Mexicans and Mexican Americans of the area. She describes Mexican workers' homes as a "breeding place for filth and disease" (p. iii). Maddux further writes that the Anglo community stopped any type of integration of the Mexican children into Anglo schools. She added that the Anglo community thought that "efforts to educate the Mexican children are a waste of time and money. They resent Mexican childrens' association with their children and say they are dirty and repulsive" (p. 29).

Schools were also seen as a way to assimilate Mexicans and Mexican Americans into American culture. Some Anglos "felt that schools were a vital element of the 'Americanization' process for the 'wetback' or 'greaser,' and that Americanization 'would serve to promote and enhance the Anglos' way of life.' Thus, schools were seen as a necessary component in assimilating the young *Latino* student" (Chávez, 2007, p. 31; see also Donato, 2007).

Regardless of these beliefs, Mexican children were usually segregated again into schools away from White children. This was supposedly done because these children spoke a language other than English. "Mexican children were routinely prohibited from speaking Spanish in school, to 'Americanize' them, or they were segregated from White students based on language" (City of Fort Collins, n.d.). "Even on the playground, students were punished for speaking in Spanish" (Ruiz, 2001, p. 24).

Adult Programs

Classes for adults began in *La Colonia* in 1921, run by a womens' club in Greeley. They taught English and citizenship/naturalization classes to adults. These classes and schools were called The Americanization School. Classes were free and took place in the evening, three nights each week in the winter (Darling, 1932; Lopez et al., 2007). In 1927, the Greeley School Board of Education began paying for the school, hiring and paying teachers. The school became part of the

Greeley educational system. Darling (1932) writes that the "average attendance was about forty adult students who were very earnest and appreciative and attended despite distance and weather" (p. 88). Although the Greeley School Board of Education stopped funding the school in 1932, other groups helped, and classes continued at a teachers' home (Darling, 1932).

Other Public Schools

We will mainly use the terms *Latina* and *Latino* from here on. This term is used instead of Mexican and Mexican American because, after the 1920s and 1930s, more people from Central and South America came to the U.S. "*Latina*" and "*Latino*" encompass Mexicans, Mexican Americans, and Central and South Americans.

As more *Latinos* moved to Greeley, more and more of them moved out of *La Colonia* and into other neighborhoods in Greeley. Their children began going to Lincoln and Central Elementary Schools. These schools grew in *Latina* and *Latino* attendance to 50 percent and 25 percent each by 1945 (Donato, 2007). However, *Latina* and *Latino* students graduated at a much lower rate than White students. In 1935, *Latina* and *Latino* students made up one-half of one percent (.5 percent) of students graduating from high school, although they were more than 9 *percent* of the total student body. Still, by 1960, there was little improvement in the graduation rates. *Latina* and *Latino* students made up only 2.3 percent of students graduating from high school, although they were more than 11 percent of the total student body. Donato (2008) added:

> It was a great victory for Mexicans and Hispanos from sugar beet towns to attend high school, a greater accomplishment to graduate, and a marvel if they made it to college" (p. 86).

He adds that only one *Latina* attended the Teachers College at Greeley (later called UNC) in 1920 and only twenty-seven in 1960.

Theresa Solis remembers this segregation, although she attended an integrated school, Greeley Central High School, in the mid-1960s.

I can say that growing up, where you were in a segregated area of town and trying to go to school, you knew that the buses wouldn't cross to pick you up, as they would for other kids. That was really difficult because I had to walk all the way from almost past the Rodarte Center, all the way to Greeley Central every day (two miles each way). And plus some of the experiences that I had to encounter in school.

Some of the kids, they could get some kind of assistance. My mom did for us because there were nine of us. They would always make derogatory comments. When I would take a burrito for my lunch sometimes, they would tell me, "Oh, that's so unhealthy; you're eating that with your hands."

I wouldn't say anything. But then, what happened a few times? Some of the kids came up to me and asked me if I could trade their lunch for mine. They wanted my burritos!

I thought, "Wow, that is interesting!"

And then, when we would eat lunch, there was always: this side was Mexicans, that side was Whites (T. Solis, 2023).

Post-World War II Schooling

Right before and after World War II (WWII), which would be in the mid- to late 1940s, "a small but growing *Latina* and *Latino* dissension with the inequality and injustices so prevalent in schools began to emerge" (Chávez, 2007, p. 37; see also Donato, 2007). Mexican families, including many who served in the military in WWII, began advocating for better schooling for their children. They said it was unfair that *Latinos* fought for the U.S. but were then not given the same educational and job opportunities for which they had been fighting (Donato, 2007).

Desegregation Efforts

The League of United Latin American Citizens (LULAC) started in 1929 in Texas. This organization began to work to desegregate the public schools. LULAC filed and won lawsuits in California and Texas to desegregate the public schools. In the *Mendez v. Westminster* court case in 1946, *Latina* and *Latino* parents sued the Los Angeles schools to allow their children to attend the same schools as White students. *Latina* and *Latino* parents stood up for their children and won the case. Right after the Mendez case, the governor of California desegregated *all* public schools in California!

The *Mendez* case led to Brown v. the Board of Education, the landmark U.S. Supreme Court case that desegregated public schools in 1954 for all children (LULAC, 2024). It is important to note that the same lawyer, Thurgood Marshall, argued both the Mendez and the Brown cases. This shows important, strategic teamwork between *Latinos* and African Americans in the fight for equality in the schools. It is also important to note that the governor who desegregated California's schools was Earl Warren. He was later appointed to the U.S. Supreme Court and wrote the opinion for the Brown case. He wrote that "separate but equal is inherently unequal."

Long before these important court cases of Mendez and Brown were in the courts, in Colorado, Latina and Latino parents were suing the school district in Alamosa, Colorado. In the 1914 case, Maestas v. Shone, Mexican and Mexican American parents won the right for their children to attend the same schools as White children (Meltzer, 2020). Thus, *Latina* and *Latino* parents, as early as 1914, were fighting for their children to receive an integrated, quality education.

As schools became more and more desegregated, more and more *Latina* and *Latino* children attended these integrated schools. However, their academic progress remained behind White students. Gonzales Guerrero, Jr. noted that the state of Colorado was not properly educating *Latina* and *Latino* children until the *Chicano-Chicana* Movement of the 1960s and 1970s.

Toward the middle of the 1970s, González Guerrero, Jr. movingly explained, 85 percent of Mexican American students were being pushed out of schools. "Pushed out" means that the school environment was racist, not welcoming, and not supportive. Typically, *Latina* and *Latino* students had to give up their culture and "act White" to succeed. The curriculum was infested with negative stereotypes about *Latina* and *Latino* identity and culture. Because of this, many *Latina* and *Latino* students were ashamed of their identities and culture, as they could not fit the stereotypical model of being White, Anglo-Saxon, and Protestant. To add to this, both Catholic and Protestant private education used the same models for assimilation as the public schools.

> *It would be a miracle if you graduated. It was not until the 1980s that the graduation rate improved, but not by much because even today, many* Latino *students still must take remedial courses in reading, writing, and math when applying to college. Most are in limbo when it comes to pursuing a career. Many have no idea what their talents are or what they want to do (Gonzales Guerrero Jr., 2024).*

Fast forward to 2023, the high school graduation rate for *Latinos* in the Greeley-Evans School District was 82 percent compared to 88 percent for White students (CDE, 2024). Graduation rates "rose dramatically for multiple reasons, including new school strategies, improved economic conditions, and the fierce determination of families" (Robles, 2022).

Some progress was also being made in higher education, although *Latina* and *Latino* students' graduation rates were still behind White students. The University of Northern Colorado (UNC) was designated a Hispanic-serving institution. This designation supports *Latina* and *Latino* students with different resources, such as money and programs to help them succeed in college (University of Northern Colorado, 2024). Information from the Colorado Department of Higher Education (CDHE) showed a huge increase in enrollment and graduation rates for *Latina* and *Latino* students in four-year universities and colleges in Colorado over twenty years (CDHE, 2024). This increase was for both undergraduate and graduate students.

Enrollment and Graduation Rates
for *Latino* Students in Colorado

Dates, Population Percentage, and Increases	2001	2021	% increase
Latino enrollment – undergraduate	9,176	27,247	197%
Latino enrollment – graduate	1,162	3,304	184%
Latino graduation from 4-year universities - undergraduate	1,281	5,689	344%
Latino graduation from 4-year universities - graduate	268	1,205	350%
Latino graduation rates (graduation as a percent of enrollment)			
Undergraduate	14%	21%	
Graduate	23%	36%	
White graduation rates (graduation as a percent of enrollment)			
Undergraduate	18%	26%	
Graduate	39%	40%	

Source: Colorado Department of Higher Education Database Search tool (https://highered.colorado.gov/Data/Search.aspx)

The Educational Background of Our Historians

Our historians have high school diplomas and most have attained college degrees as well. Of course, many of those degrees shaped their careers throughout their lives. Most went through Greeley public schools, and some graduated from charter schools such as University High.

After marrying her high school sweetheart, Martinez Rocha moved to a small town in Wyoming. While there, Martinez Rocha became a widow and moved back to Greeley with her four children. As a single parent, she earned an associate of arts (A.A.) from Aims Community College in Greeley, a bachelor of arts (B.A.) in social science with an emphasis in English as a second language, and a master's degree in interdisciplinary education with an emphasis in culturally and linguistically diverse education, both from the University of Northern Colorado (UNC).

And after my husband passed, that's what I was doing. I came back and went into education. I think education is what I always wanted to do because our plan initially was for him to get educated, and then I would get educated. But when we moved, we were kind of in a rural area. But when he passed, I went and got my education because I thought it was really important. Like, my mom empowered us, I wanted to empower students. I wanted to work with a lower SES. Latina *and* Latino *population. And it just feels great that you touched the lives of students and made them feel better about who they are and where they come from. And the relationships that you make with your colleagues, the children, and your families are just priceless (Martinez Rocha, 2023).*

She remembered her K-16-plus schooling experience in the following ways.

In my early education, I had no idea about preferential treatment in the classroom. However, as I recall, boys were called on much more than girls. I attended schools with a majority percentage of Mexican American students. I did not experience racism in schools in Southern Colorado; sexism did exist. However, when I moved to Northern Colorado during high school, I was exposed to how Anglo students got preferential treatment in the classroom and extracurricular activities. When I was applying for scholarships, my counselor advised me that I should become a homemaker or take some secretarial courses.

Many years later, I attended higher education as a fairly young widow and a non-traditional student. The professors I had were quite supportive. I always gravitated toward those professors who saw my potential and wanted to help me succeed. In my college experience, I was fortunate to have professors and mentors who looked like me and were proud of our culture and heritage. I was excited they offered courses that helped me learn about our history. I was never taught anything about our existence until college. It's like we were erased from history; we didn't matter enough to mention (Martinez Rocha, 2024).

Nickie Archibeque holds both a B.A. in business administration and a master's degree in adult education and development from Regis University. Hernandez has a B.A. in ethnic studies and community leadership and a master's degree in curriculum and instruction. She also received a secondary teaching license from the University of Colorado at Boulder (CU).

Damion Córdova graduated with a Bachelor of Science (B.S.) in math and economics from West Point Military Academy in New York. He also earned his master's in business administration (M.B.A.) from CU Boulder. When Damion was interviewed, he gave information about his parents, Roberto and Betty. His father has since passed away, but it was important to include some of Roberto and Betty's experiences because they have had such a significant impact on the *Latina* and *Latino* community in Greeley.

When Damion grew up, Roberto and Betty always stressed the importance of education. Dr. Roberto Córdova was the first *Latino* to earn a Ph.D. in Spanish linguistics from the Hispanic Studies Department at CU Boulder. He then worked at UNC teaching Mexican American history, Spanish linguistics, and conversational Spanish for over twenty-five years. Betty earned her bachelor's in education at CU while her husband earned his Ph.D. She then earned her master's in psychology and counseling from UNC. Damion explained:

> *She wanted to break that cycle of* Latinos *not believing that they could achieve bigger and better and greater things, especially in the field of education. She was the first* Latina *guidance counselor at Greeley Central High School; she worked there for about thirty years (Córdova, 2023).*

A political science major at CSU, Baca earned a B.A. degree there. She also received an honorary doctor of humane letters from UNC and an honorary doctor of law from Wartburg College in Waverly, Iowa. She taught history and civics before entering politics.

Bacas' parents' dream was to send all three of their daughters to college. She remembered:

And so my father always said he would give us a quarter if we got Bs and fifty cents for an A (Baca, 2023).

Baca was a studious student and thought of herself as a nerd back then. She knew that her mom and dad wanted her to go to college and receiving a scholarship would be her only way to get there. Because she lived in La Salle, in the 1950s, she caught the bus to College High (later named University High), which at that time was UNC's lab school. Earlier, her mother had also gone to College High when James Michener, the famed author who wrote the book *Centennial*, was a student teacher.

The teachers at College High School were professors and college students who were getting their education degrees and needed to do student teaching. That's where my mother wanted us to go because she remembered this student teacher who taught her civics or history. She said he could just paint with his words! The author (who was) a UNC graduate student, wrote (the book) Centennial, *and his name was James Michener! She was in awe of him. And so, after he wrote the book* Centennial, *there was a reception for him up at the capitol in the governor's office. And because of my mother, I was invited to the reception, as he remembered my mother! My mother was a very beautiful young woman. And so, I think that was why he remembered her and gave me a signed book for her.*

She wanted us to go to College High School because she had such an amazing educational experience there. When my mother lost her parents, she missed a lot of school. When she got back to school, she needed help … And that was James Michener, who helped her catch up with the rest of the class! … I don't have a lot of happy memories as a child, but the experiences that I had burned a hole in my heart to try to make a change so no other kids would have to experience that.

My life's experiences were the greatest gift I ever received because they caused me to work hard, get a scholarship, go to college, take risks, and continue to work hard. ... You have to change; you have to turn the challenges you face in life into positive experiences because we all face challenges. But if we turn them into gifts that we learn from, regardless of what those challenges are, we can learn and overcome them. I believe most challenges we can overcome with the help of others. And so my goal was to try to help others overcome those challenges (Baca, 2023).

For Gama:

It was my choice when I was eighteen years old in 1980. I applied to go to UNC for the journalism program, and I was majoring in journalism. I ended up dropping out, but that was why I arrived in Greeley. Just loved it. Stayed ever since.

I graduated high school. I went to UNC here in Greeley for two and a half years, and then I attended AIMS Community College for about a year. Then, unfortunately, I dropped out because I thought I did not need a college education to be a professional writer. That's probably the biggest regret of my life. I was that close to getting a degree, and I didn't get it. But everything happens for a reason. In the early 1990s, I started going back to Aims night classes, graphic arts and art design, and I took a class in HTML coding, which now a fourth grader could take and learn. But it was enough to teach me to create websites on my own, and that's what led me to start a digital marketing agency. And we were fortunate enough to be able to afford to buy a computer back then. And I'm entirely self-taught. So, Aims and UNC have had their influence on me (Gama, 2023).

Colorado College in Colorado Springs granted Gonzales-Soto a B.A. in sociology, and she also earned a juris doctorate (J.D.) from the University of Denver's College of Law. She is a licensed attorney.

I always knew from the time I was in high school that I was going to go to law school. I always knew, not because I thought being a lawyer was going to make me rich or powerful, but I knew from growing up, the value in being informed. (Gonzales-Soto, 2023)

(Romero) Horning earned a B.A. in elementary education, a master's degree in interdisciplinary studies, second-language learning, and a certificate in public school administration from UNC. She has been a long-time educator in Greeley.

She attended the Valley RE-1 school district that encompasses La Salle and Gilcrest, CO. She remembers that elementary school mostly went well; her teachers were kind and caring, and she was a good student. However, in fifth grade, (romero) Horning, was shocked to hear one of her classmates say, "You're not like those other Mexicans," while looking at some other migrant students.

This attitude from students continued into junior high, as she felt disregarded by some of them. She also remembers that the bus driver was especially mean to the students of color. When she entered high school, she concentrated on her studies and did not date.

Sometime later, she discovered that she was "off limits" to some of the families. Some of their parents of the White boys prohibited their sons from dating her because she was Mexican.

She thought her counselor in high school was a wonderful person. He was very helpful and supportive and encouraged her to excel in her studies. He helped her prepare for college by filling out forms and finding scholarships. He was able to obtain a grant for her that paid for most of her college. When she attended UNC, she did not live in the dorms, so she felt somewhat disconnected from other students. She met someone in the early 1970s and got married.

The University of St. Thomas in Houston, Texas, granted Gonzales Guerrero, Jr. a B.A. in philosophy, a master's in divinity, and another master's in theology. A third master's degree in applied theology and a Th.D. (equivalent to a Ph.D.) in applied theology was granted to Gonzales Guerrero from Harvard University. UNC granted him his fourth master's degree in teaching Spanish.

Mendoza earned an A.A. in criminal justice from Aims Community College, a B.A. in criminal justice, a minor in Spanish, and a master's degree in criminal justice from UNC. Coming to the U.S. when she was thirteen, Mendoza found school very challenging as, among other issues, she did not speak English. Her parents decided to keep her back in seventh grade. She received a lot of help from her English as a second language (ESL) teacher, and she found that the small group support helped her immensely. She recalled:

> Throughout middle school and high school, I met caring teachers who encouraged me to never give up. Many times, I told the teachers that I didn't want to stay in school. During one of those times, Mrs. Lane, my ESL teacher, told me that if I learn one word a day, one day I can become an interpreter and help others who don't speak English. I laughed at this idea, but she planted the seed. I remember going home that day to make my own dictionary: a small notebook where I made three columns, one for the word, one for the spelling, and one for the pronunciation.
>
> By the beginning of eighth grade, I had the courage to go to the concession stand and ask for an Italian ice on my own. Although not the most challenging task, that day, I realized that I had the skills to communicate in English and that only my fear of speaking was holding me back. By the end of eighth grade, I was interpreting and translating for others. Our landlord called on me to help him communicate with his tenants, most of whom were Spanish speakers. My neighbors took me with them to look for jobs and fill out applications. Every time I filled an application out or interpreted for someone, I got better.
>
> Although I faced a lot of challenges and adversities as a new immigrant and as a new student in the U.S., I chose to focus on what I can do today to be better tomorrow. I interpret, fill out forms, and volunteer every time there is an opportunity. For me, this is a way to pay it forward and a reminder of how far I've come and how much one word a day can be the gift that keeps on giving (Mendoza, 2023).

Montalvo dropped out of high school in the tenth grade and took on various jobs before returning to school to pursue a degree in social work from New Rochelle College, New York. The phone company she worked for at the time paid for her schooling. She attended night school while working full-time.

However, in her K-12 schooling experiences, she remembered being behind in school because her family was always moving and working in the fields, at times not even attending school. She remembered:

We were traveling, and then something happened with the trailer. I think the tires blew out. We ended up in Arkansas, and my dad went to work for a pig farmer. We didn't go to school there because we were the only Mexicans.

She began attending school regularly when they moved to Greeley but didn't feel supported by her teachers.

When I was in the eighth grade, I was doing so good they moved me to the tenth. When I would go to the teachers sometimes because I couldn't understand what they wanted us to do, they would tell me, "You need to pay more attention and read your book."

I was always trying to understand what they wanted, but they were so rude and so mean. They didn't care about the students. They didn't care about the Mexicanos. *They were just passing them. You know, I think that's something that needs to be focused on. Everybody should learn (Montalvo, 2023).*

Crediting the *Chicano* Movement advocacy in college admissions for increasing *Latina* and *Latino* students, Montoya came to UNC and earned a B.A. His mother only completed eighth grade, his father only sixth grade, and his grandparents did not attend school at all. Therefore, supporting their childrens' education was especially important, as they attended all of Montoya's school conferences and sports activities. He is proud of being a first-generation college graduate and is especially proud of his daughter, who earned a B.A., M.A., and Ed.D. in education. His granddaughter received her B.A. in the spring of 2025.

After graduating with a bachelor of science (B.S.) in sociology with an emphasis in criminology and a minor in psychology from CSU Pueblo, Nieto took the law school admission test (LSAT) on a whim. She passed and went on to earn a juris doctorate (J.D.) from the University of Colorado, Boulder. At the time of the interview, she was a judge and lawyer.

Perez graduated high school and then attended the University of Nebraska on a track scholarship. The demands of running track became too great, so he gave up his scholarship and worked forty hours a week to earn his B.A.

In grade school, we were taught English. Our parents consented to that because they wanted us, as young Latino boys, to progress, and they gave up their language—or sacrificed their language, their culture—for us (Perez, 2023).

Sanchez had a nursing career that spanned nearly fifty years. She received her licensed practical nurse (LPN) from Aims Community College School of practical nursing in Fort Collins. Additionally, she earned her registered nurse (R.N.) and bachelor of science in nursing (B.S.N.) degrees, as well as a master's of public health (M.P.H.) from the University of Northern Colorado (UNC). She also obtained her doctorate in education and human resource studies from CSU. Regarding her schooling experiences, Sanchez remembered:

One significant memory from my elementary education in Texas is the prohibition against speaking Spanish. There were signs discouraging its use, and both teachers and peers enforced this rule. I often felt afraid of being reprimanded, which was tough since Spanish was my first language and I didn't speak English when I entered first grade (Sanchez, 2024).

Duran Silva always desired an education. She studied by flashlight at night but missed a test to go to the ninth grade because her family traveled so much to make a living in the fields. Therefore, she decided to quit school. Later, her Catholic faith led her to a convent in Minnesota, where she received her high school diploma. She then enrolled in a junior college and went on to earn a B.A. in social work from St. Mary College in Bismarck, North Dakota. After returning to Greeley, she received a B.A. in elementary education from UNC. Her K-12 school memories are of enduring discrimination and racial remarks. Her clothes and food were made fun of, and she stated:

All I wanted was to learn English and get an education (Silva, 2024).

Taes Grimm went to school K-12 in north and central Greeley. She felt she had a good experience in elementary and junior high but felt there were few people in high school who were supportive of her desire to become a nurse. She was told she was not college material and she should be a secretary, so that's what she did. Later, she attended Aims and graduated with an A.A. and a B.A. from UNC in nursing. She felt that her experiences in college were positive, feeling supported in her quest to become a nurse (Grimm, 2023).

Adriana Trujillo worked as an exhibit assistant at the Greeley History Museum at the time of the interview.

I started off studying art and art history and then anthropology. When I did research on decolonization, I felt a responsibility to represent the Indigenous populations and the people who have been marginalized. And I didn't know where it was going to take me. I just went down that path and ended up here. I'm doing an internship at the museum and decided to stay there because I realized I can represent what's missing in the museum' the underrepresented groups. I can be that voice for them. I can try to represent them there, and that's what I'm trying to do. And it's definitely my passion (Adriana Trujillo, 2023).

Ana Trujillo graduated with a secondary education degree. While teaching in Fort Lupton as a English language development (ELD) high school teacher, she worked on a master's degree in higher education and leadership. Her future desire is to help others in pursuing a college degree.

I'm an English language development teacher (ELD) teacher at the high school level. I guess my experience as a young child working in the fields is what led me to where I am now, my dad's words about showing me how to work and not wanting me to work in the fields like he did his whole life. He wanted something better for us. That's what took me to education.

I thought, "I'm going to instill that into my daughters, that how important an education is for you to be able to make a decent living" (Ana Trujillo, 2023).

Velasquez is a retired lawyer who received her A.A. from Aims, a business degree from UNC, and eventually her J.D. from the University of Denver Law School. She remembered:

When I attended school, when I was in elementary and even high school, I can't think of any teachers who took an interest or who even encouraged that, even encouraged me. There really isn't anyone. After I graduated from high school, my first job was as a legal secretary ... working for an attorney in Greeley. And I think that he influenced me, I think, maybe, into going to law school, even though it was years later. But that was my first job right after graduation from high school. His name was John O'Hagan.

I didn't get an education until after marriage and children. I was a non-traditional student. I started at Aims Community College, which I think is a fantastic community college. After I graduated from Aims, it wasn't enough. I transferred to the University of Northern Colorado, and I earned a business degree. Even with a four-year degree, it seemed as though something was missing. It just wasn't enough. I decided to continue, and this is with a family: my kids and my husband. So I decided to go to law school (Velasquez, 2023).

Rodriguez-McNeill went to school in Natalia, Texas. She did not finish high school due to migrating to Colorado to work in the fields. Later, she received her GED and took courses to be a legal secretary and in accounting and early childhood education. She became a Head Start health coordinator and then decided to go to nursing school. She got her LPN license and director's license and became a supervisor of nurses and nurses' aides at Sunrise Community Health Center. When asked about what language she spoke as a child, she recounted her schooling experiences as well.

Spanish, only Spanish. I had a hard time. When I started school, I didn't know a word of English, and the teachers were really mean. They would hit you with the rulers on the hands, the palms, and on the back of your hands if you spoke Spanish. I ended up in a closet. A lot of times they put you in a closet and hit you because you didn't speak English. I remember being very rebellious. I still spoke Spanish. I didn't care if they hit me or not. I spoke Spanish because my dad didn't speak English. My mom didn't know very much English either (Rodriguez-McNeill, 2023).

Schooling for Vázquez was in his home country of Mexico. He explained:

We were in the second group to attend sixth grade, which is equivalent to the same grade in elementary school. No grades beyond that level were offered at the rancho *(small Mexican town). Outside of the* rancho, *more advanced grades were offered. I was one of the more advanced students. I had just turned eleven years old when I completed sixth grade. The teacher came to our home and asked if I could leave home to study. She believed in my potential because of my schoolwork. She said she would pay for my studies outside the* rancho. *Because I was so young and I needed to work to help the family, they didn't let me go. At that time, if I had been given the opportunity, I would have wanted to be a teacher. That is also what my teacher wanted me to study at the secondary level in* Tlatenango de Sánchez Román, Zacatecas, *and then go on to a "normal" (college). My family struggled to buy me my history and geography books. I learned about almost all the rivers of the world. I also have a daughter who also likes to study history (Vázquez, per Garcia Martinez, personal communication, December 10, 2024).*

Given the opportunity, Vázquez would have liked to study history and geography. History was his strength, but he also liked to study about the world. He knew most of the larger rivers throughout the world. However, there was little possibility for him to pursue education because his family was so poor. In those days, they had to buy the books, and they were expensive; twelve *pesos* was a lot for his family to pay back then. Because Vázquez did not have the opportunity to go to school, he passed on the importance of education to his family. Vázqueza's daughter is currently working on her Ph.D.

Martinez lived in Walsenburg, CO, and went to Catholic school from grades one through eight. He remembers that the Catholic nuns used different disciplinary methods, like physical punishment. He said that one of the nuns kept a big paddle in plain sight on her desk. The nun would have them bend over her desk and use the paddle on them. However, he enjoyed his friendship with the other Mexican-American kids. Even though discrimination and racism were present, all he wanted was an education.

After dropping out of high school, Martinez received his GED and then enrolled at Southern Colorado State College in Pueblo, Colorado. He felt there was a great deal of discrimination during his short tenure at the college. During his freshman year, he was drafted into the military and deployed to Vietnam. One of his big regrets is that he didn't finish college.

Other historians who earned a high school diploma or general equivalency diploma (GED) were Francisco Cortez, Abraham Garcia, Patriticia Garcia-Nelson, Ben (Mitch) Gonzales, Gabriel A. Lopez, Maria Sanchez, Rhonda Solis, Theresa Solis, and Stacy Suniga.

Ben (Mitch) Gonzales did attend UNC but dropped out because he and his wife, Ruby, were expecting their first child. While growing up, Ben (Mitch) lived on the west side of town. The schools there did not have a large percentage of *Latinos*. Thus, he felt the sting of racism many times. In kindergarten, an older student called him a "spic" (a derogatory name for a Mexican), so Ben (Mitch) punched him in the face. This was not the last time he used his fists to stop racial slurs or bullying. At each school level, he was not backing down to the bullies. He felt that once he stood his ground, the bullying stopped. At one point, he even had to defend his sister. But he always thought there was a pattern or pecking order that would happen: a new kid Ben (Mitch) would have to fight. Later, he and the bullies would become friends.

By the time he enrolled in high school, he decided he wasn't going to put up with any bullying there either. He remembers one situation when he was on the golf team. Before every meet, the student golfers competed to see who would golf at the weekend meet. He beat out his competitor. The coach told him he had decided to take another golfer, who just happened to be the son of one of his teacher colleagues.

Ben (Mitch) replied, "Oh no, you're not. I won fair and square, if you sit me out, I'm complaining."

Because his family had some clout in town by that time, his father, Ben, complained. Ben (Mitch) ended up golfing for the team.

He also remembers that many of his *Latino* friends only went out for individual sports like wrestling and track because of the favoritism in the other team sports. Some of his older *Latino* friends were all-conference football players one year but were benched the next year when they hired a new coach. He always played the White kids first.

Cortez also shared some of his schooling experiences.

Trying to learn how to speak English because, at home, Spanish was the only language spoken. I also remember playing with other kids during recess time, swinging on the swings, riding the merry-go-round, and falling off and developing friendships with other Mexican kids. Some kids ridiculed my clothes, and I endured racist name-calling. And, I remember working in the fields after school. Then my parents moved to Porterville, California. The good memories were playing sports and making the track team. I enrolled at Porterville Junior College and was there for one year. While in high school and college, I worked picking apples and oranges because we were poor and to help the family. I wanted to continue my college career to become a social worker, but Uncle Sam called. I entered the military in 1968 and was sent to Vietnam, and that denied me a college education (Cortez, 2023).

Rhonda Solis graduated from Greeley West, and her two children are also graduates of District #6.

I'm a Spartan, and that's something I'm really proud of. My kids are also products of public education, which I think inspired me to run for the local school board, where I served for eight years.

And then, right after that, I ended up running for the state board. And again, it's because of education, and although I didn't go to college, I've recognized how important education is and our right to vote is in equalizing our abilities here in the U.S. I do whatever I can to assure, promote, and encourage those opportunities for kids (R. Solis, 2023).

Attending Billy Martinez Elementary School and Franklin Middle School and graduating from Northridge High School, Vega Ruiz then earned a B.A. in business administration from Adams State College in Trinidad. He said he connected with Adams State because he still wanted to play soccer, and they awarded him a scholarship for his last two years.

A long-time educator, Watson received her B.A. in elementary and bilingual education and a master's degree in early childhood education from UNC. Growing up, she said that education was a priority, a number one value in her family. Because her father was a professor at UNC and her mother was an elementary school principal, she said that education always influenced her.

Treviño graduated from CSU with a degree in zoology. At the time of the interview, he attended Aims Community College for an A.A. in computer information systems with a certificate in cybersecurity. He said he was inspired to study zoology by his grandfather.

We'd go out to the fields, and they always wore long-sleeved shirts and the hat and everything. My grandfather would always tell me to stay underneath the pickup truck to stay out of the sun. He'd go, "I don't want you to get sick. I want you to just stay under the truck," but when he would take a break or something, he would start showing me all the different animals and what they did in relation to where they lived. That's what started getting me into science, into biology, which is where I ended up getting my degree in zoology. It was because of him that he showed me all these relationships, and I just got really interested, and I wanted to find out more about them as I got older" (Treviño, 2023).

Deb Suniga graduated from Greeley West High School and received her B.A. in sales and marketing from Mesa State College in Grand Junction. However, other family members did not attain that same level. She explained:

My grandmother and a lot of my uncles and my aunt stopped going to school in the eighth grade because they didn't have money for clothes (D. Suniga, 2023).

Beginning at Aims, Wendirad earned an A.A., a B.A. in education and communication, and a master's in Spanish from UNC. Wendirad said her mom had always wanted to go to college and told her to value her education to attain a better life. That is the reason why they left Mexico.

Johnson has a degree in interior design and a teaching certificate. However, even though she never took a teaching job, she applies her education every day.

I moved here, and unfortunately, that took me to a different course. But I believe that even though I never taught, we still teach in everyday life. Whether it's talking about resources or access to information,

The Rodriguez teens in the onion fields in Lucerne, CO.
Left to right: Daniel Rodriguez, Teresa Rodriguez-McNeill, and Pedro Rodriguez, Jr.
Photo courtesy of the Teresa Rodriguez-McNeill Collection.

whether it's helping someone understand a specific topic or providing insight. How we can help or what is out there for them to tap into is how I use what I've learned (Johnson, 2023).

UNC granted Clarence Lopez two degrees, one in business and one in sociology. He continued studying to earn a real estate license.

I studied for the real estate exam, passed the exam. I was licensed and began selling real estate. I also felt like this was an area where I could help my Mexican American community. So I began selling real estate and the majority of my buyers and sellers were Mexican Americans from North and East Greeley or the Spanish Colony (C. Lopez, 2023).

Romero earned a teaching degree from UNC, after which he applied for and received a national fellowship to Kent State University for an M.A. He received an additional fellowship for a doctorate at the University of Illinois, but before completion, he was called to California to train migrant workers.

For many of our historians, getting a high school degree was difficult, let alone getting a college education. For example, Taes Grimm shared that she attained a degree from UNC.

I wanted to become a nurse when I was in high school. I went to go see the counselor, Mr. Gardner. He said that I wasn't smart enough to go to school (Grimm, 2023).

But as evidenced, these historians had grit and determination, and they were resilient in the face of racism and terrible treatment in school.

NARRATIVES FOR CHAPTER 3
The Damion Córdova Family

I think people fear what they don't know, but then they also fear educated people of color. As my father always said, "Education is the great equalizer. Knowledge is power." —Damion Córdova

Damion Córdova's parents are Roberto and Betty Córdova.
Here he is in a red football uniform hugging Betty, his mom.
Photo courtesy of the Damion Córdova Collection.

Dr. Roberto H. Córdova (1946–2022) and Betty J. Córdova were exemplary representatives of their Mexican American and Indigenous heritage. They were both involved in the Chicano Movement, the *Candelaria* Association, *El Voto Latino*, and Greeley *Fiesta*, and they helped establish the League of United

Latin American Citizens (LULAC) for youth and adults. Betty participated in the 1960s United Mexican American Students (UMAS) sit-in at CU Boulder for *Chicano* rights. Dr. Córdova was also involved in the Black-Brown Coalition at the University of Northern Colorado (UNC) during his tenure as a professor there. Damion and his sister, Nicole, have been involved in LULAC because of their parents' activism.

Damion's family has a long line of family members serving in the military. Damion's great-uncle Herman, who was his father's mentor and Betty's brother, served in World War II. His grandfather also served as a combat medic during World War II. Damion stated:

One of my uncles on my father's side served in the Korean War. My cousins served in the Vietnam War. My father served twenty years in the Army National Guard, and I served twenty-eight years in the U.S. Army.

Damion described his service.

A lot of my time in the military was spent training soldiers. I was an instructor for the general staff officer college at Fort Leavenworth, Texas. That really helped to solidify my purpose in life, which was to share my knowledge with others, vis-à-vis teaching.

After Damion's military duty, he joined the Greeley LULAC Adult Council, where his father was the president and his mother was one of the officers.

Our primary focus was to engage Latino youth in education by establishing youth councils throughout Colorado at the middle and high school levels. We'd also fundraise for scholarships ... (and) hold a LULAC youth conference at UNC.

The Córdova family is a strong example of hard-working, determined individuals who persevere and stand up for underrepresented groups despite societal obstacles. Damion emphasized:

We are more powerful than we believe. We have to become informed and united and involved ... and when we vote, we can shape what happens in this community.

Damion's said his mother, Betty:

... has faith, and she's hopeful that young Latinos *will continue to fight for equal treatment and equal rights.*

The Córdova family's contributions to a more educated community continue to pay rich cultural dividends.

—ADRIANA TRUJILLO

Juanita Martinez Rocha

Education is the key to our freedom, to our future. By getting educated, we're getting into different roles; we're not just laborers and construction workers. —*Martinez Rocha*

The Martinez Rocha Family.
Back row: Jalene Rocha, Jodi Rocha, Julie Rocha. Front row: Joe Rocha III, Joe Rocha Jr., Martinez Rocha. Photo courtesy of Yolanda Martinez Rocha.

Juanita Martinez Rocha's mother, an influential figure, taught her honesty, integrity, generosity, and pride. She often told her children, "We may be poor, but we're not dirty. Be proud of who you are." Religion was a cornerstone in their lives, and Martinez Rocha's faith has aided her through adversity. Growing up, her parents spoke English to their children and Spanish to each other.

My parents were part of that generation that got punished for speaking Spanish in school, so they didn't want us to endure those same punishments and those same biases.

Martinez Rocha desired to pass on the empowerment and pride her mother instilled in her. She earned a degree in education with an endorsement in bilingual education. She later received a master's degree in interdisciplinary education with an endorsement in culturally and linguistically diverse students.

My goal was to work in a school that served children of lower SES and second language learners.

In the 1970s, she and her husband joined the American GI Forum, attending numerous boycotts and protests to expose injustices and support farm workers' rights. The *Chicano* Movement provided Martinez Rocha with direction and empowered her to speak out and help others. In 1994, Martinez Rocha met civil rights activist Dolores Huerta.

She was just so humble. She took a genuine interest in who you were. And that really touched me.

After moving back to Greeley in 1991, Martinez Rocha joined Hispanic Women of Weld County.

That has been my heart because when I came back as a widow with four kids, they empowered me. They encouraged me; they supported me.

She has also served on the board of Habitat for Humanity and A Woman's Place. She is a judicial performance commissioner for the state and the treasurer of the Mexican American History Project Greeley.

As Latinos, we need to get our voices out there, our information, our contributions, and our feelings. As a people, we need to unite.

She wants to see more *Latina* and *Latino* candidates running for city council and school boards and working in decision-making positions—*Latina* and *Latino* city leaders who will advocate, integrate, and create positive change in Greeley.

We are very talented, we are educated, we are smart. Right now, we're not the majority, but soon we will be. We're going to be a force to be reckoned with, and people are going to have to listen.

—BETH BULLARD

Kathleen (Romero) Horning

Education is the great equalizer. If children can see themselves as learners, as readers, that is an equalizer in the community because then they see opportunities. They see the world beyond their home … The doors can open. —(Romero) Horning

Kathleen (Romero) Horning's story reflects the values of hard work, education, and service to others. Her grandparents on the Romero side "lived in poor housing," and by the time her father was thirteen, he was "loaned out to a farmer in the Timnath area and worked as a hired hand." Unfortunately:

… a custom with lots of families at that time, Latino or not, that eighth grade was sort of the end of your formal education, and they were actually farmed out.

While working as laborers, her grandfather, father, and his brothers were frugal, which allowed them to fulfill their family goal of owning a farm.

Marriage of Kathleen (Romero) Horning's Parents, Joe and Mary J. Romero, in 1924. Photo courtesy of Kathleen (Romero) Horning.

Despite their childhood, (Romero) Horning's parents defied the odds. Her father, regardless of not having an education past eighth grade, was elected to the RE-1 school board and later became the school board president. Her mother completed her GED at Aims Community College as an honor student. (Romero) Horning explained:

We were encouraged to set our sights beyond high school (and) to expect to go to college.

(Romero) Horning's two fourth-grade teachers gave her hope of becoming an educator, specifically in her realization that:

Until that point, I really didn't know that there could be Latinas *who were teachers.*

(Romero) Horning not only became a classroom teacher but was also a human resources coordinator and a school principal.

She had the opportunity to work at more affluential schools but chose to work in Title I and bilingual schools because:

I wanted to make a difference in the lives of kids who maybe wouldn't have had that opportunity otherwise.

(Romero) Horning's approach:

No matter what a child's day might have been like before, I wanted their day in the classroom to be the best. That every day was an opportunity for them to create a better life for themselves.

Both (Romero) Horning and her mother emphasized the importance of providing opportunities for children without putting a lid on them based on their family background or the color of their skin. (Romero) Horning serves on the board of Weld Trust's Education Advisory Committee, which supports caretakers in building literacy for their children from the time they are infants. Through Nest to Wings, she provides resources to prepare high schoolers for college and trade schools. These resources are integral in a community that has a "deep history of separate and tolerate," which is why (Romero) Horning stated:

I would love to see Greeley as a community growing past its acceptance level, more to an embrace and celebrate level.

—ADRIANA TRUJILLO

Penny Gonzales-Soto

I love Greeley. I wouldn't give it up. I may be pissed at it every once in a while, right? I may not be happy all the time about it, but Greeley is my home. Greeley is where I grew up. Greeley is where I have wonderful memories, horrible memories, but memories. It is my hometown, no matter where I go. —Gonzales-Soto

Penny Gonzales with mother and siblings in 1987.
Back row: Candy Gonzales (sister).
Second row: Jose Gonzales (brother) and Penny Gonzales Soto.
Third row, Betty Gonzales (mother) and Angel Mendez (brother).
Front row: Nick Mendez (brother).
Photo courtesy of the Penny Gonzales-Soto Collection.

Penny Gonzales-Soto was born in Greeley after her family moved from the *Las Animas* area. She comes from a fourth generation Mexican American family. Her mother was a certified nursing assistant for thirty years and raised five children on her own. Gonzales-Soto has fond memories of attending the Fourth of July Parade and the different events at the Greeley Stampede. While her family was financially unable to visit places such as Elitch Gardens or Disneyland, they created warm family memories by attending local activities, which they continue to do until the present time.

Encouraged to attend college by an Upward Bound counselor at CSU, Gonzales-Soto completed her B.A. at Colorado College in Colorado Springs. Later, she and her family, which included a two-year-old daughter, moved to Denver so that she could pursue her law degree. She completed her law degree from the University of Denver in the year 2000 and came back to Greeley, where she took a position with Catholic Charities.

While working with Catholic Charities, she participated in a program that supported immigrants and refugees in the Greeley community. Her many years of working with the immigrant and refugee community in Greeley allowed her to realize that even across cultures and nationalities, we all have many commonalities that bind us together. Gonzales-Soto is a strong supporter of becoming more inclusive and appreciating our differences and commonalities. She is "passionate about empowering immigrant and refugee families to make informed decisions when it comes to their legal avenues and their futures." She is now the director of student legal services at CSU in Fort Collins.

Gonzales-Soto strongly believes that the contributions made by the Mexican American community in Greeley have not been recognized. While there has been some recognition for a few deserving leaders, many others have not been recognized. In her words:

I think Greeley was built upon the backs of Mexican Americans. I think it has not been acknowledged. Who has built the buildings, right? Who is doing the repairs? Who is doing the outreach? Who is recognizing the need for more mental health services? Who's recognizing the need to rejuvenate the north side of town? Who's thinking about the small businesses that are in town, which are predominantly Mexican Americans, immigrant communities? It has been the Mexican American community.

—DR. MADELINE MILIAN

Susie Velasquez

When it comes to what really counts, say jobs, I don't think that we're where we should be. —Velasquez

Susie Velasquez's parents' fiftieth anniversary 1927–1977.
Back Row: Leo Velasquez, John Velasquez, Felix Velasquez, Siguiel Velasquez, Abenicio Velasquez.
Front Row: Junior Velasquez, Mary Velasquez Chavez, Rosella Velasquez Valencia, Aurelia Romero Velasquez, Benito Velasquez, Susie Velasquez, Frank Velasquez.
Photo courtesy of the Susie Velasquez Collection.

Susie Velasquez's Northern Colorado ancestry dates to the early 1800s. Her grandparents worked as sheep herders and laborers, and her father worked on the railroad. The family moved to Millikin, Colorado, in the early 1950s, when her father went to work for the sugar factory in Johnstown. In the summers, her mother sorted potatoes to earn money for school clothes while Velasquez, the youngest of eleven children, joined her older siblings in the fields picking beans and cherries.

Family traditions included regular Sunday meals, listening to Mexican music, and preparing *posole* for holiday gatherings. Prayer and attending mass were cornerstones in Velasquez's mother's life. When her mother could no longer read from her prayerbook, Velasquez read it to her and later recorded it for her mother to listen to. Her mother's prayer book and altar are treasured possessions that she displays in her home.

After graduating from high school, Velasquez moved to Greeley, married, and began a family. She attended Aims Community College as a non-traditional student and earned a business degree from UNC. Despite those achievements, she felt there was more to learn, so she attended law school in Denver.

Velasquez's served on the Greeley Dream Team, Habitat for Humanity, the Colorado Civil Rights Commission, and as the director of affirmative action at the University of Northern Colorado. She was the first *Latina* Public Trustee in Weld County, serving for thirteen years, and was appointed president of the Public Trustee Association by three consecutive Colorado governors.

When asked to reflect on Mexican American representation in Greeley, Velasquez, an attorney, used statistics to explain her thoughts.

Statistics don't lie. Take, for example, in 2022, the city of Greeley, their full-time employees were 843. Of that, 56 percent were White males, 22 percent were White females, 13 percent were Hispanic males, and 7 percent were Hispanic females.

That is unacceptable. Latinas are 7 percent of the city of Greeley, and our population is about 40 percent, according to the census.

Velasquez believes that *Latinos* have contributed significantly through their decades of work in agriculture and the food industry.

We're putting food onto people's tables.

However, she hopes to see more *Latinos* in positions of power in business and government. She feels that more representation at those levels will create greater employment opportunities for *Latinos*.

How are we going to create wealth if we don't have good jobs? I think there's a lot that needs to be done yet.

—BETH BULLARD

Vivian A. Watson

*I knew from eight years of age that I was going to be a kindergarten
teacher, just like my mom. —Watson*

Vivian Leal Watson's Family.
Back Row: Saul Larsen, Bill Whitehead, Mark Watson. Second Row:
Carlos Leal III, Carlos Leal, Vivian Leal-Watson, Valerie Leal-Whitehead.
Front Row: Vicki Leal-Larsen, Johnson Leal, Nadine Leal.
Photo courtesy of Vivian A. Watson.

Education was the number one priority in the Leal family, a fact evident in
Vivian A. Watson's parents' extensive educational careers.

*My parents influenced my life, as did Earnie Andrade and the people
they surrounded themselves with.*

Watson's mother, Alicia, was a kindergarten teacher and a leader in bilingual
education. She started some of the state's first bilingual programs in Johnstown
and Pierce and traveled the state supporting bilingual programming. She later
became the principal of Billie Martinez Elementary School.

Her father, Carlos, directed the Colorado Migrant Council, served on the
school board and city council, and was a professor at the University of Northern

Colorado. Watson fondly recalls their home being an open house for her father's students and the community and the significant impact her parents made on the educational community in Greeley.

Growing up in Greeley, Watson often felt as if she was living in two different worlds: not Brown enough for the Brown people and not White enough for the White people. She commented that friends often said things like, "Well, you're not like that."

Like what? She'd think to herself.

Watson earned an elementary/bilingual education degree and a master's in early childhood and taught kindergarten in Greeley for thirty-three years. She is a self-described Greeley girl but feels the community doesn't recognize the contributions or achievements of *Latinos* in Greeley as it should.

When I was teaching all those years, I felt like I had a title over me, and I was a little more accepted. I was treated better when in teacher clothes. I think Greeley is a little bit of a racist community at times. I think there's a lot of what we call in education "White flight."

Travel was also a priority for the Leal family. Watson and her siblings spent summers in the back of the family's station wagon, traveling throughout North America.

It was important for us to learn about other people's cultures. They were teachers, so we had to keep journals of our travels. One summer, we went well into Mexico, visiting relatives in many states ranging from poor to quite wealthy. We saw it all.

Watson recalled having her first shrimp dinner in a small house on the beach in San Blas.

They went out to the ocean and came back with a bucket of shrimp and dumped it onto the table. We loved it, and to this day, I love shrimp. It was just amazing.

—BETH BULLARD

Nancy Wendirad

I'm a product of bilingual education. —Wendirad

Family of Nancy Wendirad.
Left to right: Gladys Sánchez (sister), Jaime Sánchez (brother), Nancy
Wendirad, and Eulalia (Lala) Carmon (mother).
Photo courtesy of Nancy Wendirad Collection.

Nancy Wendirad, born in *Hidalgo del Parral, Chihuahua*, Mexico, considers herself a *Mexicana*. Her family, seeking more opportunities, came to Weld County as part of the *Braceros* Program. After the program ended, her father went to work for the railroad, and later, the Chrysler assembly plant. Her mother worked as a seamstress and homemaker.

Raised primarily by her maternal grandparents and mother, Wendirad learned the value of truth, respect, responsibility, education, and hard work. Traditions were passed in stories, sayings, and recipes. Wendirad recalls sitting in the courtyard after dinner, listening to stories. A frequent *dicho* (saying) in her family was *"En boca cerrada, no entran moscas"* (flies don't enter a closed mouth, or literally, sometimes being silent is best).

When I came to the U.S., I did not speak English, so I went through the ESL program.

Wendirad entered an international program at AIMS Community College to continue her studies. After working for District 6 as an attendance liaison, she returned to school and earned degrees in education and communications, an ESL endorsement, and a master's degree in Spanish from the University of Northern Colorado.

As a high school Spanish teacher, Wendirad is often saddened when she meets Mexican American students whose knowledge of the Mexican language and culture has been lost. She wonders if the loss could be attributed to the times when people were punished or ridiculed for speaking Spanish.

Wendirad instills in her students the importance and advantages of knowing the Spanish language. She points out an aspect of Colorado history that many overlook through the quote, "I did not cross the border. The border crossed me." The quote refers to the Treaty of Guadalupe Hidalgo and the lost land that was once Mexico. It's a reminder to her students that people of Mexican descent have lived in the Greeley area for centuries.

When Wendirad first came to Greeley, she felt division and asked why there weren't more events held to learn about Mexican culture. The response she received was: "Greeley is a city of wide streets and narrow minds." As time passed, she saw the community begin to recognize Mexican culture, but she feels a lack of true understanding remains. She hopes to see Greeley become a cultural melting pot, a place where all cultures can be understood and shared through music, dance, art, cuisine, and story.

—BETH BULLARD

CHAPTER 4

Civic Engagement in Greeley

Civic engagement is defined as working to improve the community and using knowledge, skills, and values to help to do so. It includes actions that make life better, both in politics and in other ways, such as working on community boards, volunteering to work with youth in not only athletics, and also attending and graduating from college, etc. Thus, how have *Latinas* and *Latinos* participated in the Greeley community over time?

Latinas and *Latinos* have helped the Greeley community in many ways, starting with *La Colonia* in the 1920s and continuing today. The Mexicans and Mexican Americans who came in the 1920s to work in the sugar beet fields faced discrimination and segregation from White residents. However, they were resilient and worked hard to build their community and their lives.

Some of these contributions were discussed in earlier chapters. Chapter 2 discussed the *Salón*, an important place for the *La Colonia* community, and how it later became the Guadalupe Center that helps homeless people today. Chapter 3 explained how *La Colonia's* residents worked to move the Gipson School closer to their neighborhood so their children could attend more easily. Parents in *La Colonia* also fought for school integration and better education, giving their children more opportunities for a better life. Chapter 3 also mentions Alvin Garcia's store and its central role in the community's success.

Local Elections and Political Participation

Mexican American politics have not evolved as fast as the population has evolved. For many years, there were very few *Latinas* or *Latinos* elected to the Greeley School Board and Greeley City Council. However, they have been active in politics and advocacy for a long time. In the early 1900s, Mexicans in *La Colonia* faced discrimination and segregation. They were not allowed to enter White businesses, and signs reading "Whites Only" and "No Mexicans Allowed" were placed in many store windows. Because of advocacy from *La Colonia* residents and the Mexican Consulate, these signs were removed in 1926 (Lopez et al. 2007).

Even though *Latinas* and *Latinos* had lived in Greeley for many years, very few were elected to local government before the 1970s. Greeley has never had a *Latina* or *Latino* mayor, and right now, there are no *Latinas* or *Latinos* on the city council. To be involved politically is very important because whoever controls politics controls the money coming into the general fund through the tax system (Carmichael & Hamilton, 1967). Many times, White residents want to be in control of this element of a democracy because whoever is in control decides how and where the money will be spent.

The lack of Latina and Latino representation in Greeley is similar to the state of Colorado, where few have been elected to government positions. Baca started her political work in the 1960s as a student activist at CSU in Fort Collins. In 1979, she became the first *Latina* elected as a Colorado state senator, and she continues her activism today by serving on the CSU's System Board of Governors. Representation improved a bit more in the 1980s when Federico

1983 Colorado Senate Committee meeting on Polly Baca's Senate Bill 139. This bill increased the potential consequences for banks violating banking laws and regulations.

Peña became Denver's mayor in 1983. Ken Salazar was elected to the U.S. Senate in 2005 and later became U.S. secretary of the interior in 2009. Most recently, he was the ambassador to Mexico in the Biden administration. His brother, John Salazar, was elected to the U.S. House of Representatives in 2005. These elections showed that *Latinas* and *Latinos* were gaining more influence in Colorado (History Colorado, n.d., para. 22). However, there has never been a *Latina* or *Latino* governor of Colorado.

In what follows, past and present *Latina* and *Latino* leaders are discussed, including elected and appointed officials, as well as the civic involvement of the historians who were interviewed.

Mary "Martha" Benavidez was the first *Latina* to serve on the Greeley City Council. She was appointed by the mayor in 1973. Tomás Romero was the first *Latino* elected to the city council in 1981. He was a Vietnam veteran and a *Chicano* activist in the 1970s.

Montoya was active in politics for many years in the Greeley area. He helped Tomás Romero's campaign when Romero won a seat on the Greeley City Council in 1981. Montoya also worked on Charlie Archibeque's campaign for City Council in 1991, and Archibeque served for sixteen years on the city council. Montoya himself was on the Greeley School Board from 1983 to 1991. In the late 1990s and early 2000s, he also helped Avery Amaya and Sherry Calvillo get elected to the city council. During President Clinton's time in office, he was invited to the White House to give advice on *Latina* and *Latino* issues. In 2005, Montoya became an advisor to U.S. Senator Ken Salazar.

Carlos Leal was also on the city council in the late 1990s and early 2000s. Before that, he served two terms on the District 6 School Board, including one term as president. Diana Vasquez was appointed to the District 6 School Board and served from 1992–1993. Clarence Lopez served on the Greeley Housing Authority as vice-chairman.

Other important public servants include Richard Martinez, who was the first *Latino* elected as Weld County Sheriff. Gil Gutierrez became the first *Latino* County court judge in 1997 and was later promoted to district court judge in 2002. From 2012 to 2017, Nieto was the first *Latina* to serve as a municipal court judge in Greeley. Steve Moreno was elected as the at-large Weld County commissioner from 2014 to 2018. Before that, he served twelve years as Weld county clerk and recorder, winning the maximum amount of three terms. Rochelle Galindo was elected to the city council in 2015. She ran unopposed for Ward 1 and served until she was elected to the Colorado House of Representatives for District 50 in 2018.

Stacy Suniga was one of the first *Latina* Democrats on the Greeley City Council. She shared her experience.

> I was on the city council for a few years (2018 and beyond), and I felt very frustrated. I often disagreed because I didn't see much effort to help people in need. The focus was more on helping people with money and power (S. Suniga, 2023).

During her time on the council, she faced threats.

> My life was threatened once while I was on the city council. But when you threaten me, you just make me stronger. It makes me even more committed to my cause (S. Suniga, 2023).

When asked about the impact of her activism in the Greeley community, she answered:

> It really brought, I would say, empowerment in the sense that we believe that we can make a difference and bring our community together to edify them. Like I said, just getting out the vote is huge because Latinos are so disenchanted. The district we had before was very, what's that word, "gerrymandered" (a manipulation of a voting or congressional district so as to favor one political party over the other). Voters were kind of drowned out. We want to change that.
>
> We want to empower and tell Latinos that you matter. You're a part of this community, your voice. If you don't use your voice, you will still

remain in this suppressed feeling. You know? We have 40 percent Latino here in Greeley. There's no reason why a Latino can't be on the city council. Without the pressures, we get drowned out by the money and that kind of stuff. If we can bring our voting numbers up, we can have a person or two in every committee, council, commission, whatever it is. And that is my goal. I think about my past and what has happened in my experience. I'm committed to that goal—of not only edifying Weld County and Greeley but the whole Congressional 8th District. That's what I'm focusing on (S. Suniga, 2023).

Stacy Suniga and Deborah Suniga (Stacy's partner), along with others, started the *Latino* Coalition of Weld County.

One of the reasons that we started the Latino *Coalition of Weld County is that we don't have representation. We need to have a voice; we need to have representation. It comes to initiatives. I mean, Stacy's testified over eight times for the redistricting (redrawing the congressional districts), and when it came and we won, that's why we worked so hard to get Yadira Caraveo elected.*

If we can get the vote out and we can get our community educated and let them know that they do have a voice and their vote does matter, we can make a difference. Look what happened this last election season for (Congressional District) CD 8 with Stacey testifying for the commission. We got our first Latina *in CD 8, Yadira Caraveo, and it's a two-year seat. Work is not done. We have to continue because we could get more people on the school board in 2023 (D. Suniga, 2023).*

Along with Stacy and Deborah Suniga and the *Latino* Coalition of Weld County, Rhonda Solis was also very instrumental in getting a new Congressional District Eight (CD 8) created.

Adams and Weld County are now together to form one district, and we just elected our first congressional person from Colorado, a Latina, *Yadira*

Caraveo. Both she and I were running and campaigning in CD 8 for these offices. I will be the first person to serve on the state Board of Education representing CD 8 … I made history. … And the first representative at the federal level from the state of Colorado, (Yadira) who's a Latina. That's huge! … I am the only Latina on the state school board (now) (R. Solis, 2023).

Many historians mentioned that Rhonda Solis encouraged them to be more involved in politics. Mendoza joined her campaign for the Colorado State Board of Education in the fall of 2022. Mendoza was excited that Rhonda was one of the first *Latinas* to run for that position. This inspired her to be more involved in the future.

For Rodriguez-McNeill:

We don't get into politics anymore because I think I'm going to say that I'm going to leave it up to the brave women like Rhonda Solis. You know, the younger ones who are more educated than we are. We struggled to get educated. You know, I wouldn't be speaking English if I hadn't struggled.

I do little things like campaigning for Obama, campaigning for David, and campaigning for different people that I feel have the same interests that we do (T. Rodriguez-McNeill, 2024).

Currently, Dr. Brenda Campos-Spitz serves on the District #6 School Board. She was elected in the fall of 2023. In the fall of 2024, Ryan Gonzales was elected to the Colorado House of Representatives for District 50, which serves the Greeley area.

Next, resistance to unjust employment conditions, oppressive education situations, and cold, uncaring treatment in the community will be discussed.

The Sugar Beet Worker Strike in *La Colonia*

There is little information about political activism from the years after World War II until the 1960s, when *El Movimiento* (the *Chicano* Movement) spread across the country. However, it is documented that the residents of *La Colonia* had already started a tradition of standing up against injustice and oppression.

The Sugar Beet Worker Strike of 1932 is an example of how workers fought for better wages and living conditions. The workers began organizing in 1930 and went on strike in 1932. They demanded not only higher wages but also fair hiring practices, the right to negotiate as a union, better housing, clean drinking water, and garden spaces (Vargas, 2013). The strike led to violence against Mexican and Mexican American workers, arrests, and even threats of deportation. Many residents of *La Colonia* left the area because of the strike (Lopez et al., 2007).

Even though the strike lasted only two weeks, it had a lasting impact on the Greeley community. It helped build a strong sense of unity and confidence among Mexican and Mexican American residents, which continued through the 1940s and beyond (Vargas, 2013).

The *Chicano* Movement in Denver

In Denver, Corky Gonzales was a leader of *El Movimiento*. He started the Crusade for Justice, a civil rights group, and worked with Cesar Chavez and Dr. Martin Luther King, Jr. to fight for justice and equality for *Latinos*.

In 1969, students led a protest at Denver's West High School after a teacher told students, "The reason *Mexicanos* are stupid is because their parents are stupid and their grandparents are stupid" (Holdman, 2023, para. 16). The protesters demanded that the teacher be fired, that bilingual education programs be created, and that *Chicano* and *Chicana* history, culture, and contributions be included in the school curriculum (Esquibel, 2015). Over three hundred students and families joined the walkout, which became known as The West High Blowout.

The protest was peaceful at first, but it turned violent when the police arrived wearing riot gear. Officers used clubs and tear gas against students, and Corky Gonzales, along with other leaders, were thrown to the ground and arrested. Young women were dragged into police vans, and the situation quickly became chaotic due to police violence (*Chicano* History and Culture, n.d., para. 10).

Over the next week, more than 1,500 middle and high school students across Denver joined the walkouts. Police dressed in riot gear used more tear gas, helicopters, and even asked the FBI for help to stop the protests. In the end, the protests were successful. The racist teacher was removed, bilingual education programs were introduced, and *Chicano* history and culture were added to the curriculum. Esquibel (2015) explained that the activism of these students and leaders continues to influence politics and civic life today.

> El Movimiento *has inspired today's young* Chicanas *and* Chicanos *to get involved. In just one of many examples, the Colorado* Latino *Forum, headed by state officers Julie Gonzales, Gia Irlando, Lisa M. Calderón, and Dulce Saenz, addresses issues of voting rights and access, criminal justice, economic development and housing, education, energy and environment, human and health services, immigration, and LGBTQ issues within and beyond the* Chicana *and* Chicano *communities (Esquibel, 2015, p. 21).*

The *Chicano* Movement in Northern Colorado

El Movimiento spread to Greeley and Northern Colorado as well. *Latinos* who returned to Greeley from World War II and the Korean War in the 1940s and 1950s saw that *Latinos* were poorly treated. "They remembered how they felt when they returned home, rejected and scorned by the Anglos for whom they had fought" (Cumming, 2020, para. 90). *El Movimiento* in Greeley was led by Jose Calderón, Ricardo and Priscilla Falcón, and many others. They led protests, marches, and walkouts throughout Greeley and Weld County in the 1960s.

> *For Falcón and his peers,* Chicano *struggles were rooted in a legacy and culture of resistance to US imperialism, which included the conquest of much of the American Southwest, formerly part of Mexico. Rather than assimilation, the necessity of* Chicana/o *political independence and* Chicana/o *nationalism was at the forefront of their organizing (G. Sánchez-Esquivel, 2024, para. 4).*

Much of their work led to violence against *El Movimiento* activists. Ricardo Falcón was murdered in 1972 by a racist man at a gas station in New Mexico. Falcón was traveling to a conference of *La Raza Unida* Party (LRUP), an organization centered on *Chicana/o* equity and civil rights, in Texas. His murderer was found not guilty by an all-White jury. This added to the injustice and violence of his murder. In nearby Boulder, six *El Movimiento* members were killed in two separate car bombings in 1974. No one was ever arrested or charged with these crimes.

Al Frente de Lucha (meaning at the forefront of the struggle) Community Center became an important location for organizing protests and unifying the Greeley *Latina* and *Latino* community (Cumming, 2020). Priscilla Falcón and Ricardo Romero, activists in *El Movimiento*, have been organizers and leaders for many years.

In this next section, some of our historians share their experiences with *El Movimiento*.

In his youth, Romero was involved in multiple protests and marches. First, he was at the Washington, D.C. Poor People's March in 1968. This gathering was an effort to address the economic injustices suffered by poor people in the U.S. at the time. He also marched with Cesar Chavez, protesting the treatment of farmworkers in California and was involved with the Kitayama Carnation Strike in Brighton in 1968. The workers at the flower plant were protesting inhumane working conditions, low wages, and their right to unionize. After over two hundred days of protesting the plant, Romero and the strike organizers— Guadalupe "Lupe" Briseño, Rachel Sandoval, Martha De Real, Mary Sailas, and Mary Padilla, among other strikers—were tear-gassed as they chained themselves to a gate to the plant. Later, Romero and others were sued by Kitayama for $175,000. However, they were represented by an assistant dean at the University of Colorado at Boulder at the time, and they won their case.

The Kitayama Flower Plant did not continue to unionize after the strike, but the working conditions improved following the strike's conclusion. Wages increased, and workers were allowed bathroom and water breaks.

Montoya was also very much involved with the movement in his teens. He attended protests, strikes, and boycotts with his father. He was a part of the Coors boycott, where *Latinos* were protesting hiring practices (not hiring or promoting *Latinos*) at the Coors plant in Golden, Colorado. When Montoya was fourteen years old, he also joined the Kitayama Carnation Strike. Further, he remembers the bombing of a police station, a school, and the burning down of a clinic in Brighton. Montoya's father, Press, was actively involved in the community during Press's youth and helped to investigate the Fort Lupton Police Department for their arrest percentage of Anglos versus *Latinos*. After the investigation found that there was a huge disparity, the Fort Lupton City Council refused to take any action. This led to weekly protests involving the University of Colorado Boulder students, Ricardo Falcón, Corky Gonzales, and Ricardo Romero. Montoya became a Brown Beret (a pro-*Chicano* para-military organization) and member of the Crusade for Justice, an organization that offered the *Chicano* community job training, a food bank, and bilingual schools that encouraged cultural pride.

When Damion Córdova was asked the question, "Were you affected by the *Chicano* Movement of the late 1960s and 1970s," he said:

Indirectly, yes, because of my parents. They were around during the Chicano *Movement. As a matter of fact, it was Corky Gonzales who actually was the impetus for my father becoming a community activist. My father was doing his undergraduate work at Western State College up in Gunnison, and in his last year there, he found out that Corky Gonzales was going to be speaking down in Denver. My father drove in their old beat-up 1970-something Volkswagen to Denver and heard Corky Gonzales speak. And that's when my father got the bug about community activism.*

My mother was more of the MEChA (Movimiento Estudiantil Chicanos de Aztlan: Chicano *Student Movement of Aztlan) and UMAS (United Mexican American Students) participant. And so while she was up at CU Boulder, she participated with* MEChA *in the sit-ins at the administration buildings at CU demanding better rights for* Chicanos. *For me personally, I wasn't affected or impacted, but indirectly I was because of what it did for my parents and how it spurred them on to become community activists, which—again—they passed on to my sister and I. We became part of LULAC (League of United Latin American Citizens) and worked with them as well (Córdova, 2023).*

A community group met to discuss the history of Al Frente de la Lucha and its contributions to the Chicano Movement. Mural by Aurelio Tekpakalli Diaz, May 12, 1984.

The *Chicano* Movement also had a strong impact on Clarence Lopez.

Yes, I was strongly (impacted). I am who I am today because of the Chicano *Movement. I was in my early teens in high school during the* Chicano *Movement, the Black movement, the social rights movements, and the Vietnam War protests. As a young teenager, I participated in lots of the protests that were going on at that time. For instance, when I was in eleventh grade, we were protesting and picketing Safeway and King*

Soopers and Jerry's Market. We were also boycotting grapes and lettuce and in support of the United Farm Workers struggle with Cesar Chavez.

We protested against the Vietnam War. This is with (others from) the Chicano Movement. They were kind of aligned with the protests against the Vietnam War.

We also marched on Dr. Bond's office from UNC. He was the president of UNC at the time. We marched from the University Center up on the hill of 20th Street and 11th Avenue and marched down to Dr. Bond's office. We were protesting because we wanted the university to hire more professors and Latinos, people who looked like us, and professors of color, who were Brown like us.

1979 Monfort strike picket line. Teófilo Bustillos is on the viewer's right in the black beanie, coat, and jeans.
Photo courtesy of the Angelina Bustillos Collection.

We also picketed The Greeley Tribune, *the local newspaper. I was a senior in high school. We were protesting because we felt that The* Tribune *was giving the Latinos bad press. It was always things that were happening, crimes instead of the good things that were happening in our community. We wanted them to hire* Chicanos *on their staff, especially a reporter who would report the good things happening.*

I was part of the Al Frente de la Lucha, *a grassroots organization that still exists today in Greeley. I'm still part of* Al Frente de la Lucha. *And we were bringing grassroots issues to the table, such as wanting the City of Greeley to install sidewalks and other needed infrastructure in North Greeley.*

Again, there were no sidewalks in parts of North Greeley, and there were still some houses that did not have plumbing. We supported the farm workers that were working out in the fields east of Greeley. So yes, the Chicano *Movement did have a strong effect on me. It's kind of made me who I am today (C. Lopez, 2023).*

This activism from the 1960s and 1970s continued to spur on community activism throughout the years.

Bustillos remembers her father, Teófilo, being involved in the 1980s strike against Monfort of Colorado. The beef packing plant closed due to the strike but reopened in 1982 with a union contract.

Monfort had a very large Latino *workforce, and they weren't paying their workers a fair minimum wage. So, the workers decided to picket. Unfortunately, the strike went on longer than what my dad had envisioned. He joined the picket line but knew that he had to feed his family as well. After a few weeks, he decided, "Well, I'm going to have to look for employment elsewhere."*

And that's when he found his job at STC in Louisville. And we moved to Longmont to be closer. But once the strike was over, my dad was proud to know that they did get a higher wage for the hard, hard work that they did (Bustillos, 2024).

In 2015, students at the University of Northern Colorado protested the ending of the Mexican American Studies Program. The university restored the program in response.

Beginning in 2013, Garcia-Nelson and others protested the oil and fracking industry in Greeley.

I think I need to start off with the most controversial thing. Weld County is a very industry-heavy county when it comes to oil and gas. My son goes to Bella Romero Elementary School, which is on the east side of Greeley, where we had the installation of a full oil and gas facility less than seven hundred feet from the playground. It's really been my mission for the last five years to get those wells shut down. Not just simply because it's dangerous, but because it has been an example of environmental racism, a very blatant example of environmental racism.

That site was originally going to go behind Frontier Academy. When you look at the demographics of the two schools, at the time of the approval of the permits, the demographics were Black and White. We had Frontier, with about 78 percent of their students who were White. Less than 20 percent of their students had free and reduced lunch. And when we go to Bella Romero, over 80 percent of our students are identified as Latino or Hispanic. A majority of the school had free and reduced lunch (Garcia-Nelson, 2023).

Garcia-Nelson and others worked very hard to have citizens vote on the 2018 Colorado Proposition 112, Minimum Distance Requirements for New Oil, Gas, and Fracking Projects Initiative. This law would have forced the oil and gas industry to drill more than 2,500 feet from schools and other nearby buildings. The voters of Colorado did not vote the law into place. However, the fight for a clean environment, safe distances from drilling, and protection for students' health continues.

Although she is too young to have participated in the *Chicano* Movement, Rhonda Solis believed:

I have benefited from all the marches. I've benefited from learning about the stories of the people who were involved in the Chicano *Movement. And it really has given me a feeling of pride and almost like, you know, a pass of the baton of this is what we did, these are the doors that we opened, and now it's on you, and what are you going to do with it? I feel a huge responsibility to carry on that legacy (R. Solis, 2023).*

Businesses in *La Colonia*

Since the early days of *La Colonia*, *Latinos* in Greeley have contributed to their community, not always by holding political positions but by starting their own businesses. "Rather than sit on the council or school board, *Latinos* are turning their attention to entrepreneurship, saying business opportunities are the way to improve the lives of *Latinos*" (Aguilera & Whatley, 2016, para. 15).

Many *Latina* and *Latino* businesses started because of segregation and discrimination that began long ago. As mentioned earlier, many businesses had signs that said, "No Mexicans Allowed," which "kept Colony residents from getting even a hamburger in town" (Deutsch, 1992, p. 111). Mautner and Abbott (1929) wrote about the segregation faced by Mexican families in the Arkansas Valley. This was likely similar to what *La Colonia* residents experienced.

The definite impression was gained that these families are not wanted in the towns or around places where Americans gather and that the colonies are designed to keep them to themselves... There are Mexican pool rooms, Mexican barber shops, Mexican stores, Mexican halls (Mautner & Abbott, 1929, p. 113).

Residents of *La Colonia* were also prevented from patronizing businesses run by Anglos. Because of the restrictions, they started their own businesses, although there is very little information about *Latina* and *Latino* businesses in the early days. The *Greeley Daily Tribune* (1934a) shows a nine-line advertisement for a "Spanish Beauty Shop," which offered services "for Spanish patrons." The same beauty shop advertised again five days later, writing, "Exclusively for Spanish-American trade" (*Greeley Daily Tribune*, 1934b). No other *Latino* businesses could be found in the newspaper.

Latina and *Latino* Businesses Today

As mentioned before, residents of *La Colonia* in the 1920s and 1930s started their own businesses because they were not allowed to shop at White businesses. Over time, the number of *Latina* and *Latino*-owned businesses has grown. One example is Montoya's real estate business.

The NoCo (Northern Colorado) Latinx Businesses/Services website (NoCo, n.d.) lists eight types of businesses in the Greeley/Ft. Collins area, with more than twenty-five businesses included. The Northern Colorado *Latino* Chamber of Commerce has over 110 members (https://nocolcc.com/). These include businesses such as law, finance, real estate, retail, landscaping, and construction.

There is no exact information on the economic impact of these businesses in Greeley. However, the U.S. Federal Reserve estimates that *Latina* and *Latino* businesses contribute over seven hundred billion dollars to the U.S. economy each year (Mills et al., 2018). This is a big increase from the single hair salon that advertised to *Latina* clients in the 1930s.

A few of our historians own their own businesses. Jenny Garcia has had a long-time restaurant in Greeley.

> *I own Jenny's Malt Shop and Diner in Downtown Greeley. I've always been an entrepreneur. I've always worked pretty much for myself. And what led me to this was where we used to go when we were young; there was a restaurant in Gilcrest that was pretty much like mine. We used to go there all the time. The only thing you don't do at my restaurant is you don't go there and dance to the oldies like we used to. And I always said*

when I could, this is what I want to open up—a 1950s shop—and I did it over thirty-six years ago. Tropical snow was there for about twenty-five years, no, maybe longer. We've been there for thirty-six years. Since 1988, when I opened up, I was on West 10th for about a year and a half, and then I closed for about half a year. And then I found this building where I'm now, and I've been here the rest of the time. I love it (J. Garcia, 2023).

Ben (Mitch) Gonzales' family has also run a furniture store in Greeley for over fifty-four years.

It started out as Ben's Furniture, TV, and Appliances in the 1960s. And we've kind of made it more into furniture and less into TV and appliances, but it's done really, really well, and it's supported a lot of families (B. M. Gonzales, 2023).

His father retired in 1998. Ben (Mitch) and his friend Lincoln Gallegos have successfully run the business since then.

Since 1978, the Durans have operated Duran Excavating/CG & S Company in Greeley, completing projects exceeding eighteen million dollars in size. In addition to commercial projects, these projects have included community-focused projects such as Kyger Reservoir Fishing Improvements Project in Windsor, Anythink Nature Library Infrastructure in Thornton, High Point Park and West Fork Regional Trail in Denver, and the Boys & Girls Club of Weld County Teen Center.

Both Clarence Lopez and Vega Ruiz own thriving real estate businesses. Nieto provides legal services as an attorney. She specializes in juvenile delinquency, truancy, family law, civil protection orders, and municipal, criminal, and domestic violence law. Gama is a pioneer in digital marketing. She was the first *Latina* in Greeley to own this type of tech business.

Civic Engagement in the Greeley Community

As discussed in this chapter, *Latinas* and *Latinos* in Greeley have taken collective action since the early days of *La Colonia*. Community activism and civic engagement have always been part of this movement. An organization like the *Latino* Coalition of Weld County, which promotes diversity and inclusion, has supported the community for many years. However, many organizations have served the *Latina* and *Latino* community over the years. We focus on three that are closely connected to civic action and support for women and our youth.

Al Frente de Lucha Community Center began in the 1960s as a center for activism. Its mission is to be an "anti-colonial organization dedicated to the struggle for the self-determination and liberation of all oppressed people" (*Al Frente*, n.d.). *Al Frente* runs a youth collective and a retreat in Tierra Amarilla, New Mexico. One of our historians, Hernandez, worked with Dr. Pricilla Falcón, a professor at UNC, at this retreat. The program was a seven-day cultural immersion camp.

The Greeley Dream Team has been supporting *Latina* and *Latino* students since 1987, helping them continue their education after high school. The organization was started by community leaders, including Montoya and Gil Gutierrez. They wanted to address the high dropout rate among *Latina* and *Latino* students. The Dream Team'a mission is to "mentor, empower, and educate today's youth to transition to college and become tomorrow's leaders" (The Greeley Dream Team, n.d., para. 1). The program provides academic advisors and mentors to over 1,800 students in the Greeley School District.

Hispanic Women of Weld County (HWWC) has been around since 1988. Charlotte Rodriguez, an employee of Aims Community College at that time, established a career day to support *Latina* career advancement and recognition. From there, Charlotte founded HWWC to support women in Weld County with nurturing and networking at monthly meetings, college scholarships, and support in overcoming barriers that interfere with their ability to live up to their potential. Diana Vasquez was HWWC's first president.

In what follows, our historians detail their own community advocacy and civic action. Jenny and Abraham Garcia worked with the Nu Alpha Kappa fraternity at UNC.

Alvin Garcia, Abraham Garcia's father, sponsored his annual Christmas Party for over six decades. Today, Jenny and Abraham sponsor the party which takes place at Our Lady of Peace Catholic Church.
Photo courtesy of the Abraham and Jenny Garcia Collection.

Well, I call it El Nako *because that's the name of our shaved ice that we made for them. They're the ones who started that one! Every year we do a carnival that they put on for kids. I like doing that because I like being involved with kids. Alvin (Abraham's father) really instilled that in me, you know, helping kids. I like working with them, and we give as much as we can (J. Garcia, 2023).*

They also help with the annual Christmas Party at the Guadalupe Center at *La Colonia.*

Then the Christmas party with the kids. Of course. Even though we couldn't put on the party itself every year, whatever we get donated, we give to the Guadalupe Center. Then we give to families Christmas baskets, gift baskets, food, and still give presents to kids that come to us. Families come to us and ask for donated toys, so we still do that (J. Garcia, 2023).

For Garcia-Nelson:

I've been involved with my community since I was a young kid. When I was younger, I was very involved with Our Lady of Peace, and so I volunteered as a Catechism teacher. I believe I had like three classes of first graders and two classes of elementary school kids that did their first communion. When I did my confirmation, I was the youngest person in my class.

I'm a member and board member of Hispanic Women of Weld County and also the president of the Young Democrats of Weld County. I'm also the treasurer for the Democratic County Party. I also like to do various other community service projects. I run a group of volunteers, and we do lunch at the Guadalupe Shelter once a month, and just any way that I can find to serve my community, I'm going to be all for it (Garcia-Nelson, 2023).

Ben (Mitch) Gonzales and his family have also been very active in the Greeley community for many years. He has been a Greeley Elks Club member for thirty-five years. He was also a member of a committee that raised money for projects around Greeley. These projects include the Greeley Ice Haus (ice rink), the Greeley Recreation Center, and the expansion of the Rodarte Community Center. He was the only *Latino* on that committee. In addition, Ben (Mitch) has been involved in many *Latino* organizations like the *Dieciséis de Septiembre* events (September 16 Mexican Independence Day) and the *Cinco de Mayo* (May 5) events. His family also runs golf fundraising contests for the League of United Latin American Citizens (LULAC) and other *Latino* organizations in Greeley.

Ben (Mitch) has also been the president of the Rodarte Community Center board for many years.

I started coaching baseball when my kids were little and started a base-ball program at the Greeley Rodarte Center. I took that one team to eight teams. That was all fundraising. I mean, the city never really helped us with that, other than letting us use the fields. For quite a number of years at the Rodarte Center, which helped at that time, we had a really, really good board. I had a lot of help from like Hispanic Women of Weld County, and we were able to walk to the neighborhoods on the north and the east side and get people aware of the new two AA ballot (new ballot measures) to help do things like an expansion at the Rodarte Center. They now have a gym. When I first was on that board, it was a building that was probably no more than twelve thousand square feet. Now they've got a dedicated boxing room, and they've got a dedicated gym! They've got a nice facility out there for the kids on the north side (B.M Gonzales, 2023).

Before going to law school, Gonzales-Soto worked with the elderly in Greeley. She also worked at Catholic Charities for a program called Supporting Immigrant and Refugee Families after she graduated from law school in 2002. The program ran a resource center for immigrants. This center offered information on life skills, learning English, and safety for children while in automobiles. While there, Gonzales-Soto successfully united migrants, immigrants, and refugees from many countries to help improve their life situations. Today, she continues to meet with and advocate for the immigrant community in Greeley. She attends legal clinics and offers legal advice. Gonzales-Soto cares very much about helping immigrant and refugee families make decisions about their legal paths and their futures.

Johnson also strongly believes in helping the community in many ways:

I'm a public servant by heart. And helping the community—that's important to me, to be able to help. And I think that also got ingrained in me as a younger child, seeing my dad helping adults with disabilities. And my mom also. I call her a "philanthropist" because I don't have a term for when my parents are out there asking for help to assist a cause or when my mom tells me, "Hey, take off your tennis shoes because we're going to give them to this person who needs them," things like that (Johnson, 2023).

Johnson has served on many boards, and Governor Polis appointed her to two of them: the 19th Judicial Performance Commission and as vice-chair of the Regional Air Quality Council. The Regional Air Quality Council helps ensure the air quality stays safe by working to reduce greenhouse gases and control emissions. The 19th Judicial Performance Commission evaluates judges to to make sure they are fair and just. Johnson is also on a statewide board called Colorado *Latino* Leadership Advocacy and Research Organization (CLLARO). She is also a board member and public relations representative for Hispanic Women of Weld County, and serves on the board of Friends of A Woman's Place, which supports survivors of domestic violence. Her most recent appointment is to the board of Operation North Star. The organization works to empower individuals in the community with tools and resources needed to do well in their learning environments. At the time of the interview, she was a member of the Evans City Council.

Clarence Lopez has been a realtor for thirty-nine years. He supports and advocates for his community in real estate.

When I first became licensed as a realtor in 1985, I felt like this was the area that I wanted to help my community. This is when I talked about working and selling homes to the Mexican American community and the immigrant community who were coming here from Latin America. I felt that this was the niche that I wanted to create for myself, and I felt I could help my community.

In 1985, I joined the Greeley Housing Authority. I was the vice chairman of the Greeley Housing Authority for five years, from 1985 to 1990. Our goal, you know, as the housing authority, was to provide decent, safe, and affordable housing for low-income families. I felt like this was an area where I was also serving my community, the lower-income families who couldn't afford to buy a home at that point. They needed a place to rent.

In 1994, there were about six of us Chicano *businessmen and one* Chicana *businesswoman on our committee as well. We formed the Northern Colorado Hispanic Chamber of Commerce. We felt there was a need for representation for the* Latino *business owners in Greeley. We felt the Greeley Chamber of Commerce was not servicing the needs of the* Latino *business community nor supporting our needs. Because of that, we formed the Hispanic Chamber of Commerce, which became the* Latino *Chamber of Commerce (C. Lopez, 2023).*

When Gabriel A. Lopez talked about the book *White Gold Laborers: The Story of Greeley's Spanish Colony,* written with his wife, Jody, his excitement jumped off the page of his interview transcript!

Clarence Lopez served as a member of the Housing Authority of the City of Greeley. Back row, left to right: Jim Boyle, Clarence A. Lopez, and Jon Helwick. Front row, left to right: Ronald J. Lambden and Charlotte Rodriguez. Photo courtesy of the Clarence Lopez Collection.

I had to; I love that story. I love the history of Spanish Colony and the (Greeley) Grays, and it's just an amazing history. And actually, Jody and I did the book. We wrote the book and did all the research and everything, but the book itself is what made it popular. And we're all over the U.S., and then we're also in Australia and New England. A store there sells our books! The stories represent people's lives, the older ones, and so that's what made it popular. We are spokespeople for it. But we've been enjoying it. Don't get us wrong. We like traveling (G. A. Lopez, 2023).

Martinez has been a part of the American GI Forum (a civil rights organization run by *Latino* veterans). He has also been involved in the American Legion (an organization of American war veterans). He was the vice-commander of American Legion Post 18 and was legionnaire of the year in 1999. After he joined the American Legion, Henry and his friend Frank Martinez began the "Last Fire Base." This group of Vietnam veterans was recognized as an official unit of the U.S. government. In this job, he and others led bingo games every week. They then donated the money to the Veterans Memorial here in Greeley. They gave a lot of money to the animal shelters for pet food and supplies. In addition, they gave scholarships every year to deserving members of their organization.

Martinez Rocha has had a lot of experience with community involvement as well.

I think I started when my kids were young. I was their Brownie leader, their Girl Scout leader, and then, their catechist. The first organization my husband and I joined together was the GI Forum, and we were very active there. I became the chairperson for the American GI Forum Women when I was twenty-two. I think I was the youngest chairperson who they had ever had. We did a lot of good for the community. We were also involved in the League of United Latin American Citizens (LULAC). When I moved to Greeley, I joined the Hispanic Women of Weld County

(HWWC). That has been my heart because when I came back as a widow with four kids, they empowered me. They encouraged me; they supported my family and me. I have been an active member for thirty-three years and a two-time past president (Martinez Rocha, 2023).

At the Hispanic Women of Weld County Breakfast in 2019.
Left to Right: Stacy Suniga, Dolores Huerta, Martinez Rocha, Baca, Ally Johnson, Rhonda Solis, and Priscilla Falcón.
Photo courtesy of the Juanita Martinez Rocha Collection.

Martinez Rocha has also been part of the Habitat for Humanity Board for four years. While she was on this board, Martinez Rocha went to *Tuzla* and *Santiago*, Mexico, to help build houses. HWWC members have also helped build Habitat houses in Greeley for many years. She is on the board of directors for The Greeley Dream Team. This program mentors, empowers, and educates today's youth to transition to college. Martinez Rocha is also a member of the Assistance League, a philanthropic group that supports the community with low-cost clothing and home goods, among other services. Another board that Martinez Rocha has worked on and is very important to her is A Woman's Place:

a shelter that supports women who are victims of domestic violence:

> *My mom was a battered woman; I do this in honor of her memory. I'm currently on Friends of A Woman's Place Board, which raises money to support A Woman's Place shelter. I'm also a part of the Judicial Performance Commission, a state commission. We evaluate the judges on their performance, and we recommend improvements if needed. Then the judges who are approved through our commission can appear on the ballot for re-election as a judge in the 19th District.*
>
> *I'm on this Mexican American History project, which I think is an amazing project. When Emma (the project's coordinator) approached me about being on this committee, I thought it was quite an honor because I think that, as* Latinos, *we need to get our voices out there, our information, our contributions, and our feelings to be known. I'm on a subcommittee of the oral history program and serve as treasurer (Martinez Rocha, 2023).*

Montoya has been active in the Greeley community for many years. After moving to Greeley and graduating from UNC, he became a juvenile probation officer. Throughout his career, three different governors appointed him to important positions in the state. He has worked with young people, serving as an educational leader at the Colorado Commission of Higher Education. He also served on the state's real estate commission. Montoya also played an important role in building the Greeley Recreation Center after Tomás Romero asked him to join the new Greeley Recreation Committee. He also increased *Latina* and *Latino* representation by recruiting Romero to the school board. This made history, as it was the first time that two *Latinos* served together on the school board.

Montoya helped hire District 6 Superintendent Tim Waters in 1986. Waters came from Arizona and brought an inclusive mindset to the school district. During Waters' leadership, *Latino* community leaders, such as Ernie Andrade

Rodarte Community Center, named for Jesus Rodarte, is a center of youth-focused activities with a boxing gym, STEM Summer Scholars, and After school Programs. Jesus Rodarte was instrumental in getting the center built. It began as a 12,000 square foot building and now has an addition with a full gym.
Photo from Clarence Lopez.

and John Pacheco, were promoted. John Pacheco later became the only *Latino* superintendent in Greeley's history. Montoya also supported women on the school board, helping to stop the long history of an all-White, all-male board. He served two four-year terms on the Greeley District 6 School Board. He was one of the founders of the Greeley Dream Team, a nonprofit organization that helps middle and high school students continue their education. At the beginning, he helped raise one million dollars to begin its mission in helping students attain skills to be successful in higher education. Today, after thirty years, the program has a 100 percent student success rate in high school graduation and college attendance. In the last six years, Montoya has worked for Jobs of Hope. This is a nonprofit organization that supports and gives housing to former gang members and incarcerated men who want to rejoin the community.

For thirty-five years, (Romero) Horning has been dedicated to education and improving the lives of children. She has worked hard to ensure that all children, no matter their family's income or skin color, have access to educational opportunities. She chose to work in low-income schools, believing that every child deserves a chance to learn and succeed. (Romero) Horning also volunteers at her church and serves on the Weld Trust Educational Advisory Committee, a foundation that supports literacy and career advancement. She is also a board member of Nest to Wings, an organization that helps students go to college or trade schools.

For over nine years, Nieto has been involved with A Woman's Place, serving on the board and as a past president. She is also the co-chair of Friends of A Woman's Place. Nieto volunteers at many organizations, including local food banks, the Relay for Life—an event for raising money and awareness of cancer —and the local hospital NICU, which helps families with newborn babies in the hospital. She is also involved with Grace Upon Grace, which gives diapers and hygiene products to low-income families, and is a district chair of the Boy Scouts Pine Derby. Nieto is a member of Hispanic Women of Weld County, a past president of the Greeley Dream Team, and a past vice president of the Colorado Municipal Judges Association.

Perez has worked in community action programs and migrant programs in Nebraska. In Greeley, he has been an active member of the chief of police's *Latino* advisory committee. On that committee, he strongly advocated for body cameras to improve police accountability. Before that, Perez also served on a state committee that fought for the same cause, helping make law enforcement more accountable and just.

For Theresa Solis, working to improve the community is in her family's DNA. In the late 1940s, her mother helped raise money to build Our Lady of Peace Church. This was after her family was discriminated against in other White churches. Later in her life, she worked with an attorney to help improve the working and living conditions of agricultural workers in the area. An abusive farmer threatened her with a gun, so Theresa organized media coverage to further the cause. She showed that the farmer was exposing his workers to difficult living conditions: no electricity or running water, no proper shelter, and unpaid wages that they had earned.

She shared:

I still do work for some of the people because where I live now, on the east side, it's an HOA. I found out that a lot of the people there were from Mexico, and some of them were undocumented. They were frightened, so I approached some of them and asked what was wrong. They told me that some people on the HOA board had charged a man a thousand dollars for parking an inch over the curb! And then another gentleman had put in a handicap ramp, and they made him move the ramp to his garage. He'd have to come out the side way (instead of his front door). Then, other people told me they were being fined, and they would have to pay cash.

As a consequence, I started working on it, and I did a lot of research. It took me hours! I spent a lot of time working on that project, and I went to look at city records. I visited different offices here in Greeley, and I found out, looking at secretary of state records, that the HOA was not registered, and they were getting money from people when they were not a valid HOA. What I did was I filed complaints, and then I finally met with the attorney general in Denver. The HOA had to reimburse some of the people (T. Solis, 2023).

Stacy Suniga has worked with the community to open a homeless shelter called The Room at the Inn.

Then I got into my heart work. In the late 1990s, I had an encounter with a homeless man, and I've always pitied people who had to sleep out in the snow and that kind of thing. It was really snowy, like a two-degree night, so that changed the trajectory of what I wanted to do. I did some research on homelessness and then gathered my faith community. First working through my faith community and then the community at large, and other faith groups, we started the homeless shelter Room at the Inn, opening its doors in 2001. It was for families and children. I did that; that was my first type of community work, which was organizing and bringing together faith groups to work together and then provide these services (S. Suniga, 2023).

Along with his parents, brothers, and *Latina* and *Latino* instructors from UNC, Treviño was very involved in Greeley's *Candelaria* Association. This association brought to light and addressed issues in the *Latina* and *Latino* community of Greeley.

Like Treviño, Damion Córdova, his father, Roberto, and his mother, Betty, have also been very involved with the *Candelaria* Association.

Yeah. my parents, Roberto and Betty Córdova were involved in the Candelaria Association back in the day, as well as LULAC, the League of United Latin American Citizens (Córdova, 2023).My father was also involved in the Black, Hispanic, Latino, or the Black/Hispanic Coalition (a group of diverse student groups) up at UNC. I went away for college and military duty. I came back and actually joined the adult council here, the LULAC Adult Council in Greeley. My father, Roberto, was the president, and my mother, Betty, was one of the officers as well. What we really did was about education, community activism, and our primary focus was education for Latino youth. And so, most of our focus was on engaging Latino youth through the establishment of twenty-six different youth councils throughout the U.S. and throughout Colorado in middle schools and high schools. And then we'd also do some fundraising for scholarships.

Then, every year, we would hold a big LULAC youth conference up at UNC. A lot of the LULAC youth from the middle schools and high schools would attend that conference where we could actually bring them to campus, show them what it feels like to be on a college campus, and have them go through conference workshops just like a person would if they're going to a conference workshop for their job. And we'd have different presenters, Latinos, Latinas, you know, from different walks of life stressing the importance of education, and they would share their stories. The whole idea was, "Hey, look, if I can do it and get here, you can do it too. And that we've done, and we've paved the way, so let's get you going" (Córdova, 2023).

Wendirad has also been involved in the community in many ways. She has overseen organizing meals at the Guadalupe Shelter for the homeless. Wendirad is also involved with her church and was a member of the UNC Scholarship Committee. She also serves on the UNC Alumni Board and is a host for the Family and Friends Program.

Romero is a long-time educator, activist, and organizer. He has a multi-year profile in community involvement. To begin, Romero is one of the founders of the American GI Forum in Brighton, Fort Lupton, and in Greeley. The GI Forum is a *Latino* organization focused on veteran issues, education, and civil rights. Along with Carlos Leal, Romero also founded the Sunrise Clinic in north Greeley. This clinic serves low-income patients. According to Romero, there are nine other similar clinics in the Northern Colorado area. The *Candelaria* Association is another organization that Romero was instrumental in starting. He also worked with Peak and Envision to improve parent education and bring more support for students, including those with special needs.

We found things that needed to be done, things that needed to be changed, discrimination cases, things of that sort. Yes ... very involved. And then, I was also one of the founders, with Carlos Leal involved ... with the Hispanic Coalition, the Black, Hispanic Coalition at UNC (Romero, 2023).

Community involvement for Rhonda Solis includes serving on the Greeley District 6 School Board for two terms or for eight years. She has also served as a CASA advocate, where she worked with children who are in the court system because of abuse and neglect. Hispanic Women of Weld County (HWWC) is an organization that is near and dear to her heart; she has been a long-time member and a past president. For two years, from 2023–2025, Rhonda represented Colorado's District #8 on the State Board of Education. She is one of the first *Latinas* to be elected to the State Board.

Velasquez has contributed to her community in many ways.

I have a list ... I served on the Greeley Dream team. ... served on the board of directors of Habitat, went to Mexico, where we helped build homes, and went to two different villages. ... I was also the commissioner (appointed by Governor Ritter in 2007) on the Colorado Civil Rights Commission. We heard illegal discrimination complaints. I also served as the director for action. I was the person who investigated the discrimination complaints of students and faculty and staff at UNC (Velasquez, 2024).

Rodriguez-McNeill was involved in the "movement."

You know, with Jose Calderón, and then they built a little tiny place like Al Frente de Lucha. *It was little, you know, and then they wanted to charge to use it, you know? But anyway, we worked on that project. We worked for the celebration of September 16 and* Cinco de Mayo *because, at that time,* Cinco de Mayo *wasn't celebrated. We'd have it in the park, and we also celebrated it at the state armory. The state armory was our dance hall at that time (Rodriguez-McNeill, 2023).*

For many years, Rodriguez-McNeill has volunteered to teach *Ballet Folklorico* to thousands of children. Her dance group has performed at many events in Northern Colorado and Denver. They are a regular part of celebrations like *Cinco de Mayo*, Fourth of July, and *Dieciséis de Septiembre. Ballet Folklorico* is a traditional Mexican folk dance. Each dance comes from a different region of Mexico. The dancers wear bright, colorful skirts with ribbons. Male dancers wear short jackets and dark pants, which are decorated with silver ornaments.

Rodriguez-McNeill shared:

I have a dance group ... I started the dance group a long time ago. I've always danced, and when my kids were growing up, they wanted to learn. I taught them, and we danced together as a family with my sisters and kids (Rodriguez-McNeill, 2023).

Vega Ruiz has coached local soccer teams for over fifteen years. Since 2014, he has served on the Habitat Family Selection Committee, helping families to fulfill their dreams of home ownership. As a re-

The Bella Romero Education Fiesta was established 1996. Francisco Cortez presents ballet *folklorico* dance award medals to children. Photo courtesy of the Francisco Cortez collection.

altor, Vega Ruiz is part of the Associate Leadership Council for Keller Williams. He is also on the executive board and serves as treasurer for the Northern Colorado Chapter of the National Association of Hispanic Real Estate Professionals (NAHREP). Additionally, Vega Ruiz is the vice-chair for the City of Greeley Parks and Recreation Advisory Board. He helps improve parks and recreational programs for the community. One of his goals is to guide and mentor young people.

For us, it was more like once you get through high school, once you're done with high school, you have the opportunity to choose whether or not college is for you. We always harped on it. It's business, college, or, military, right? There are opportunities out there, and you can make an impact (Vega Ruiz, 2023).

Vega Ruiz was asked how these organizations had an impact on him and the community. He said that his focus was on helping others, educating, and leading by example.

Habitat has been one that I grew up near, one of their early developments in town. And I know that my family was never qualified or were able to get our application accepted. That experience, for whatever reason, has sparked an interest in helping other families (who apply for a home through Habitat) (Vega Ruiz, 2023).

Watson's father, Carlos Leal, did a lot for the community over many years. Carlos was a professor at UNC and became a role model for many *Latina* and *Latino* students. He worked with other *Latina* and *Latino* activists like Romero, where they worked to recruit, retain, and graduate *Latina* and *Latino* students at UNC in the 1970s and beyond. He served on the Greeley City Council and on the District #6 School Board. Watson's sister, Valerie, was also a member of the school board.

Charles Archibeque, father of historian Nickie Archibeque, while serving on the Catholic Charities Board of Greeley, helped found the *Plaza del Sol* and *Plaza del Milagro,* which provide housing for migrant workers. He was also a member of the Weld County Airport Board and the Colorado Department of Transportation Commission. For sixteen years (four terms), Charles served on the Greeley City Council. He worked with others to start Island Grove Village (low-income housing community) and the Guadalupe Center. Both are important housing resources for the community.

Nickie Archibeque also wanted to help *Latinos* in Greeley. She joined the City of Greeley Human Relations Commission to learn how the city supports different communities. She also took over her father's position on the *Plaza del Milagro* Board. Her daughter, Hernandez, another one of our historians, started her community involvement as a teen in the Greeley Youth Commission. This experience helped her understand the importance of giving back. While studying at CU-Boulder, Hernandez became student body president and worked on community organizing. Because of her efforts, two laws were passed, allowing undocumented students to qualify for in-state tuition (ASSET). She also convinced the CU Board of Regents to accept ASSET students, even after they had first rejected the idea.

Montalvo has worked as a caseworker for Catholic Charities. She has contributed to her community by working at the food bank doing food stamp outreach and assisting the elderly. She has also been involved with the Hispanic Women of Weld County.

Military Service

Serving one's country is undoubtedly the highest form of civic engagement. Some of our historians and/or their families have unselfishly sacrificed their time, energy, mental health, and separation from their loved ones in order to serve their country. Like many military families, some of our historians' families have made the ultimate sacrifice.

We asked our historians two questions about their military experience. The first was: "Have you or anyone in your family served in the military?" The second question was: "How were you or your family members treated when you came back to regular life?" Here are some of their answers to the second question.

Watson answered:

When Dad came back and my uncles came back, it was still a time in history where it didn't matter if they had served for our country; they were still treated horribly. They shared a lot of those stories where they were just still poor Mexicans. Nobody, nobody put them up on a pedestal like they do today. My son didn't experience any of that, and my father-in-law shared stories (that were not discriminatory), but he and I think it was because he was not a person of color. His experience was very different. Dad and my uncles experienced something very different. But that was back in the late 1950s and early 1960s, and racism was alive and well. It was during Martin Luther King's time. They were not treated well (Watson, 2023).

Vázquez came to the Greeley area when he was seventeen. He told stories that happened in and around Spanish Colony.

I was told stories of other Mexican Americans. You see, there was a time we couldn't cross the train tracks around the Spanish Colony, Eaton, and Kersey. If we went to town to bring groceries, they would wait at the tracks to beat us up when we returned. … Sometimes the Mexican Americans would get drunk and go to town in force, and they were given a beating and thrown on the other side of the road (Vázquez, 2023).

Vázquez said he felt freer only after World War II ended. He remembers that most places treated people better, but one restaurant, the Greeley Inn on 8th Avenue, did not.

The restaurant did not want to serve the Mexican American military men who had just returned from the war. Even though they wore their uniforms, the restaurant still refused to serve them. The soldiers thought their uniforms should be respected. When they were not served, they broke the dishes on the table and left. The waitresses were also not kind to them (Vázquez, 2023).

Other historians, like Velasquez, had family members fight in Vietnam. She brought up the terrible effects of Agent Orange.

My husband served in Vietnam and is now suffering the effects of Agent Orange. He was in Vietnam, two tours of duty in the Marines, and right now, we're hopeful as he started a new treatment, but he has leukemia caused by Agent Orange. He has 100 percent disability through the VA (Veterans' Administration). And, we're hopeful that this treatment is going to help him because there is no cure. There's no cure for Agent Orange.

He's literally dying for his country, but all they can do is try to extend his life.

In Vietnam, they used Agent Orange to spray the trees because of the Vietcong who were hiding in the jungle. They sprayed Agent Orange to defoliate the trees because then they'd be able to see the Vietcong. Well, they were spraying the people of Vietnam. They sprayed our soldiers (too)! ... and now there are thousands, maybe millions, of people in Vietnam suffering the effects of Agent Orange, and so are our veterans (Velasquez, 2023).

Treviño's uncle also had experience with Agent Orange.

I had an uncle who was in the military. He was in the Army, and he served over in Vietnam. When he came back, he had been exposed to Agent Orange, so he had a number of health issues (Treviño, 2023).

Henry Lee Martinez served in Vietnam from 1968 to 1969 in the U.S. Army 173rd Airborne Brigade.
Photo courtesy of the Henry Lee Martinez Collection.

As with most wars, many who return, and their family members, experience mental health issues. Silva brought up these issues, such as post-traumatic stress disorder (PTSD), that many of them suffer.

They came back with bad health, real problems. My husband, I'm pretty sure he had PTSD because he would wake up in the middle of the night shaking and trying to run because, I imagine, he was dreaming he was still in the service, and I think that messed him up (Silva, 2023).

Martinez Rocha agreed.

And then, when my husband (Joe Rocha) came home as a Vietnam vet again, they were ostracized, criticized. They were spit on. He had a difficult time. I remember when a siren would go off and he'd jump out of bed! You know, because he was afraid, it took some years of adjustment, but I think more than anything, what really bothered him is that they risked their lives for this country. And then, they came back home, and they treated him like crap. That's why I think he got so involved with the Veterans Outreach Program. He said that he wanted to help vets adapt to life again because they were having trouble getting jobs and buying homes. They didn't care if you served your country or not as long as you were Brown (Martinez Rocha, 2023).

Some of the historians also talked about the injustices they face while in the military. Martinez remembered the differences in receiving awards and medals.

Oh yes, yes! But the thing that made it bad is that you have to work twice as hard for them. If you were Mexican, you had to work twice as hard to get that decoration. If you were a White guy, you got it right away, right off the bat. They put you in for it, you got it. If you're Mexican, you had to go through the same scenario twice to get one! You had to get wounded twice to get a Purple Heart! You had to get shot at five times to get a self-defense medal ... so there was bias and prejudice in Vietnam (H.L. Martinez, 2023).

Damion Córdova served much later than most of our older veterans. He had more positive things to say about his time in the military.

I think for me, in my generation of individuals serving in the military, I didn't see as much discrimination in the military because your life depends on somebody else and their life depends on you. You don't care what color person is, or their religious background, or their practices. You don't care because you have to look out for each other (Córdova, 2023).

Ben (Mitch) Gonzales also thinks that more minorities today are having increased positive experiences in the military.

My son is currently a master sergeant in the U.S. Air Force, and he's been in for about fourteen years. … And my son has got quite a few commendations, and he's risen through the ranks pretty rapidly for the time he's been in. As I said, it's flipped. But now I think the military, since Truman integrated the military in the late 1940s, I think the military is ahead of, I mean, you see a lot more Black and Latino generals that you would've never seen in the 1950s and 1960s. I think the military's changed quite a bit. And I'm proud of my son for being in the military (B.M. Gonzales, 2023).

Perez had a similar experience as Córdova. But he also experienced some of the same unfair treatment as Martinez.

In the military, I felt comfortable because we had to have each other's back. And my experience was in the Vietnam War, and I think young Latinos, Chicanos, the Mexican Americans were overly represented in that war, as were the Black members of our community (Perez, 2023).

Perez further spoke to the difficulty he faced when he returned from the service.

And then when we came back, I felt that I did my duty, I did my time in the service.

Joe Perez served in Da Nang, Vietnam (1971). Photo courtesy of the Joe Perez Collection.

I just wanted to get back and be back home where it was safe and sound and leave the war behind. But during one of my high school reunions, I reconnected with some of my high school friends—Latinos. And of the thirteen Latinos who graduated from high school, nine of us had served in Vietnam.

We said, "Wow, what were they *trying to do?*"

If we're not going to be proud of this, and we're not going to let people know, this is going to be forgotten!

We worked on building a memorial. Number one, our first phase was to build a memorial for the young Latinos who were killed during Vietnam. And there were a number of names that came up from not only the barrio but the Valley, we call it the Valley of the Community of Latinos. And we built a memorial to recognize their service.

And then we said, "Wow, I wonder how many of our uncles and relatives have served in the service?"

And we came up with over six hundred names!

Wow! We didn't even know! So we built a memorial and put the names of those six hundred names to recognize and honor the fact that from this small barrio in this valley of Western Nebraska, Latinos had contributed so much to American society (Perez, 2023)!

Cortez also spoke to the hard times he experienced after he returned from Vietnam.

When I was in service, when I was overseas, they called me a spic (a derogatory name for a Mexican American); that came home with me. And when I put my uniform on, I was proud of my uniform until they spat on me. It doesn't matter. It didn't matter. I mean, I could have lost it, but I didn't. I just put my uniform away. And then, when I went to work here in Colorado, I was homeless for three years. I lived out of my car, or I stayed with friends. I dated women so I could find a place to stay. And, yeah, wages were crap. I was making a buck and a half for construction (Cortez, 2023).

We end this section of our veterans' experiences with a quote from Martinez. He spoke to how many of those Vietnam vets felt in the 1960s and 1970s.

I don't think Mexican Americans were treated any differently than everybody else. Vietnam veterans were all treated the same. As a matter of fact, Vietnam was nothing compared to the humility and the low-down feeling I felt when I came home. That was the hardest part of Vietnam for me: when I came home. I was delayed. I had survived the war, survived several wounds, and come home, and oh, I had felt so glad to be home!

Then we landed in Fort Lewis, Washington. We went to the airport, and there was this old lady. She was running after me, trying to kick me and spit on me. Also, after we landed in Fort Lewis, we left the gates to the bus. There were people with signs that said, "Go back! You're Not Welcome, Baby Killers! Go Back! You're Not Welcome Back in America!"

You know, and I'm (thinking), "What the heck's going on?"

I was just in a combat zone. I'd never, never heard what was going on here, stateside. I didn't know all this was happening! That was really the biggest let-down of my military career.

I'm going to expand on that a little bit. One of the things that made it even worse was the fact that we went by ourselves and came back by ourselves. We didn't go as a unit. None of the people who went over to Vietnam went there as a unit. You had a plane full of people, but they were all assigned to different units. Once you landed in Vietnam, everybody split up, and you were by yourself again until you got to wherever you're going.

Same way going home. "Your duty was up. Goodbye. Have a good life. We'll see you."

They said, "You, go home by yourself."

There was no unit cohesion, no unit celebrations to come back. And then to have the people themselves actually treat you the way they did. You know that really affected me mentally the most (H.L. Martinez, 2023).

Jacob Duran, U.S. Navy.
Photo courtesy of the
Jacob Duran Collection.

It is very sad to hear about the experiences of many veterans, especially those who served in Vietnam. When Latino Vietnam veterans came home, they faced even more discrimination. However, some historians shared positive military experiences. We will also honor one of Greeley and Weld County's most respected veteran, Joe P. Martinez.

Among the forty-four people interviewed, over one hundred of their family members have served in the military. Some of the historians who served include Henry Lee Martinez, Joe Perez, Francisco Cortez, Jacob Duran, and Damion Córdova. Many of them served with honors.

For example, Martinez earned a Purple Heart, a Flight Medal, and a Vietnam Service Cross. Also, Jenny Garcia's sister was one of the first *Latinas* to become a lieutenant colonel. She worked at the North American Aerospace Defense Command (NORAD) and the Pentagon, where the U.S. Department of Defense is located.

Josie Duran spoke proudly of her Uncle Joe, who was awarded a Congressional Medal of Honor and a Purple Heart medal, saying that he was "pretty valiant!" She feels sad when she hears about his bravery because she never got to meet him.

Private Joe P. Martinez was drafted into the Army when he was twenty-two years old. He is one of the most honored service members in U.S. history. There are statues of him in Bittersweet Park in Greeley, in Ault, Colorado (his hometown), and in Denver.

Private Joe P. Martinez (July 27, 1920–May 25, 1943) was the first Mexican American and first Coloradan to receive the Medal of Honor, the highest military decoration, for his heroic actions in the Aleutian Islands during World War II.

In 1945, the U.S. Navy renamed one of its ships the *USNC Private Joe P. Martinez*. This ship carried soldiers to Korea during the Korean War.

In the 1970s, the city of Pueblo, Colorado, named a street after him, Joe P. Martinez Boulevard. The state of Colorado also renamed a former military reception center in Greeley in his honor. A Disabled American Veterans' chapter in Colorado and an American Legion Post in California were also named after him.

The Army honored him in 1977 by renaming the Welcome Center at Fort Ord, California, Martinez Hall. The base is now closed, but Martinez Hall still helps veterans as a transition center.

Finally, part of Colorado Highway 85, beginning on First Street in Ault to Main Avenue in Eaton, is called the Private Joe P. Martinez Memorial Highway. (Hubbard. J. (2023). Navy Vet Honored for Getting Colorado Highway Named for War Heroes. Available at: https://kdvr.com/news/problem-solvers/serving-those-who-serve/joe-p-martinez-memorial-highway-col-stan-cass/)

Private Martinez died in action in the Aleutian Islands, Alaska, on May 25, 1943. He was the first Mexican American and the first person from Colorado to receive the Congressional Medal of Honor. This is the highest military award in the U.S. for bravery. He received it in 1943 after he died; his family accepted it for him.

He also earned other medals, including the Purple Heart, the Army Good Conduct Medal, the American Campaign Medal, the Asiatic-Pacific Campaign Medal, and the World War II Victory Medal.

Joe's bravery was heroic. In 1942, Japanese forces took over the Aleutian Islands in Alaska. This was the first time a foreign enemy had occupied American land since the War of 1812. The U.S. was worried that Japan might use the islands to attack the West Coast, so the military needed to remove the Japanese quickly.

In May 1943, the mountains of the Aleutian Islands were still covered in snow. Private Martinez stood up and moved forward up Holtz-Chichago Pass. He fired at Japanese soldiers hiding in foxholes while gunfire and grenades exploded around him. Joe called on his fellow soldiers to follow him. Inspired by his courage, they did. Together, they regained ground as they climbed the mountain.

Even though it was dangerous, Joe kept leading the soldiers. Sadly, during the second advance, he was badly injured and died. His bravery helped the Army take back the pass, which was an important step in removing the Japanese forces from the Aleutian Islands in Alaska (https://military-history.fandom.com/wiki/Joe_P._Martínez, May 15, 2024).

Like Josie Duran, the *Latinos* of Northern Colorado are also very proud of Joe's courage, bravery, and leadership. If Japan had been able to use the Aleutian Islands as a base, they could have won the war. WWII might have ended very differently.

In conclusion, *Latinos* have greatly contributed to our community and this country through our civic involvement. Johnson believes we need to be more vocal. She also said we should be acknowledged for our contributions to civic engagement.

> I think there's a lack of acknowledgment. That's one of the things that I feel that I try, and I don't think others do very well is amplifying the voices and highlighting our contributions. I started this Instagram and Facebook page called Latinos *Making Waves* for that same reason because I noticed that we weren't being highlighted. There are so many Mexican Americans, Latinos, and Hispanics who have been doing phenomenal work for a long time, but no one knows about them. Representation matters, and kiddos want to see people who look like them doing great work because they also want to know that they can too. And without that representation, I mean, how are you supposed to know that it's something that can possibly happen to you? (Johnson, 2023).

Rhonda Solis explains that being more involved in the community and politics is very important for the future of *Latinos* in Greeley.

You need to be part of the system to change the system. And I say we need it all. We need to draw attention with marches and protests, especially when we see big things happen. Like what was happening at our meat-packing plant around COVID-19 and employees actually dying. We need to get more people to run for office. And I know sometimes it's hard to get involved politically, but when you look around, everything is political, and someone is making the decision for you. You have to decide: are you just going to be on the sidelines, are you going to be on the menu, or are you actually going to be at the table? I want to be at the table! (R. Solis, 2023).

Even though many older veterans had very difficult times in the military, they have worked to help other veterans have an easier time returning to normal life. For example, Martinez started a group called the Last Fire Base. It was made up of Vietnam veterans who held weekly fundraisers in Greeley. They used the money to help veterans and also gave scholarships to members of their group.

Martinez Rocha's husband, Joe Rocha, helped veterans through the Veterans Outreach Program. Perez also worked hard to build a Veterans Memorial in his small Nebraska community.

Many *Latino* veterans have turned their difficult experiences into hope. They work to make things better, not only for other veterans but also for future generations.

NARRATIVES FOR CHAPTER 4

Polly Baca

I often say the greatest gift God ever gave me was being born a female child to a poor Mexican American family in a bigoted community ... it was the pain of that bigotry that drove me to try to do something about it, so I was absolutely determined to prove that Mexican Americans were as good as anybody else. —Baca

Polly Baca at the 1968 Democratic Convention in Chicago. She worked on Robert F. Kennedy's presidential campaign.
Photo courtesy of the Polly Baca Collection.

Polly Baca, a female trailblazer and politician, has worked tirelessly to create change for underrepresented communities at the highest levels of government. Experiences from her childhood and her father's teachings influenced her trajectory in life. Baca recalled:

It was very difficult growing up in Greeley, CO, as a child in the 1940s and 1950s because of the bigotry.

Boys would throw rocks at her and call her a "dirty Mexican." She recalled seeing store signs that said, "No Mexicans or dogs allowed." Regardless of the rampant racism, her family defied the odds through community work. Baca's father, José Manuel Baca, helped establish Our Lady of Peace Catholic Church and was the first to lead Greeley's Credit Union for small loans. The Baca and Nuanez families also established the first Mexican grocery store in Greeley, which was located across Lincoln Park on 9th Avenue.

Regardless of her parents not completing high school, their dream was to see their three daughters graduate college. Baca graduated in the top 10 percent of her high school class, earning a scholarship to attend any state school of her choice. She attended CSU and was the first in her family to leave home to attend college. Her father iterated the importance of understanding the political system, which led her to obtain a teaching degree in political science in 1962.

Baca has broken the glass ceiling as the first female Colorado Mexican American in various ways. She was the first chair of the Democratic Caucus of the Colorado House of Representatives from 1976 to 1979.

Baca's great, great uncle, Juan Antonio Baca, was elected in 1878 to the Colorado State Senate, and it took one hundred years for a Mexican American woman, Baca, to be elected to the Colorado State Senate in 1978. She served from 1979 until 1987.

She also served in the House of Representatives from 1974 to 1979. She was the first co-chair of the National Democratic Convention. A major contribution Baca made was the creation of the Latin American Research and Service Agency in 1964. Baca was their first CEO. She is also represented in the National Hispanic Hall of Fame and the Colorado Women's Hall of Fame.

Baca's success was due to her persistence, hard work, and commitment to making a difference. She is exemplary of the impact one can have despite *and* because of society's obstacles.

—ADRIANA TRUJILLO

Jacob and Josie Duran

Get along with us. All of us. We all have the same blood running through us. —Josie Duran

Jacob and Josie Duran.
Photo courtesy of the Jacob and Josie Duran Collection.

Jacob and Josie Duran's lives exhibit the stories of hard work, resilience, and dedication to their families and community. Josie's family moved from Taos, New Mexico, to Ault in 1927 to work in the beet and cabbage fields of Northern Colorado. This first-hand experience instilled a profound understanding of labors' value to Josie—one that she would never forget. By the time she was fourteen years old, Josie was already contributing to her family's income by going to work herself. Despite the long, laboring days her family endured, they still maintained a home filled with warmth, love, *tamales,* and green chile.

Jacob's story began in Fort Collins, Colorado, eighty-three years ago. His family also had a history of migration following the work of the land. They moved from New Mexico to Nebraska and finally to Colorado in the 1920s—all in the pursuit of better opportunity. Jacob's father worked in the fields and a sugar factory, displaying a determination to provide for his family: Jacob and his nine siblings. Despite navigating the challenges of growing up in poverty, Jacob fondly recalls a childhood filled with kindness, love, and happiness.

Education was a luxury neither Josie nor Jacob could fully attain. Josie had to leave school in the eighth grade to work, while Jacob left in the eleventh grade to join the Navy. Jacob's and Josie's lives intertwined in their twenties when they moved to Greeley, Colorado, in the mid-1960s. Jacob worked for the Pink Wilson Company, eventually co-founding the CGNS Company, a ditch company they ran for forty years. Josie's career spanned working in restaurants, at the Bayly Manufacturing Company, and with a tax accountant. Josie and Jacob Duran's professional achievements highlight their resilience and determination to overcome obstacles and create lasting change for their community.

Both Jacob's and Josie's families have deep military ties. Jacob's father served in World War I and his brothers in World War II, the Korean War, and Vietnam. Jacob himself served in the peacetime Navy. Josie's family also had several veterans, highlighting their dedication to their country and community. The most famous is Josie's uncle, Joe P. Martinez. He was given the highest military award, the Congressional Medal of Honor, for his bravery in battle during World War II.

Living in Greeley since 1965, the Durans have witnessed the city's growth. While appreciating their peaceful neighborhood, they acknowledge the prejudices they endured in their earlier years. However, they remain hopeful for progress, recognizing both good and bad in people. Their advocacy for Mexican American recognition in Greeley showcases their desire for a more inclusive future.

Jacob hopes for a community where Mexican Americans thrive and gain acknowledgment.

Well, there are a lot of businesses owned by Mexicans or Spanish-speaking people now, so hopefully it continues to get better.

Jacob and Josie Duran's lives show strength, loyalty, and a strong commitment to their community. Their story reflects the enduring spirit of those who make lasting changes against the odds and strive for a fairer society.

—Caleb Flore

Lori Gama

I think I can claim that I'm a pioneer in the industry, especially in Northern Colorado, being the first Latina to start a marketing company that is still in operation after twenty-eight years. —Gama

Lori Gama, president and founder of DaGama Digital Marketing Agency.
Photo courtesy of the Lori Gama Collection.

Lori Gama, president and founder of DaGama Digital Marketing Agency, is a pioneer in Colorado's digital marketing industry and a proud advocate for her community. Born in Oakland, California, Gama arrived in Greeley in 1980 to pursue higher education. While taking an HTML and graphic arts class at

Aims Community College, she saw the potential of the Internet as a powerful tool for businesses. She decided to launch a company specializing in web design and online marketing. In 1993, DaGama Web Studio became the first *Latina*-owned digital marketing agency in Colorado. Gama's entrepreneurial success is deeply rooted in the values instilled by her family. Raised in a close-knit household, she was taught to go the extra mile.

My grandmother and my mom told me, "Always do your best, do the right thing, and always tell the truth."

These lessons shaped her character and propelled her to succeed in a male-dominated industry.

Gama, a Mexican American who was raised during a time when assimilation was encouraged, embraced her cultural identity. She fondly remembers family gatherings filled with *mariachi* music, Mexican food, and celebrations that strengthened her connection to her heritage. Now, she strives to represent her community and encourages other *Latinos* to step into leadership roles. Noting the importance of representation, she said:

I hope that our role will grow a lot more in positions of power and decision-making boards.

In addition to her business accomplishments, Gama is a dedicated community leader. She serves on the boards of United Way of Weld County and the Women's Fund of Weld County, while also supporting nonprofits such as the Greeley Dream Team and Habitat for Humanity. She shared:

Now that I'm in a position to give back, I'm really honored and grateful to be able to do that.

Gama sees Greeley as a city evolving toward greater inclusivity and diversity. She envisions a future where Mexican Americans and *Latinos* have a stronger voice in shaping the community, and she remains committed to paving the way for others to succeed.

—Caleb Flores

Ben (Mitch) Gonzales

I'm very proud of our family. We've built ourselves up, educated ourselves, and become community leaders. So, I've got a lot of really good role models to thank. —Ben (Mitch) Gonzales

Ben (Mitch) Gonzales is very proud of his family.
Left to Right: Shanae Gonzales,
Ben (B.J.) Gonzales, III, wife Ruby Gonzales,
Ben Mitch Gonzales, Jr., Cory Joe
Photo courtesy of the Ben (Mitch) Gonzales Collection.

When the Gonzales family moved to Greeley from La Junta, CO, in 1967, their first experience was not a positive one due to housing discrimination. While his mother wanted to live in the Hillside community, most Mexican Americans were shown low-income housing on the north side of town. They eventually found a house in Evans, but this first impression was a stark contrast to the life they had in La Junta. There, Mexican Americans constituted a large percentage of the population and were less exposed to housing discrimination or derogatory terms such as being called "spic" to refer to those who came from Spanish-speaking homes. They attended schools with many other Mexican American students.

His mother's family lived in the northern New Mexico/Southern Colorado area for five generations. They were farmers who owned property in Raton, New Mexico. His paternal grandfather came from northern Mexico around 1925 to work as a miner, while his paternal grandmother's family has been in the U.S. for four generations. Ben (Mitch) credits his parents for being the most influential people in his life as they provided a stable, supportive religious home that built the foundation for his own future family. He speaks proudly of his children and all their accomplishments.

Ben (Mitch)'s father worked for the Gambles Corporation, a conglomerate of retail stores, and was transferred to Greeley as part of his sales position. Before his sales job with Gambles, his father worked in the onion docks, followed by a job manufacturing mobile homes. But in 1969, his parents opened Ben's Furniture Store, which has been a successful family business in Greeley since its opening. The store has been an important part of the family, and Ben (Mitch) has very warm memories of his growing-up years at the store. After his father retired in 1998, Ben and his friend Lincoln Gallegos took over the management of the store, which continues to be a central part of the family.

Community involvement has been extremely important to Ben (Mitch)'s life, and he has a long history of contributing to multiple non-profit organizations, sports activities, boards, and committees. He was instrumental in developing and growing the baseball program at the Rodarte Community Center.

Ben (Mitch) laments that the contributions made by Mexican Americans to Weld County are often overlooked and that there is still limited representation of *Latinos* on city, county, and school boards. He hopes that we can support more *Latinos* to become involved in civic service so that boards can become more inclusive.

—DR. MADELINE MILIAN

Alicia Johnson

The community is important. Elevating voices, helping people get to where they want to be, and connecting them to the right people—that's how we move forward together. —Johnson

Taking the oath of office administered by Judge Steward for the city of Evans, Councilwoman Johnson with Isaac (son), and Zuri (daughter). Photo courtesy of the Johnson Collection.

Alicia Johnson never planned to go into politics, but when she saw that her community's voices weren't being heard, she knew she had to do something about it. She became the first *Latina* elected to the Evans City Council, making history and proving that representation matters.

Born in Greeley in 1980, Johnson's journey began with her family's immigration story. Her father, born in Zacatecas, Mexico, and her mother, from the Dominican Republic, worked hard after immigrating to the U.S. to build a life and learn English. Growing up bilingual, Johnson often acted as her mother's translator and navigator, helping her navigate life in a new country. She joked:

I was the Google Maps before Google existed.

Her greatest inspirations were the strong women in her family, especially her Tía Edy and her mother.

My Tía Edy always told me, "You're beautiful, and you deserve to take up space."

Her mother, despite the struggles she faced, raised three daughters to be strong, independent women.

She always told us that life is hard but you keep moving forward.

Johnson carried these lessons with her when she decided to run for Evan's city council.

I wanted a platform where I could help more people because I noticed there was a need and a lack of representation. I decided to run, and I did it.

Though she initially lost, a vacancy opened, and she was appointed. The following year, she ran again and won—a true illustration of determination. Being the only *Latina* voice on the council has come with trials, but Johnson knows how important it is to show up and speak up.

It's one voice, at least there's one voice, right? It's hard to create quick change when you have one voice, but small steps still move us forward.

For Johnson, public service isn't just a job—it's a calling.

For me, my path led to public service, helping people. Not only do you want to do good in life, but you also want to give and help others in need. The community is important. Elevating voices, helping people get to where they want to be, and connecting them to the right people—that's how we move forward together.

Beyond politics, Johnson is a proud wife and mother to two children. She serves on several state and local boards and also founded *Latinos* Making Waves, a platform that highlights the contributions of Latinos in Northern Colorado.

Johnson's story is about more than politics—it's about representation, resilience, and paving the way for future generations. She has already made history, but for Johnson, this is just the beginning.

—CALEB FLORES

Henry Lee Martinez

The future is out there; all you have to do is reach out and grab it. That has been my philosophy since I was growing up. Whenever opportunities arose, I tried to capitalize on them. —Martinez

In the small town of Walsenburg, Colorado, the stories of its residents show their strength and honor. One of them is Martinez, a soldier who was drafted into the U.S. Army at twenty-two and served in Vietnam from 1968 to 1969. He left for Vietnam two days after his son, Martin, was born. Martin later followed his father's path by serving in the U.S. Army as well. Military service is a family tradition, as Martinez's father also served in the U.S. Navy.

Jose Elias Martinez, father of Henry Lee Martinez, served in the U.S. Navy. Photo courtesy of the Henry Lee Martinez Collection.

Martinez was drafted during the Vietnam War despite his request for a deferment to continue his education at Southern Colorado State College in Pueblo, Colorado, while several of his classmates received approval for their deferments. He adapted, focusing on personal growth, and completed advanced training, including paratrooper jump school, and was deployed with the 173rd Airborne Brigade.

He encountered discrimination as a Mexican American soldier, as his Anglo counterparts frequently received medals for actions that were of lesser significance. He received numerous prestigious honors: the Purple Heart, Cross of Gallantry, Bronze Star Medal, Air Medal, Civil Defense Medal, National Defense Medal, Combat Infantry Badge, and the Vietnam Service Medal.

After his service, he became an active community member and was involved in organizations like the American GI Forum and the Greeley *Fiesta* Committee. He was honored as Legionnaire of the Year at the American Legion Post 18. At Kodak, he founded the Veterans Network of Kodak Employees Chapter.

Upon his discharge from the U.S. Army in 1969 and on his journey home, passing through the airport, a woman chased after him, attempting to spit on him and kick him. Meanwhile, others in the crowd held signs labeling soldiers as "baby killers" and expressed their disapproval of Vietnam veterans. He was shocked to learn of the negative sentiments and media portrayals of the war, which he was unaware of during his time in combat. The lack of any celebratory welcome for Vietnam veterans upon their return was a profound disappointment. Martinez retired at age fifty-seven and lives with his wife Linda in Greeley, Colorado.

—Dr. Maria Sanchez

Joe Perez

Our heritage comes from Mexico, but my family roots have now dug deep into the U.S. and into the American culture. I'm more of an American than I am Mexicano, *but my culture and everything about me is* Latino. —*Perez*

Joe Perez, born in Scottsbluff, Nebraska, grew up in a *barrio* in Western Nebraska. Family, faith, and culture were priorities. Perez felt blessed to have hard-working, involved parents and grandparents who were community leaders.

I grew up very safe, enjoying my child-hood in the barrio *and grade school. It wasn't until junior high and high school that I confronted the realities of life.*

Perez and other *Latinos* experienced incidents of subjugation through name-calling and the refusal of job opportunities.

Joe Perez served in Da Nang, Vietnam (1971).
Photo courtesy of Joe Perez.

Nobody appreciates being name called, particularly a "greaser," a "wetback," or being told to go back to Mexico.

Those instances shaped Perez's understanding and strengthened his identity. Education and the opportunity to advance himself became essential pursuits. When reflecting on his time in the military, Perez stated:

In the military, I felt comfortable because we had to have each other's back, and my experience was the Vietnam War. I think Latinos, *young* Chicanos, *young Mexican Americans, were overly representative in that war, as were the Black members of our community.*

After his tour in Vietnam, Perez, happy to be away from the conflict, moved to Greeley, seeking job opportunities. He served in the National Guard, worked for the City of Greeley, and was active on the Greeley chief of police's *Latino* Advisory Committee, where he advocated for body cameras.

When reflecting on *Latino* culture and contributions in Greeley, Perez remarked:

> *I see it as beautiful and progressive. I see that with my eyes. The Anglo community sees us a little differently, and that's sad because there are a lot of good* Latinos *in Greeley. We just have to speak up and be proud of our contributions. Whether they be in education, in medicine, in our community service, or even as church members.*

He is optimistic and believes the future holds countless possibilities.

> *Our youngsters, the number of students who we are graduating from high school and colleges are increasing, and they are seeking professions that are going to contribute to American society. I think that's great. As* Latinos, *we should be proud of both our culture and contributions.*

—BETH BULLARD

Rhonda Solis

Part of my journey has really been learning more about my heritage—being proud of that—and healing some of the family patterns and pathologies that have gone on for generations. —Rhonda Solis

Rhonda Solis grew up in a dysfunctional family, which caused an identity struggle with her heritage. She's worked hard to flip the narrative of her childhood for herself and future generations. Her involvement with the Hispanic

Rhonda Solis was sworn into the State Board of Education for Colorado's 8th Congressional District in 2022, taking her oath on the Bible of her grandmother, Mary Padilla. Photo courtesy of the Rhonda Solis Collection.

Women of Weld County helped her better understand where she comes from and how to be a strong Brown-skinned woman.

Rhonda, an award-winning activist and advocate, feels a responsibility to continue the legacy of those who opened the doors of opportunity before her. She's served on numerous boards and commissions and, in November 2022, became the first representative elected to the State Board of Education from Colorado's 8th Congressional District. Rhonda believes all children should be educated to the best of their ability and, upon graduation, be career or college-ready.

When reflecting on the industries that have made Greeley, Rhonda believes there's more to be done to "Recognize the generations of people of color that have worked these jobs." Shedding light on the need to celebrate the migrant workers who made Greeley's success even achievable.

We can do better; we need to do better.

Rhonda believes your vote is powerful. She considers drawing attention to problems with marches and protests and having representation in government championing issues equally important. Rhonda wants many more strong people of color in government leadership positions on boards, commissions, and councils. Knowing the effort will need to be conscious, deliberate, and consistent, she suggests creating paid positions at various levels of government to address equity, inclusion, and access for everyone who contributes to the wealth of the community. She's concerned that moving the needle on inclusion will be difficult without a focused lens and voice.

Regarding racism, Rhonda describes gut-punch moments. Times when, no matter what you've done or achieved, you're judged solely by your skin color. She advises her children against the negative impacts of acting out of anger.

In those moments, you're going to have to pick better or bitter, and I hope you pick better.

She feels sharing *Latina* and *Latino* stories and achievements can instill a sense of pride so gut-punch moment can diminish.

—BETH BULLARD

CHAPTER 5

Social Justice Issues in Greeley

Previously, stories about Mexicans and Mexican Americans who moved to the Greeley area to live, work, and raise their families were presented. Many of these stories are connected to social justice. "Social justice" means fairness in how money, jobs, education, and rights are shared among all people. The United Nations (2006) explains social justice as making sure everyone has fair opportunities and equal rights.

The United Nations (2006) described six important parts of social justice.

- Fair sharing of income (money people earn)

- Fair sharing of property and wealth

- Fair chances to get jobs and earn money

- Fair access to education and knowledge

- Fair access to healthcare, safety, and social support

- Fair chance to participate in government and community decisions

This chapter discusses the social justice issues that *Latinas* and *Latinos* have faced for many years. Their hard work in the fields and the community has helped build Greeley and its economy. However, because of unfair treatment, they did not always benefit from their hard work. This unfair treatment, called *discrimination*, happens when people are treated differently because of their ethnicity, gender, race, age, or sexual orientation. *Latinas* or *Latinos* have experienced discrimination because of their ethnicity since their arrival in the 1920s.

Yet, *Latinas* and *Latinos* have endeavored to make Greeley a more equitable place, *equitable* meaning fair to all. Their actions helped shape Greeley into a city that values diversity, parity, community, and inclusion. They have stood up for their rights in many ways, from showing quiet dignity to protesting unfair treatment. These hard-working people also fought against unjust treatment, such as segregated schools and signs that said "No Mexicans Allowed" in the local business windows. Because of their strength and determination, *Latinas* and *Latinos* have won many battles for equality and continue to work on parity.

Today, Greeley is the fastest-growing city in Colorado. Between 2022 and 2023, Greeley's population grew by 3 percent, more than any other city in the state. The second-fastest-growing city, Loveland, grew by only 1.9 percent (U.S. Census Bureau, 2024).

La Colonia

Chapter 1 of this book discussed the beginning of *La Colonia* community in the 1920s. In 1924, the GWSC created *La Colonia*. This was not surprising because GWSC wanted Mexican and Mexican American farmworkers to stay in the area instead of migrating to other states to work the fields. By doing this, the company made sure it had a strong and experienced workforce to work in its sugar beet fields. This helped GWSC make a lot of money, in part, because of the consistent workforce.

However, GWSC did not give these adobe houses in the 1920s to the workers for free. The company gave them building materials through a loan, and the workers had to pay back the loan over five years (Donato, 2007). These adobe houses were small, with only two rooms, and they did not have electricity or indoor plumbing.

La Colonia is one example of how *Latinas* and *Latinos* have been treated in Colorado, the Southwest U.S., and even other countries. It is not surprising that GWSC named the neighborhood in that manner. This name connects to colonialism. Colonialism happens when one country takes control of another, using its land, people, and resources. It also forces its own language and culture on the people who live there (Blakemore, 2024).

Colonialism affected how GWSC treated Mexican and Mexican American workers back then. The company controlled them by forcing Anglo culture and taking advantage of their labor. Historians call this "settler colonialism." This means that Native people are removed from their land so that new settlers can live there. "To grow its power, a settler-colonial state removes Native people and tries to erase them. Then, it sends (other) families to live on the land" (Bilotte, 2020).

Settler colonialism was part of Westward Expansion, which has often been portrayed as a positive story in U.S. history. However, many people now question this idea and recognize that it involved taking land and removing Native Americans (Morris, 2019). The way GWSC used Mexican and Mexican American workers is part of this larger history of settler colonialism, which harmed Native Americans who once lived on this land.

La Colonia is also part of a bigger international story. It reflects racist attitudes and imperialism toward *Latinas* and *Latinos* around the world. *Imperialism* happens when a country expands its strength over other places. This can happen through military force or economic control to gain power.

In the early 1900s, the U.S. became very involved in Central and South America. At first, U.S. businesses, like the United Fruit Company, were interested in making money. But soon, the U.S. government also became involved for political reasons. In 1904, the Roosevelt Corollary to the Monroe Doctrine said that the U.S. would step in if Latin American countries did not pay their debts to international banks. Many of these banks were in the U.S. (Office of the Historian, n.d.).

Over time, U.S. involvement grew stronger. The U.S. sent weapons to different countries in Central and South America. It also took land to grow coffee and bananas. All of this was done to protect U.S. business interests (Falcón, 2022; Mapes, 2010; Stahl, 2021).

When we look at *La Colonia* in both national and international history, we see many social justice issues. GWSC took advantage of Mexican and Mexican American workers. They made them live in poor housing, separate from White Greeley residents, and placed them onto land taken from Native Americans. Because of this, the workers had fewer chances to earn money, own property, and find better jobs.

Photo of the Spanish Colony in Greeley, CO, captured in 1949.
Photo courtesy of the Alvin García/Gabriel and Jody López Collection.

However, as Chapter 1 explains, the people of La Colonia worked hard to build good lives. They helped Greeley grow and develop. To challenge the negative beliefs that White residents had about Mexicans, they wrote a constitution. Many White people thought Mexicans were lawless, dirty, and lazy (Lopez et al., 2007). One way the residents resisted these stereotypes was by planting gardens around their homes. They wanted to make their neighborhood look more "respectable" (Bilotte, 2020).The people of *La Colonia* also built the *Salón* Community Center. This center helped bring people together and created a strong support system that lasted for many years. Weddings, baptisms, and any kind of party happened there. The community gathered there for multiple reasons but all in the spirit of supporting and celebrating each other. The Colony Trustees and the House of Neighborly Service also held meetings and activities there. The Guadalupe Community Center, an extended stay housing program for men, women, and families, now occupies *La Colonia's Salón* community center of long ago. While we cannot directly connect the community center to Greeley today, it is clear that the people of *La Colonia* built a community that continues to support *Latinas* and *Latinos* in Greeley today.

Racism and Micro-aggressions Faced by Mexicans in Greeley

As mentioned multiple times, during their time in *La Colonia*, Mexicans and Mexican Americans faced racism and discrimination from White people in Greeley. Since its founding, business owners put up "No Mexicans" signs in their store windows. Mexican students were segregated into the Gipson School, away from White children. Even in St. Peter's Catholic Church, ushers led Mexican parishioners to the sides of the church instead of letting them sit in the center.

From a social justice point of view, the way Mexicans and Mexican Americans were treated showed unfairness in having a safe environment and taking part in the community. The idea of a safe environment is important to discuss. While physical safety is one part of it, safety also means feeling secure mentally and emotionally. Discrimination and racism, whether through micro-aggressions (subtle comments that show stereotypes) or open acts of racism, can harm both physical and mental health. Research shows a strong link between racism and mental health problems like depression and anxiety (Pichardo et al., 2021). This link is not because of a lack of health care but is related to the ongoing need to defend against racial attacks.

Studies have found that experiencing discrimination over time increases the risk of mental health issues. Exposure to discrimination can also lead to negative changes in personality, such as higher levels of anxiety (Williams & Etkins, 2021).

Another important social justice issue related to racism and discrimination is a *stereotype threat*. This affects people from any group that has negative stereotypes (Steele and Aronson, 1995). A stereotype threat happens when someone worries that they might do or say something that will confirm a negative stereotype about their group, whether it's based on race, ethnicity, gender, or other factors. For example, a stereotype of a Mexican or Mexican American or *Latinas* and *Latinos* is that they are lazy and dirty.

Research has shown that stereotype threat affects students and workers, including *Latinos*, African Americans, and women. It can have serious negative effects on academic performance, work success, and mental health (Gonzales et al., 2002; Totonchi et al., 2021; Turochy et al., 2023). Because of this, it limits opportunities for good jobs, education, and knowledge, making social justice issues even worse for *Latinas* and *Latinos*.

The people of *La Colonia* did not just accept the unfair treatment they faced. They took action through advocacy, community, and perseverance. One way they did this was by building Our Lady of Peace Catholic Church to serve their community. Most of the money to build the church came from the local residents themselves, and today, it is a symbol of hope for the *Latina* and *Latino* community in Greeley.

Mexican parents also fought for their childrens' rights by asking to end segregation in public schools. This effort led to the closing of the Gipson School and allowed their children to join other schools in Greeley. Through their determination and hard work, these *Latina* and *Latino* residents and parents helped shape Greeley into the diverse and welcoming community it is today.

Historians' Experiences with Social Justice in Greeley

Many of our historians spoke about experiencing discrimination. This happened not only in school but also in their everyday lives. Discrimination is defined as unfair treatment of people based on ethnicity, gender, sex, race, age, or sexual orientation. Many of our historians have faced discrimination based on their ethnicity or being *Latinas/os*.

Watson explained:

Now that I'm retired and don't have that (teacher) title with me and I'm getting older, the racism is right there. Every day you feel it. And I remember also as a teacher, when I went into stores, I was so much more accepted if I looked like a teacher, dressed like a teacher, and had my teacher name tag on versus on a Saturday morning after just getting up, pulling my hair back, and going into the store with sweats on. The racism is there.

You have to work extra hard, and it always reminds me because I live in two very different worlds. Even right here in Greeley, that line, in that movie, Selena, *where her father says, "You know, Mija, we're not Brown enough for the Brown people, and we're not White enough for the White people!"*

That's how I feel sometimes, especially as I get older. But even when I was younger, I felt like our friends would say things like, "Well, you're, you're not like that!"

Like what?

And I was very, very, very shocked just a couple of months ago at my book club full of educators discussing a book on racism. I said something, and one of the teachers from across the room said, "We're not talking about you. You're not like the people ..."

An educator! I was shocked! People just don't understand. And it's alive and well. Okay? (Watson, 2023).

When Vega Ruiz was asked, "Have you experienced discrimination in Greeley?" he answered:

Unfortunately, yes. I have three examples of that.

One of them, my wife and I have a home in West Greeley. One evening, we said, "Hey, we haven't checked the mail in a long time."

There's a cluster of mailboxes, and it's about two blocks away. We decided to take our dog out. Honestly, it had been about a month or so since we had checked the mail. I took a little backpack, right? I know what I'm getting ready for. Oddly enough, as we were walking back, we were followed by a police car. Apparently, they called the cops on us in our own neighborhood! It was interesting! We got followed up into our house. They made sure that we went into the house, and then they drove around the block a couple of times to make sure it was our house! It was very interesting. I'm sure that that wouldn't have happened if we didn't look a certain way.

The other two are again, all these are recent. Downtown, my wife and I really enjoy going downtown. But we've come across a couple of interesting situations with a couple of businesses downtown. ... She loves karaoke, they do karaoke, but she was not allowed to do Spanish karaoke or in any Latin type of music. I was shocked when we were told that, and we've been told that multiple times now. And when I asked, questioned it, I said, "Well, what's the reason?"

They just said that ownership has a strict policy. They are not allowed to play that type of music! Go figure! On a different occasion, same place, I would probably stop going there, honestly. A friend's form of identification was a Mexican passport, right? The document that gets you into the U.S., and unfortunately, at this same place, it was not accepted as a legal ID (Vega Ruiz, 2023).

Bustillos shared an experience as a 2020 census worker.

Yes, so the recent census, there were a lot of myths with regards to who could participate and who couldn't. And so, for me, it was important to help ensure that the Latino *population was accurately represented. I tried to find ways to volunteer. I couldn't find any. The only way I was able to participate was to actually work for the census. So, despite having a full-time job, I agreed to work part-time for the census, and I was very clear as to my purpose. I wanted to be sent to where there was more of a* Latino *population, more of a monolingual Spanish-speaking population. And for whatever reason they didn't, they would send me to rural Weld County. And, unfortunately, I was called names. I was asked to leave the premises. Assumptions were made as to why I was there. Assumptions were made as to what I was trying to do with the census. And really, I was just trying to do my job and collect accurate data.*

But unfortunately, here in Weld County, there are parts that are not very welcoming to people of color. And the more I went outside of Greeley to the rural areas within Weld County, the more I experienced it. And it wasn't a pleasant experience.

I gave that feedback to the census people and would constantly ask, "Why are you sending me there? That's not why I joined your team! This is not my purpose."

But they use some weird, automated computer system that randomly sends you to areas for you to do.

And it got to the point where I didn't feel safe going anymore by myself. So, I would have to take my husband, and he would stay in the car. Because I worried, okay, if something happens to me out here in rural Weld County, by the time someone finds me … It's not safe.

And I hated that I had to go through that, and my daughter asked me, "Well, Mom, why do you continue to do it?"

And I said, "Well, because I'm hoping that maybe there might be that one day that the purpose of why I signed up will actually come forward. That I will meet the family who's reluctant to participate because they don't speak English and because they've been given wrong information."

And so, unfortunately, that didn't happen, but my daughter has asked me if I will do it again, and I honestly don't know because it was a very, very bad experience (Bustillos, 2023).

Rodriguez-McNeill spoke about an experience she recently had at a downtown Greeley store.

I have seen a lot of changes. A lot of changes where, you know, there was a lot of discrimination in Greeley. There still is, but it's not as bad as it used to be. We were followed in the stores. My sister was even asked to empty her purse. And we were taught not to steal. They said that she had stolen something, and she hadn't. And so that was at Woolworth. I don't know if you remember that, Woolworth (a chain of department stores that first opened in downtown Greeley in 1910). Yeah. And there's still stores here in Greeley that follow you. They think you're going to steal.

I encountered one just recently. Just last year, I went to a store in Greeley, and they followed me. I carry a little purse, and I was looking for a gift. I went there at the last minute to buy a birthday gift.

These ladies were following me, and I said, "Why are you following me?"

And one said, "Oh, can I help you?"

You know, like they were going to help me!

I said, "Don't be following me because I'm not going to steal anything! I'm going to buy a gift."

And then that was okay. But then, they followed me again, and I felt really uncomfortable.

I say, "You know what? I'm never coming back here again."

And I used to spend a lot of money there. Yeah. So this, it still exists (Rodriguez-McNeill, 2023).

Stacy Suniga told a very sad story about segregation.

When my uncles were smaller, they couldn't swim at the local pool, which was the only one (in town). And that was in the Island Grove Park. They had signs on there saying "No Dogs and No Mexicans." When they wanted to go swimming, the boys would go to the sand pits. One day, while they were there, a cousin started to drown, and then one of their brothers, my uncle, jumped in to save him. And both boys didn't survive.

There was a kind of a movement within, with a teacher at the local public schools who took one of my uncles with his son to go to the swimming pool. But they wouldn't let my uncle in. This teacher approached the city council and really made that change. And after that, the Hispanic kids could go swimming, but it took the loss of two lives to understand that segregation was wrong. And not that I think that anybody will tell you that bigotry has stopped, but those are small steps that make a difference (S. Suniga, 2023).

Theresa Solis discussed one of her artifacts that she brought to the interview session.

Oh, yes. I have a photo here of our Lady of Peace Church, and this is the church that my parents donated to; my mom donated her wedding rings. And my dad donated some of his religious medals and other people put things in there too ... My aunt told me they all had to get together to build this church because of all the discrimination they were facing in the other churches. When they'd go to a church, they always had to sit in the back. Even if there were empty spaces in the front where they could sit, they weren't allowed to. They had to stay in the back of the church. And my aunt said that ... I don't know if I should say that the priest ... he was very, very rude and mean to them. They all got together and had bake sales and whatever they could do to get the money to help build this church, Our Lady of Peace Church (T. Solis, 2023).

Rhonda Solis shared a couple of racist incidents pertaining to the dentist's office she works in.

I think a lot of times we think that it's just normal until you get older, and it's, "Oh my gosh, that was, that was racist!"

There were times I was followed around in the stores and the time that I worked for that female dentist. She would send me to go get supplies with an office check. And they would have to call her to make sure that it was okay that I had that check.

I also worked at the front desk at that (dentist's) office, and I had a rancher come in. He had dentures made, and he was going to pay for them with cash. But he refused to give me the cash. And it really was those gut-punch moments, that's what I call them, where you've jumped through all the hoops, you've done everything you were supposed to do, and yet, there's still someone that will treat you differently because of the color of your skin (R. Solis, 2023).

Although Martinez Rocha's memories of discrimination in her schooling experiences occurred in the late 1960s, it is important to document. This feeling of not belonging for many *Latina* and *Latino* students is still prevalent in the schools today.

> *I personally haven't experienced it much, but I remember in 1967 when I first moved here. I came from Southern Colorado and the Pueblo area. There, we were the majority, so we ruled. We were the popular kids in school. We were all elected* Latino *officials. We just kind of ran the county because in that part of the state, we were in the majority. Other people of other races were our friends; we just all got along.*
>
> *But when I moved to Greeley, I really saw segregation because I went to Greeley West. At that time, it was fairly new. They bused the kids from the Spanish Colony. I remember when I came to the school, I didn't see any people of color, right away. And then after I was there a few days, I noticed that there was a table back there (in the cafeteria) and it was just* Latinas, *and they were just segregated from everybody else. Some of them didn't feel comfortable, and they didn't feel like they were welcomed in other parts of the school. And I just thought, "Oh my gosh," and then they started to tell me that there were those signs in the restaurants just a few years before then that said, "No Dogs, No Shoes, No Mexicans Allowed!"*
>
> *That was in the late 1960s, and that was still going on! And that didn't exist for me in my world where we came from! I just thought, "Oh my gosh!" (Martinez Rocha, 2023).*

Cortez spoke about his discriminatory experiences.

> *I was coming home from work, and a state trooper pulled me over.*
> *The first thing he asked was, "¿Hablas ingles?"*
> *I said, "Doesn't everybody?"*
> *He gave me a seventeen-dollar ticket for no seat belt. That was it!*

Then I got pulled over coming out of a gas station. The same cop pulled me over and said, "Oh, I thought you were somebody else."

"No, it's still me!"

Attitude. Yeah, there's a lot of it. It was more blatant than it is now (Cortez, 2023).

The following lengthy quote comes from Gabriel A. Lopez and speaks to the discrimination he has faced in Greeley and in Cooperstown, Ohio, at the National Baseball Hall of Fame. But it also speaks to good people who appreciate authors who put their heart and soul into documenting important history such as the Greeley Grays. When asked if he had ever experienced discrimination here in Greeley, Gabriel said:

Here in Greeley? Yes, through the explosion settlements and everything I went through, I had a lot of money and wanted to get my dad a tractor. Because he always had old beat up tractors, and I was always having to fix them. So I took him to get him a tractor. I had all the cash and everything, and nobody would wait on us. And we sat there for about an hour, then an hour and a half. Nobody waited on us. I went, okay. I walked out.

Finally, as we were leaving, the gentleman came up to us and said, "Well, what do you want?"

I said, "Nothing from you!"

And he said, "What do you mean?"

I said, "Well, I was here to buy a tractor with cash, and you guys didn't want to have anything to do with us, so we're going somewhere else!"

And we walked away from that one.

And it's still there. … education (too). When we went to the Smithsonian, they wouldn't listen to Jody and me until they found out what we've done and accomplished. And then afterwards, it was the Gabe and Jody Pony Show! They kept asking us questions, questions, and questions, but until then, we were nobody! Because we only have a twelfth-

grade education, we see it every day, all the time. What Jody and I have accomplished, it's the one time that I've been so proud of what we've done.

So, we were at Cooperstown (the National Baseball Hall of Fame is there), and they invited us up to do a presentation on the Spanish Colony and the (Greeley) Grays. We showed up, but we didn't know what the protocol was. It is a big museum, with baseball history and everything!

*We took (our) two books (*White Gold Laborers: The Story of Greeley's Spanish Colony *and* From Sugar to Diamonds: Spanish/ Mexican Baseball 1925–1969: Stories of the Greeley Grays and the Teams That Dared to Challenge Them*), two copies: one to donate to Cooperstown and one just to show people.*

We did our presentation, and the gentleman who had contacted us, Eric Stroll, said, "Gabe and Jody, I need to talk to you afterwards."

I thought we were in trouble!

We said, "Okay."

We waited. We were in this (small) room a little bit bigger than this. We sat way in the back. It's the archive room, and all the professors and lawyers and everybody were in there, and they wouldn't talk to us. They just ignored us.

Then, he (Eric) came down, and he pushed everybody aside and said, "I need Gabe and Jody Lopez here."

Then he saw us, and he said, "Jody and Gabe, come here."

Well, as we walked, it opened up. We walked between them.

They said, "Who's this?"

Us!

He took us up (there), and he said, "Gabe, in the history of the National Baseball Hall of Fame, we have six criteria in order to be part of the National Baseball Hall of Fame. If you have just one of them, we don't even listen to you. If you meet two of them, well, maybe we'll talk to you. Maybe we'll look at you. If you meet three of them, we'll talk. In history, since the Hall of Fame started, there's only been two people who ever made it! That's you and Jody! You've reached the six criteria!

Anything you write, anything you do, you send it to us! It'll automatically go into the National Baseball Hall of Fame!"

He continued, "You guys have done so much and reached such a level that at Cooperstown, we have a whole basement for you down there, a whole section in the basement for you!"

They took all our research, everything, our material that we wrote on and it's there! It's also in the Smithsonian!

So Jody and I had big heads! That was the first time we ever had our big heads puffed up so much! She had to go down first in the elevator, and then I went second. Because that elevator was not big enough! Our heads were too big! Ha ha! Couldn't put both of us in there! But that was the only time, you know, otherwise we're happy with the way it's going. We're proud of how it's going (G.A. Lopez, 2023).

Johnson expanded on the different types of discrimination she has witnessed.

I think, you know, sometimes it can be with the air quality. If there's fracking around a specific school (a school that has more students on free and reduced lunch), that's also environmental discrimination. If there is, for example, during the pandemic, the Well Recovery Grant, it wasn't translated into any other language. Considering we have a high population of Spanish speakers, that wasn't translated. I helped towards the tail end of that grant to ensure that at least we got the guidelines translated. But that's language discrimination, again, it's not language justice. Then you see, when it comes to a job, the type of job that you have, there's discrimination in that, again, not being provided the appropriate salary or less medical coverage because they can lower your hours.

Again, all of that, there's a lot of discrimination that's happening in different ways, and I think the climate of the country has definitely exacerbated that (Johnson, 2023).

Something that has not been mentioned when it comes to discrimination was brought up by two of our historians. And that is skin color or a *Latinas/os* with lighter and darker skin tones have experienced discrimination. For many, the darker you are, the more discrimination you experience, versus a lighter-skinned *Latina* or *Latino*. Wendirad tells a story of being in Downtown Greeley with her husband, who is darker, and overhearing, "Oh, look at the zebra family!"

Abraham Garcia shared his thoughts.

Back in the early 1960s, when I was in high school, I felt it, but I don't feel it now like I did back then. I think it's gotten a lot better, but to me, it kind of depends on sometimes your skin, your skin tone.

… The darker you are, I think people kind of associate you more with the Mexico or Central American part because … this has been true for a long time … my daughter even noticed that in high school because she's really light complected. So was her friend. They'd go to parties, and the Anglo girls or Whites would be talking about Mexicans. And Tess would understand. They'd kind of get in their face, and they'd be surprised because they thought they were Whites because they were light-complected. As I said, the lighter you are the more you can blend in better, and … if you're darker, you stand out (A. Garcia, 2023).

When asked if the historians thought discrimination has increased or decreased in Greeley, Treviño said this:

It's increased. It's increased, especially in the last six years since Donald Trump became president. He made it more acceptable for Anglos to say whatever they want to say. They feel more comfortable now because they have a president who speaks that way. That made it clear that you're Brown, you're Black, and you're not part of us. I've seen that increase.

I've had my sister yelled at by older White people who said, you know, "Go back to Mexico!"

And my sister said, "I was born here in the States! What do you mean, go back to Mexico?"

And they said, "Well, that's where all you people belong!"

You know, we've had situations like that. And that's only been within the last four or five years since he's been in office. You just saw that rise in discrimination nationwide (Treviño, 2023).

Martinez shared similar sentiments.

Yes, one of the examples is if you're employed somewhere and you do the job to the best of your ability and you're the one that's next in line but they pass you up because of your race. I think that is really sad, and that is still ongoing today. And today, not only in the workplace, it's happening in the military as well. It's been that way since day one. And—and it hasn't changed. Hasn't changed (H.L. Martinez, 2023).

Cortez shared:

Well, it's increased because depending on who you are, who you see. They'll say, "Go back to where you came from!"

And I say, "Yeah, we crossed a small stream! You guys crossed an ocean!" (Cortez, 2023)

Bustillos thought:

I think, like in most parts of the country, it has increased. I think that after having had a president who made it okay to talk about your prejudice against others, we started to see a lot more discrimination and hatred towards minorities. I think that, unfortunately, has gone up. And a lot of us have felt that more now (Bustillos, 2023).

On the other hand, Ben (Mitch) Gonzales said:

I think it's decreased. I mean, you see a lot more Latinos *in managerial positions. You see a lot more* Latinos *with businesses that have a little bit more influence in the community. But I mean, it always needs to be more, we need to represent our community a little bit more than we do right now.*

And like I said, that's pushing each other to get more education. Pushing each other to run for mayor, to run for city council, to run for school board spots. We need to push each other for that and support each other. And, you know, we can do it with our numbers, but we need to push each other a little bit harder (B.M. Gonzales, 2023).

Jenny and Abraham Garcia somewhat agreed with Ben (Mitch).

To me, (Abraham) I think it's decreased from when I was young versus now. But you know, you can still see it because when people speak a lot of Spanish, I see other people turn around. It's not like when you're in Vegas and there are twenty different languages being spoken or whatever and nobody cares. But over here, it's like some, well, Whites, think you're kind of making fun of them or talking about them or something like that. That's my feeling.

Jenny said:

I don't see any discrimination being in my store. And because that's the only place I'm at most of the time …(A. and J. Garcia, March 13, 2023).

Gama weighed in on how she thinks discrimination has decreased.

I think it's decreased, and I have to speak only from my experience and anecdotal information. I am married to an African American man, and I noticed it happening more so when I married him. Just walking into a room, the looks of people, some friendly and smiling, some like we weren't even there, some out-and-out dirty looks. It's there, unfortunately. It's a conservative community for the most part, though there are many progressive and liberal people here as well (Gama, 2023).

Another question was: "What is your opinion or perspective on Greeley's ability to be inclusive?"

Velasquez responded:

I think they're trying, I mean, again, we have the Cinco de Mayo, *we've got the Stampede (Greeley's Fourth of July rodeo, carnival, and parade), and now, we've got the Mexican rodeo. But I think that there are just a lot more things that could be done. But you know, until we have more* Latinos *in power, I don't think it's going to change very much. But we can be more inclusive by hiring. That, to me, is so important because again, that's how you create wealth is having a good job. If you're being held down, you're not going to be able to provide as well. You can't pass down money because you've grown up poor. We just have a ways to go (Velasquez, 2023).*

Silva's thoughts on inclusivity in Greeley:

I think that they could be more inclusive by having more town meetings with the people in authority and the different departments, like the educational people, the schools, and the people who have restaurants. Have a real town meeting where they learn from each other, their talents and their abilities. That will show they can help each other. Because we can lose a lot if we are apart. They could learn from each other and grow in their ability to create a better world. Because the problem that this world has is that we think there are people less important than we are. We ignore the other people who are not similar to us, who are less educated or speak a different language. We don't even talk to them. But if we interacted more, I think we would have a better world (Silva, 2023).

Rhonda Solis shared other ideas about how Greeley can become more inclusive.

> *Their ability to change is difficult if they don't put somebody in positions to make sure that they're conscious and deliberate about their actions and how they move forward. That means that things are translated. That means that things are welcoming. That means that we have people that look like us in administrative positions at the school board, the city of Greeley, the city of Evans, and our county commissioners. All of those levels should have people who have experience and knowledge about being inclusive, equity, and access, and that we're continually asking those questions. Are we doing everything that we can and what can we do better?*
>
> *I've seen communities with the podcast that you know, Chris Garcia and I do, it's called* Latino, Northern Colorado. *We've seen things in Fort Collins that are way advanced in outreach, in making sure that people feel welcomed and their percentage of* Latinos *is much less than ours. There are some things that we have to improve here. There are some things that we need to demand that we improve here. Those discussions need to happen, and we need representation at the city council level. There are no people of color on the city council right now. And so, without that lens, without that voice, without that push, those things aren't going to get done and people aren't going to pay attention to it (R. Solis, 2023).*

Gonzales-Soto believes inclusivity begins with having a voice.

> *… to have a voice. Those folks who know what the needs are, need to be the ones who are empowered at the local level, at the state level, and at the federal level. Right? It needs to be the ones who are the judges, needs to be the ones who are running the city, needs to be the ones on the school board, those who understand what the needs are because they've actually had a personal experience of discrimination. Because I'm very sorry, but*

if you haven't had a personal experience or know somebody who's close to you has had a personal experience, it's hard to realize what the impact is. And if you don't have that and you're a person of color, you're incredibly privileged. And if you can't acknowledge that privilege and realize that you need to listen to those who have grown up a different way and learn from it, then you're in a hard place.

But I think that's how we begin to represent and truly be more inclusive of the different populations, right? The marginalized communities, the more vulnerable communities are opening those doors because they feel that there's somebody they trust, somebody who looks like them in a position of power or a position to be able to make a change (Gonzales-Soto, 2023).

Gama thinks inclusivity is achievable.

I think it's good overall. My perspective about it, it's such a large community, relatively speaking, if you include Weld County as well. But let's just say Greeley, there's definitely hope that it can improve. I think it's just a matter of some organizations, for example, some don't even know that they should have a policy, a diversity, equitable, inclusive policy! They don't even know they should have that in place! Who's going to educate them? And that's a start right there. I see it improving. It's just, I think it's going to take a lot of work, but I think overall most people are open. I think it takes more people like, if I could share people I really admire, more people like Rhonda Solis. For example, during COVID what she did for the employees who were actually dying at a place of business here in town. Though many people would disagree with her methods. I mean, at least she was reaching out and helping, right? And then she served on the school board and did a lot of service there, and now she's on the Colorado School Board. It takes more people like her. Also, I'd like to name Stacey Suniga and her wife, Deb Suniga. Stacey had run for city council, didn't win, but then somebody had to be replaced (Gama, 2023).

Nickie Archibeque and Hernandez also gave their opinions on how to make Greeley more inclusive.

We need representation. First of all, these people need to see that we are making moves and … we need to be represented. We need to make sure we're clear headed on what our goals are. Let them know we're here, we're here to stay, and we just need to be smart about it. We need to be tactical about where we place ourselves. Like I said, in politics, we, our organizations, and honestly the new generation, we've got to use our talent. Social media, oh my gosh, technology! That's where we need to stick together as a group, and we need to stay together and move forward. If we're all climbing up the ladder, we need to help each other climb up the ladder and not push anybody out of the way! (Archibeque, 2023).

And you'll see this as a theme … to me, it's about learn, learn, turning inward, right? And starting with ourselves because I think that we experienced discrimination as Latinas and Latinos, and then when the East African population came in too, we had this different experience. I think we were also discriminatory towards them. And so I think it's about us looking inward. I think it's about the White community looking inward. I think it's all of us. Really, confronting our assumptions, our biases, and where those come from? And trying to get to the root. To me that looks like conversations, that looks like community circles. And I really go towards that piece where we need to go inward and do some of those courageous conversations (Hernandez, 2023).

And finally, Johnson expands on others' visions on how Greeley can be more inclusive.

By really trying to listen. Listen to the Latino community and what they have to say. Also, try to fix the infrastructure in the areas where a high volume of Latinos live. … Really show that you care in that way by, you know, improving things. Also, pay teachers a decent wage and have more teachers who look like the students. And ensure that the communication is also there (Johnson, 2023).

Another question that was asked of our historians was, "How do you see Mexican American culture being represented in Greeley?" Perez said:

I see it as beautiful and progressive. I see that with my eyes. The Anglo community sees us a little differently. And that's kind of sad because there are a lot of good Latinos in Greeley and throughout the U.S. And we just have to speak up and be proud of our contributions, whether we're in education, the medical field, community service, or even as church members or if we're elected. We don't have any elected officials. We do have some from the Denver area and other parts ... but I think we need to show more pride and speak out about our contributions to American society (Perez, 2023).

Clarence Lopez thinks:

I don't think there's enough emphasis by the City of Greeley to acknowledge the contributions that Mexican Americans have made to this community, starting from the Bracero Program to today. I don't see any bronze statues in any of the parks commemorating or honoring the Mexican Americans who have contributed to this community.

I don't think the city council emphasizes programs that create holidays and banners. You don't see banners depicting any Mexican Americans. I don't think there's enough acknowledgement for Mexican Americans in our community, and I think there is a need for that (C. Lopez, 2023).

Clarence Lopez also answered the question, "How do you think Mexican Americans have contributed to the success of Greeley?"

Greeley's economy is heavily dependent upon agriculture, the farms east of Greeley, north of Greeley, south of Greeley. Without the Bracero programs, without families like my father's family coming up from southern Colorado to help work the agricultural industry, Greeley's economy would not have survived.

You know our agricultural economy was built on the backs of Mexican American and Latino *labor. Another example is J.B. Swift. It used to be in Monfort of Colorado. It's the largest employer in the city of Greeley. A majority, I don't know if it's a majority, but Mexican Americans were heavily represented (there) and today, Mexican Americans are heavily represented at J. B. Swift. Without all that labor, you know, J.B. Swift couldn't keep their doors open (C. Lopez, 2023).*

Ben (Mitch) Gonzales added his thoughts on how *Latinos* have contributed to Greeley's success:

I think it's a situation where they've got to admit that without the Latino *population, Greeley, Weld County, wouldn't have worked. (Those) farms, everybody that has a business where there's heavy manual labor, be it construction, meat packing, manufacturing, realizes how important the* Latino *population in this county is. Your business, if you were a farmer, wouldn't have worked.*

There aren't a lot of Anglos picking crops out there. There are not a lot of Anglos working at places like JBS and Monfort. There are not a lot of Anglos working in construction jobs. I mean, are they represented? Sure. But if you look at the workforce, it's primarily Hispanic. Anybody who has any common sense would need to agree that without the Latino, *Greeley and Weld County wouldn't be near what it is today (B. M. Gonzales, 2023).*

The authors end this chapter with hope! Yes, many *Latinos* have faced difficult oppressive, discriminatory experiences. But yet, we rise as Maya Angelou (1978) described:

You may shoot me with your words,

You may cut me with your eyes,

You may kill me with your hatefulness,

But still, like air, I'll rise.

Angelina Bustillos

Nothing brings me more joy and pride than to speak about my dad …
he was an amazing father and friend, and anything I can do to help
highlight his legacy I will continue to try. —Bustillos

Angelina Bustillos's father, Teófilo Bustillos, came to the U.S. from *San Juan, Balleza, Chihuahua,* Mexico as a *bracero*—he was only twenty-one at the time. His six brothers also worked as *braceros.* During his time in the *bracero* program, sometimes, Teófilo worked for farmers who abused their power by withholding wages and failing to provide living arrangements that were promised.

Bustillos stated:

Carmen, María, and Angelina Bustillos at their father's gravesite.
Photo courtesy of the Angelina Bustillos Collection.

The program helped him become legal and allowed his family to be born and raised here. Despite the bad experiences, he was grateful for the program and believed that the good outweighed the bad.

Fortunately, one of the farmers he worked for sponsored him, which allowed him to obtain legal status.

Bustillos relayed:

He was a little activist himself. He loved politics and geography. He would tell us, "You have opportunities here; take advantage of those opportunities."

While he worked at Monfort, Teófilo took part in the strike of 1979. Workers were striking due to unfair wages. Teófilo joined the picket lines but had to leave the company when the strike lasted longer than his family could afford—he refused to go back.

Teófilo was excited to vote after becoming a citizen; however, he passed away before he had the chance to vote. Bustillos volunteered for the Boulder County election office to ensure that others were able to vote. She explained:

My dad used to say that regardless of your political affiliation, your participation in the voting process is your voice, and you should use it. This is because in some countries, there is no proper electoral process in place and people's votes are not respected. Additionally, women are often not given the right to vote. Thanks to my dad, my sisters and I have a great passion for the voting system.

Teófilo passed away in 1995. The values he taught his three daughters, education and hard work, are still held close. Bustillos explained:

He came to this country to provide us with better opportunities. Going to college was an expectation.

All of his daughters received an education at UNC. Other important values Teófilo passed down were:

… to be proud of our biculturalism, to keep our language and speak it well, and to be compassionate and help others.

Teófilo's oldest daughters, Carmen and María, are ESL teachers, and Bustillos is a child protection social worker—all inspired by his teachings.

—ADRIANA TRUJILLO

Francisco Cortez

I enjoyed all of it; if I die tomorrow, I have done my part. I did every-
thing I could to improve the conditions of my fellow people. —Cortez

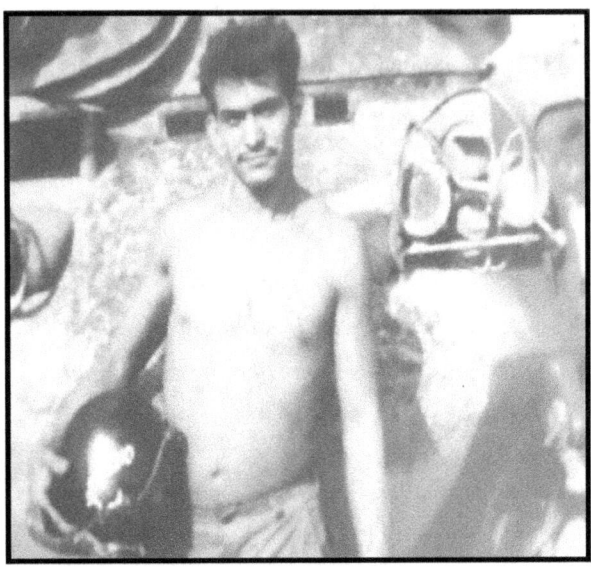

Francisco Cortez in Vietnam, on April 16th, 1969. His nickname, Poncho, is
displayed on the front of his helmet. Behind him is a forty-eight-ton tank.
Photo courtesy of the Francisco Cortez Collection.

Francisco Cortez 's life is one that displays the virtues of service, activism, and
resilience. Throughout his life and the lapses along his path, Cortez refused to
accept mediocrity and always found a passage that led to success. Cortez's story
begins in his birth town of *Del Rio,* Texas, near the Mexican border town of
Acuña over seventy-five years ago. He was raised in a blended family of seventeen siblings, and this family dynamic taught him the value of hard work and
motivation early in his life. Although he recalls childhood memories of playing
baseball or learning English by watching cartoons, by the age of nine, he was
earning a full-time wage working long hours due to the lack of child labor
laws. This necessity arose following the passing of Cortez's father, a Methodist
reverend from Plainview, Texas, and his unwavering determination to help his
widowed mother provide for their family.

Cortez's determination propelled him far beyond working labor jobs. He pursued higher education at Porterville Junior College and CSU, driven by a desire to confront systemic inequities through the study of sociology. His path, however, took a transformative turn when he chose to enlist in the military and serve in the Vietnam War. After six months of combat, Cortez sustained injuries and was offered a medical discharge. Refusing to abandon his commitment, he completed his service as a draftsman, utilizing his skills to contribute in a new capacity. Following his military service, Cortez embarked on a forty-year career in construction, leaving a lasting impact on the Greeley area through his dedication and hard work.

Cortez's work outside of his construction career was a testament to his values of equity and community empowerment. He played a significant role in establishing the Statewide Parent Coalition and advocating for educational opportunities for families who came from underrepresented communities. He also facilitated community events, such as the Educational *Fiesta* at Sunrise (now Archibeque) Park in Greeley where he provided resources for students, such as backpacks and school supplies to alleviate the stigma of receiving school supplies in a public setting.

I learned that, that within myself, the higher up you go, the less you know about people around you. That's why the Fiesta *was so important to us.*

Cortez's activism extended to broader cultural and social issues. He was deeply involved in the *Chicano* Movement of the 1970s, helping to organize events that celebrated Mexican American heritage and educated the community on its history. He viewed this work as essential to preserving cultural identity and inspiring the next generation to pursue equity and recognition.

Cortez's work in Greeley with the Mexican American community championed the importance of inclusivity and representation. His advocacy for programs and community involvement initiatives demonstrated his commitment to systemic change. Cortez exemplifies the spirit of determination and service to people, and his contributions emphasize the impact of community leaders in shaping a more inclusive and equitable society.

—CALEB FLORES

Clarence Lopez

I pray that in the very near future, we shall see young Latino *leaders emerge, leaders who will take up the reins, and begin to create the changes we would like to see happen in our communities.* —Clarence Lopez

Clarence's story begins in the San Luis Valley of southern Colorado. His parents, grandparents, and great-grandparents were born in *Chama* and *San Luis.*

Abade Lopez and Eralia Vialpando Lopez.
Photo courtesy of the Clarence Lopez collection.

Our history in Colorado dates back to 1851, when San Luis *was founded. My father always reminded us that* San Luis *is the oldest town in Colorado and that we are* chameros. *He instilled this pride in all of us from a young age.*

His father and grandfather farmed the land in and around San Luis and Chama, however, in 1942, his father, Abade Lopez, was drafted into the Army. He fought on the infamous Omaha Beach on D-Day, June 6, 1942. When World War II ended in 1945, Abade returned to *Chama.* His goal was to continue farming with his father, but "the two different parcels that my father and grandfather had been farming for many years were sold during the war." In 1946, his father married his mother, Eralia Vialpando, and they had three children. Many of the young families began moving out of the *San Luis* Valley in search of better lives. Thus, in 1951, his father decided it was time to relocate as well, and he moved his young family to Greeley seeking gainful employment.

Clarence has fond memories of his summer vacations in Southern Colorado.

My father would load us up, and we'd head off to the San Luis *Valley. We had lots of relatives there. We were welcomed for who we were as Mexican Americans. My family had value; my parents were respected down there. When I returned to Greeley, I could feel a culture change; I felt different. I didn't feel the same respect. I was now being looked at as a Mexican and not being valued for who I was as a person.*

Born in Greeley, he was raised in a predominantly Mexican American neighborhood in East Greeley. As a young teenager at Greeley Central High School, he began following and actively supporting the *Chicano* movement.

Our leaders were young Chicano *activists like Jose Calderón, Len Avila of Denver, Ricardo Falcón of Fort Lupton, Keith McNeill, and Theresa Rodriguez McNeill of Greeley. We protested in front of* The Greeley Tribune, *the Greeley Police Department, and President Dr. Richard Bond's office at UNC. We boycotted and picketed Safeway stores in support of the United Farm Workers. And we boycotted and protested the Coors Brewing Company. On one Saturday, we marched from Greeley to the Colorado State Capitol and protested. Out in front were our leaders, Jose Calderón, Ricardo Falcón, and others. I am who I am today because of the* Chicano *Movement.*

Clarence purchased his first home shortly after graduating from UNC, where he earned a bachelor's degree in business administration. A Mexican American realtor who assisted him with the home purchase inspired him to pursue a career in real estate. He recognized an opportunity to serve his community and create a niche market selling homes to the Mexican American and Spanish-speaking immigrant communities, a population that was underserved at the time.

I have literally helped hundreds of families realize their dream of owning a home.

Standing, back row, left to right: Del Lopez, Ray Lopez, Fil Lopez, Rick Lopez, Clarence Lopez. Front row, seated: Diane Lopez Berg, Kathy Lopez.
Photo courtesy of Clarence Lopez.

Understanding the need for decent, safe, and affordable housing for low to moderate-income families, Clarence began purchasing rental properties.

I rent to families and individuals that other landlords turn away. They may have negative credit issues, employment issues, or no credit at all. I feel like I am providing a service to a community.

Clarence has served on many boards and committees in the city of Greeley. For four years, he served as vice-chairman for the Greeley Housing Authority. During his tenure as vice chairman, a multi-million-dollar renovation was completed on the forty-four-unit, two-story Dominic Apartments. Clarence was one of the original eight founding members of Greeley's first Northern Colorado Hispanic Chamber of Commerce. The name was subsequently changed to the Northern Colorado *Latino* Chamber of Commerce, and it continues to operate today.

—CLARENCE LOPEZ

Pres Montoya

*I grew up in the Chicano Movement era. They bombed our police sta-
tion, they bombed our school, they burned down our clinic. All the things
that went along with that. But we stood up for ourselves. —Montoya*

Six generations strong in Greeley! Pres Montoya with his family, celebrating their deep
roots and lasting legacy in the community.
Left to right: daughter Ashley Aragon, granddaughter Alyssa Aragon.,
Montoya, grandson Alfonso, wife Diene, and daughter Kristin.
Photo courtesy of the Pres Montoya Collection.

Pres Montoya, a proud *Chicano* leader, has dedicated his life to advocating for
education, equity, and representation in Greeley, Colorado. Born in Denver and
raised in Fort Lupton, Montoya grew up witnessing the struggles of Mexican
Americans during the *Chicano* Movement era, which inspired his lifelong commitment to empowering his community. His activism began early, attending

boycotts and protests with his father, Press, including the Coors Boycott and the Kitayama Carnation Strike at age fourteen. These experiences shaped his passion for social justice and community advocacy.

Education has been a cornerstone of Montoya's work. He co-founded the Greeley Dream Team, a nonprofit that has helped hundreds of students access higher education over its thirty-year history. Additionally, he launched the RES program with Bella Romero to recruit, retain, and graduate *Latina* and *Latino* students. Recognized as an education leader, Montoya was appointed to the Colorado Commission of Higher Education, where he worked to improve access for underserved communities. His efforts have left a lasting impact on Greeley's educational landscape.

Montoya has also played a pivotal role in increasing *Latina* and *Latino* representation in leadership. He helped recruit Romero to the school board, enabling two *Latinos* to serve simultaneously for the first time. He supported the promotion of *Latino* leaders like Ernie Andrade and John Pacheco within the school district and advocated for the hiring of the first woman in the district's cabinet, challenging an all-male leadership tradition. His work has been instrumental in breaking barriers and creating opportunities for underrepresented communities.

Beyond education, Montoya has made significant contributions to social services and real estate. As a leader with Jobs of Hope, he has helped gang-affiliated and formerly incarcerated men rebuild their lives through the Hope House, offering housing and resources. In real estate, he has worked with top firms and now partners with C3 Real Estate Solutions, focusing on creating opportunities for underrepresented communities.

Montoya's life reflects his core values of education, hard work, and community service. His advocacy stems from a deep understanding of systemic inequities, as seen in his fight for justice during the *Chicano* Movement and his ongoing efforts to uplift his community. A proud *Chicano*, Montoya's story is a testament to the resilience and contributions of Mexican Americans in shaping the history and future of Greeley, Colorado.

—YVETTE FLORES

Ray Romero

The Latinos made the farm issue as big and as prominent as it is. That helped build the enterprises that exist like ConAgra and Monfort. They were always the workers but got a pittance. —Romero

1942 image of the Romero children.
Left to right: Manuel, Ray, Dale, Rosie and Helen Romero.
Photo courtesy of the Ray Romero Collection.

Ray Romero, born in New Mexico in 1939, is the twelfth generation of his family to live in what is now the U.S. His mother often shared stories of their ancestor, Bartolomeo Romero. She told them how, in 1595, he traveled from Spain with the explorer Juan de Oñate to what is now New Mexico and how Bartolomeo, a military officer, built the City of Santa Fe.

The family came to Northern Colorado in the early 1940s after Romero's father died. At age four, Romero started working in the fields to help his mother support the family. He never started or finished a school year due to his work in the fields. In school, Romero recalls that students were separated into four groups, A through D. Mexican kids typically started in group D. Each year, he moved up a group, and by the fourth grade, he was in group A. Romero's school peers were now White children from affluent families in Greeley.

I hated it because I was just not used to that.

Romero's oldest brother, Juanito, taught him to stand up for what was right. Romero incorporated his ideals into all aspects of his life. He became an advocate not only for himself but for others, and many times experienced physical violence because of it.

After graduating from college in 1964, Romero became highly involved in the *Chicano* Movement.

I was one of the persons who started the American GI Forum.

He was also actively involved in the Cesar Chavez movement and farm worker strikes. During the Kitayama Brothers strike in Brighton, Romero recalls how the sheriff tear-gassed the demonstrators who had chained themselves to the gate protesting for workers' rights.

Romero has spent his life helping people of color. He worked for the Head Start program, the Department of Health and Human Services, private agencies, the Social Security Administration, and the University of Northern Colorado.

When reflecting on Mexican American culture, Ray offered:

Well, I think that as individuals, we do live it, understand it, love it, and appreciate it. I think in terms of the Greeley community, I don't think that they're inclusive whatsoever. I don't think they really want to know who we are. I think there has always been a strong effort to keep us down.

—BETH BULLARD

Eddie Treviño

I look forward to my grandkids being able to say, my grandfather and my great-grandfather and my great-grandmother were part of this, and I'm going to continue doing this. They're involved in a lot of community activities as well. They're continuing to learn and keeping our traditions alive. —Treviño

The Treviño Family
Front row: Ruben Treviño Sr., Florence Treviño.
Center row: Eddie Treviño, Ruben Treviño Jr., Steven Treviño.
Front row: Salvador Treviño, Dale Treviño, Danny Treviño, Diana Treviño.
Photo courtesy of the Eddie Treviño Collection.

A long-life learner, Eddie Treviño attributes his love for biology and zoology to his childhood conversations with his grandfather about animals and plants. He also fondly describes how, as a young child, he used to admire nature when he rode his minibike around the farm area where his grandparents lived, which is what is now know as Centerplace in Greeley.

Treviño was born and grew up in Greeley and comes from a fourth-generation Mexican-American family. There were six boys and one girl in his immediate family. His maternal grandparents were migrant workers from Texas who would come to Colorado in the summer and fall to do agricultural work. His paternal grandparents were from Mexico. Treviño's paternal grandfather was a gardener in Greeley, who was always very proud of the plants and flowers under his care.

His father was a mechanic and a tow truck driver, and his mother was a teacher's assistant who was a strong advocate for education. His own family now consists of two sons and four grandchildren. Treviño learned to have a very strong work ethic from his parents and grandparents. Admirably, Treviño and his siblings have all obtained college degrees, including two law degrees.

Treviño's family has been active with LULAC, Rodarte Community Center, *Candelaria* Association, and Our Lady of Peace Catholic Church. The church was integral to his family's life, and he remembers attending church functions and celebrations as he was growing up. He has also visited many local schools and engaged with students on discussions related to different science topics.

Although Treviño has many enjoyable memories of his early years in Greeley, he also remembers unpleasant incidents. He shared:

> *When I went to Jefferson Elementary, it wasn't uncommon for White kids to be chasing us, throwing rocks at us, and calling us "beaner" and "spic" and everything else. That was how it was through junior high and high school. You always had your group of kids that just couldn't stand Mexicans for whatever reason.*

Treviño is very optimistic that someday *Latinas* and *Latinos* will be fully recognized for what they have done for this city. He hopes that young people, like his four grandchildren, will continue to engage in efforts to increase *Latina* and *Latino* representation and make Greeley a more inclusive city where everyone's contributions are acknowledged.

—Dr. Madeline Milian

CHAPTER 6

Conclusion

The previous chapters discussed the lived experiences of *Latinos* in Greeley, from the early days of *La Colonia* to the *El Movimiento* of the 1960s and 1970s to the modern day. The everyday lives, education, economic, political, civic leadership, and contributions over the decades have been vividly shared using the words of real people, the community of Greeley, our historians.

To review, Chapter 1 detailed why Mexican and Mexican Americans came to Greeley all those years ago. In the early part of the twentieth century and after the Mexican Revolution, many Mexicans and Mexican Americans were colonized in the U.S. (colonized means people native to the land being taken over and controlled in this case, by the White people in power) and were relegated to a life of poverty. Many, especially in New Mexico, lost their land and migrated from their small villages to Northern Colorado, where hard work in the fields awaited them. Chapter 1 also outlines the work or employment Mexicans and Mexican Americans did in those early years, with the chapter ending with what types of jobs our historians held at the time of their interview. Each chapter ends this way, documenting our historians' experiences with the chapter's topic and content.

Chapter 2 explored the religion of our *Latina* and *Latino* historians. From the beginning, the Mexican and Mexican American population has been a very religious community, which in part helped them cope with and survive the racism and discrimination they experienced. Chapter 2 also explores how our historians' culture strengthened not only their lives but also enriches the Greeley community as well.

Chapter 3 documented how *Latinos* have been educated in Greeley. This educational history begins with a segregated school called the Gipson School and continued to the present day.

Chapter 4 detailed how *Latinas* and *Latinos* have unselfishly given their time and energy to make Greeley a better place through their civic actions. Whether it be serving on the school board or other boards in the community, serving on the city council, to political organizing to give *Latinas* and *Latinos* more of a voice in their city and state government, or volunteering for the betterment of our youth, they continue to serve and advocate for their fellow *Latinos*.

Chapter 5 focuses on social justice issues that *Latinas* and *Latinos* have faced since the 1920s. This chapter explains how *Latinas* and *Latinos* have fought against unfair treatment, starting with the sugar beet workers' strike for better pay in the 1930s and continuing with the protests and marches of the 1960s and 1970s. The fight for justice continues today.

In the late 1960s and early 1970s, many Mexican Americans, also called *Chicanas* and *Chicanos*, protested in major cities across the U.S. In Greeley, a group called the Apostles for Justice and other *Chicana* and *Chicano* organizations led efforts to stop discrimination. These groups pressured employers to hire more Mexican Americans and *Chicana*s and *Chicano*s in different jobs, not just in meat plants and farm work. In the 1980s and 1990s, more *Latinas* and *Latinos* began working in professional jobs. The terms *Latinas* and *Latinos* are used for this time period because they includes Mexican Americans, people from Central and South America, and *Chicana*s and *Chicano*s. By the early 1990s, there were more *Latina* and *Latino* principals, teachers, and blue-collar workers.

However, in the 2000s, this progress slowed down. It was not because *Latinas* and *Latinos* were not qualified for the jobs because they were qualified. But many leaders at the time did not push for more *Latinas* and *Latinos* to be hired in city, state, and federal jobs. Because of this, hiring practices for *Latinas* and *Latinos* went backward, similar to the 1940s and 1950s.

This final chapter, the conclusion, also looks to the future. It shares what our historians hope will happen in Greeley to help *Latinas/os* thrive and succeed. In short, the historians want more fairness and inclusion for *Latinas/*os in the community. According to data from UnidosUS (2024), by the year 2030, 20 percent of all workers in the U.S. will be *Latina* or *Latino*. Between 2020 and

2030, 78 percent of new workers and 70 percent of new homeowners will be *Latina* or *Latino*. However, these successes have not been easy.

As we saw in the earlier chapters, *Latinas/os* have worked hard with strength and courage to achieve success. This chapter will explore how these qualities will continue to help *Latinas* and *Latinos* in the future, using the words of our historians.

Inclusion of *Latino* Culture in Greeley

Our historians had a lot to say about the inclusion and exclusion of *Latina* and *Latino* culture in Greeley. Many of their opinions were said consistently. Gonzales Guerrero, Jr. shared:

> *Well, I don't think it's represented at all. We're invisible people here.*

Cortez agreed.

> Cinco de Mayo, *it's a food fest; that's essentially what it is. You know, there's no speakers about the history of it, why it was implemented, what happened after that, and then no continuity.*

Adriana Trujillo thought so too.

> *The stereotype of Mexican culture is shown. And then I feel like the city thinks, "Okay, we represented them. We put money into their celebration. We're good for the year!"*

Montalvo added that she thought Greeley's attempts at inclusivity were because of finances and not a genuine promise for inclusion. Gama added that, except for *Cinco de Mayo*, she didn't see different *Latino* cultures shown in Greeley. Johnson said:

> *We can do better. I think we can build on that as we move forward.*

Clarence Lopez suggested that Greeley was not doing enough.

It's up to us, as Mexican Americans, Latinos, Latinas, Latinx, Chicanos, to push the city of Greeley to become more inclusive. Because right now, I don't feel like it is a real inclusive community.

A few historians talked about how *Latina* and *Latino* culture is shown in positive ways, especially today compared to the past. Nieto said she sees Mexican American culture being represented.

… in a really positive light. I feel like it gets better every year.

Garcia Martinez said that there are ways this can improve, but:

… there is more pride in the community, more representation. People are less shy about really representing their culture.

Hernandez said that *Latina* and *Latino* culture is shown more deeply.

Not only food and dance but to really see us as, as we are, as whole humans. I think that it's starting to shift with the generations.

Nickie Archibeque agreed with that.

Definitely more than when I was younger.

Garcia-Nelson added that last year was:

… the first time we celebrated Mexican Independence Day for Friday Fest! The streets were full of people! I hope that's a tradition, where we have Mexican Independence Day downtown, for sure.

Several historians, however, suggested that there was still room for improvement in sharing *Latina* and *Latino* culture in the community.
Martinez Rocha said:

We have a long way to go. It seems like it's up and down, up and down.

Mendoza added:

Sometimes when we go to some of those meetings where the big decisions are being made, there's not a lot of us. There's not enough communication of those events or how important they are to our community.

Vázquez agrees that the situation has improved with the newer generation. However, he also thinks that some families have lost their pride in being Mexican, feeling more American. Deborah Suniga said that Greeley could become more inclusive by:

… doing what you're doing now, working together. I think with us, with the Latino Coalition, working with the immigrant refugee center, working with different groups, building those bridges together and building that community, that's what we need to keep doing.

Theresa Solis agreed, saying that she:

… wants to see more community involvement and outreach on the east side of town. This is where the population is more diverse.

(Romero) Horning said that bilingual education and encouraging and celebrating both Spanish and English were real solutions to including different cultures.

Inclusion in the Economic Domain

Since the earliest years of *La Colonia* and the GWSC, *Latinas* and *Latinos* have worked in many different jobs in the Greeley economy. González Guerrero, Jr. spoke critically of this history.

Well, all the labor. The sugar industry. The barons here became super wealthy because of Mexican labor. Greeley, presently, would not make it. Neither would Fort Collins, or Denver, or anywhere if it was not for Mexican labor. Cleaning offices, teachers, principals, entrepreneurs, at the plant, everywhere we're workers. We have the most dangerous jobs. We have the least paying jobs, and the least benefits (Gonzales Guerrero, Jr., 2023).

Gabriel Lopez added:

Starting from 1919, Great Western wouldn't have made their money without Mexican American labor.

Clarence Lopez also said:

Agricultural economy was built on the backs of Mexican American and Latino labor.

Ben (Mitch) Gonzales connected this history to today's economy. He said that there were:

… not a lot of Whites working in kitchens or washing the dishes. There's not a lot of White maids. There's not a lot working at the hotels who are Anglo. Without the Latinos *in Weld County, Weld County would've been a bust. You know, for them to overlook the* Latino *community is just foolish (B.M. Gonzales, 2023).*

Clarence Lopez made more connections.

Mexican Americans helped the University of Northern Colorado. There are lots of Latinos *and Mexican Americans working at the Northern Colorado Medical Center, which is Banner Health today. We contribute heavily to the economy of Greeley.*

Many historians believe that the economic contributions by *Latinas* and *Latinos* have been improving over the years. Garcia-Nelson said:

Going down 10th Street, we can really see examples of the entrepreneurship of Latinas *and* Latinos, *in general, in Greeley.*

Montoya said that *Latinas* and *Latinos*:

… presented very well. We're the hard workers that make this town go.

Gama compared recent improvements.

It's been interesting that in the last couple years I'm seeing more women of color, men of color, especially Latinas, Latinos, *in business networking events and workshops. But I think it was really sad that up until just two years ago, I would quite often be the only Brown person in the room, you know? It's really, really good to see more* Latinas, Latinos *in these types of events, networking with their own businesses. I would still love to see twice as many, three times as many in a shorter amount of time (Gama, 2023).*

Garcia-Nelson said that economic prosperity will probably change for the better in the future. She said, looking at the businesses:

… that are starting to pop up downtown, I am noticing that a lot of the business owners are younger people, so I feel like that will definitely make a difference.

Gonzales-Soto pointed to more diverse businesses in Greeley.

I think it has become more prevalent where you're seeing more stores that are catering to populations that are not White, that are catering to populations that are identifying either as Mexican American or Hispanic or Latinx or Latino.

However, Stacy Suniga spoke of the need for more *Latina* and *Latino* businesses in the Chamber of Commerce. She said that this could happen by inviting *Latina* and *Latino* business owners:

… in their native language.

Inclusion in Housing for *Latinas* and *Latinos*
Some of the historians spoke about the past inequality in housing for *Latinos*. Cortez said that "There's different levels of housing" (for *Latinos*). Theresa Solis actually studied home mortgage data and found inequality between the eastside and the westside of Greeley. This suggests "redlining" (a bank's refusal to loan

to a buyer because the house is in an unfavorable neighborhood location or overpricing of a house so as to discourage a buyer from putting in a bid) that hurt *Latina* and *Latino* homebuyers. She explained:

> *If the people on the eastside wanted a house almost similar to what they had but located on the westside, it was overpriced. They couldn't afford it. A lot of them were buying homes on the eastside. There's quite a bit of people now that live on the eastside (T. Solis, 2023).*

Taes Grimm told a similar story about her experiences of discrimination in obtaining housing in Greeley.

> *So that was one way that I was discriminated against: even when I was married, trying to get a place to live. Sometimes they would tell you, "It's already been rented; it's not available."*
>
> *Then, when someone else went in, like even a person with my last name, Grimm, you could call on the phone and the home was available.*
>
> *I would go in, and they'd say, "No, you can't do it."*
>
> *Then he would go in, and they'd say, "Oh, yeah. We can do that (Grimm, 2023)."*

(Romero) Horning shared that her parents tried to buy a home in the Garden City neighborhood in the 1950s. However, the seller stopped the sale when he found out the family was Hispanic. She added that also in the 1950s, other new Greeley neighborhoods clearly prevented Mexican Americans from buying a home there.

Inclusion in Political/Government Domain

Many of our historians spoke of the lack of *Latina* and *Latino* representation in local government. This included politically, in leadership, and in managerial roles. Taes Grimm hoped:

> *… to see more Hispanics involved in city council, on the school board, in all of the areas that would help our people. Without bringing out any*

political parties, I think some political parties would like to see less of us and keep us quiet. But that's one thing that I think we have to try and change.

Johnson spoke in earnest about there not being enough *Latinas/os* in government.

If your council doesn't look like you, how inclusive are you? When you don't have a voice of a population that's growing, like the Latina *and* Latino *population, there's not a voice there to advocate for you or to say, "Hey, we're missing this."*

Nickie Archibeque spoke strongly about her desires for more *Latinas/os* in politics, saying "I want to see a *Latina* or *Latino* mayor. I want to see a city manager. I don't think there's any *Latinos* that sit on the city council today. That's what I want to see."

Stacy Suniga agreed.

I think right now, in particular, there is not even a Latino *on the city council.*

She said this explains her activism in the process for changing voting districts in the Colorado House of Representatives.

Ben (Mitch) Gonzales repeated her thoughts.

The numbers we have, we should have three people on city council, five people on the school board, and a lot more activity. It's a bit disappointing that we don't support each other. ... I think if we flexed our muscles, we could be a lot more inclusive (B.M. Gonzales, 2023).

Montoya agreed.

We should have two or three people on the city council. We should have them on school boards.

However, our historians also looked hopefully to the future generations. Clarence Lopez said:

I feel that as our younger generations begin to age, become educated, create new businesses, I think that just the fact that through sheer numbers, and strength of numbers, we're going to see more representation.

Mendoza said:

Latinos *have some work to do, and that's part of what we can do: be more active at the council meetings where the big decisions are being made with the government.*

Deborah Suniga added:

Educating our community, getting people out there to run for the boards, the commissions, the councils, and the younger generation, os important.

Some historians talked about representation in politics and in government services and hiring practices. Martinez Rocha said that Greeley should:

… kind of reevaluate their hiring practices. I don't think there's any Latinos *in any kind of leadership role in the City of Greeley. … I really think that the city needs to be a lot better at hiring people of color and* Latinos *in leadership roles.*

Treviño agreed.

Greeley should have much more representation within the city workplace, as well as the police department and fire department. Anything that the city government gets involved in should have much more representation.

Nieto added that Greeley needs to:

Fill more positions in the government with people of color. Greeley should also increase diversity on city boards and commissions.

Inclusion in Civic Engagement

Several historians talked about community activism and political participation together. They discussed the contributions of several *Latina* and *Latino* members of Greeley's community. Nieto talked about Rhonda Solis and her work uniting the community and talking about important issues, particularly while she served on the school board. Nieto also talked about the great work that Hispanic Women of Weld County has done to be more visible and active in the community through fundraisers and events. Gonzales-Soto said it is important for *Latinas* and *Latinos* to get real experience about the needs of the community so they can take leadership roles.

Comfortable in Greeley

Because Mexicans and Mexican Americans were excluded in Greeley in the past, shown by "No Mexicans" signs in store windows, it is important to see how *Latinas* and *Latinos* feel living in Greeley today. Adriana Trujillo said she feels comfortable:

> ... *because of the community we've created with other Mexican Americans. We have to be there for each other, and that's what makes me comfortable.*

Jacob Duran added that in the area where he lives:

> *There's no crime or theft or anything like that. We enjoy Greeley, but it's getting kind of crowded.*

However, other historians said that racism towards *Latinas* and *Latinos* was still there. Nieto said:

> ... *every day in the courts that I work in, especially the juvenile delinquency court. How many more kids I see there who are getting detained, arrested, committed—who are kids of color versus kids who are not kids of color (Nieto, 2023).*

Montalvo agreed.

A lot of the Hispanics here in Colorado get picked on by the police a lot. You know, I think that they're judged because this one is this, or this one is homeless, or they think that we're all the same, and we're not (Montalvo, 2023).

Martinez expressed hope that the situation would improve. He said:

Greeley is making an honest attempt to try to address that. I'll give them credit for that. I think Greeley is trying to make an honest attempt.

Wendirad shared that she thinks there are some events but there is still a long way to go. She said that people:

… don't need to value our culture or customs, but they need education to understand where we are coming from.

Acknowledged for Contributions

Almost all our historians agreed that *Latinas* and *Latinos* in Greeley have not been acknowledged for their contributions to the economy and the community. González Guerrero, Jr. said:

No. No. We're never consulted about anything. Not even about our kids.

Jenny Garcia said the only time she was acknowledged was for her work with the Hispanic Women of Weld County. Jacob Duran agreed, saying that some have been acknowledged but not many. Garcia-Nelson gave a specific example about the Greeley Museum.

When we look at the museum, we don't see Brown faces. I feel like that's definitely an issue, and I'm really grateful that y'all are working to change that.

Many historians mentioned the Mexicans and Mexican American laborers who worked the sugar beet fields in the early part of the twentieth century

Gonzales-Soto said that Mexican American laborers built Greeley, which has not been adequately acknowledged. She added:

> *I think there has been some recognition. I will be honest, I think the recognition is for those individuals who have played by the rules, who have lived within the White supremacy world, who are White passing. They may not look White passing, but their attitudes and their behaviors have been White passing. Those are the individuals that have been recognized, which is fine because they have done it. But I think you have a slew of other individuals that are breaking their backs, doing that work, who have not been recognized (Gonzales-Soto, 2023).*

Adriana Trujillo agreed.

> *There's nothing that acknowledges all of the migrant workers and* braceros *who have worked these fields and have provided sustenance for the entire country.*

Garcia-Nelson added that farm work was very difficult, and:

> *It takes the right kind of people, and those people have been our people. I feel like definitely acknowledging the farm workers would be a huge thing.*

Deborah Suniga pointed out that farm work is:

> *… out in the elements, but* Latino *people show up and do it. I mean, just start there. We have food in our supermarkets because of* Latino *people working in these fields, from here and east.*

Martinez Rocha said:

> *The contributions that we have made in the past have not really been looked at as contributions because they were related to agriculture.*

Gabriel Lopez suggested that this lack of acknowledgement could be because of media.

It's hard to get them going when the newspaper doesn't want to write (about us). We're fortunate to have a friend in Channel 9 News who understands it, accepts it, and wants to help.

Nieto also suggested:

I think some people don't want to put their name out there and don't want to do it. I know I've had friends that I've tried to encourage to go out there and do things, and they don't believe they're enough. They don't believe they're good enough to do it. They don't believe they're well-known enough to do it, whatever. I think there needs to definitely be some more kind of recruitment to get more people to participate in all of these organizations so that more people can see us because, if they do, I think it will only help level the playing field (Nieto, 2023).

Ana Trujillo agreed. She said that she didn't think that:

… Mexican Americans voice their success as much as we should. We try to educate ourselves, but we don't go out there and voice it.

Treviño suggested that the contributions of *Latinas* and *Latinos* have not been acknowledged:

… because it's just been the way Greeley is.

Stacy Suniga added:

We have college professors and local activists, and I don't think this community's ready to talk about them.

Theresa Solis praised *Latinas* and *Latinos* for their work on establishing the Rodarte Center. She said these people should receive more acknowledgement, individuals such as:

Pete Longoria, Sal Salazar, and there were also people from Denver who came up that would help.

A few historians said that people might be starting to acknowledge the contributions of *Latinas* and *Latinos*. Martinez suggested that there has been some acknowledgement. He said:

It's what Monfort, all your meat packing houses consist of, nothing but the Mexicano *population. There are very few Whites doing that kind of work, very few Anglos. That was a lot of hard work, and I think that's what actually put Greeley on the map (H.L. Martinez, 2023).*

Wendirad shared her thoughts about *Latina* and *Latino* recognition for their contributions to the Greeley community.

Someone told me, "Greeley is a city of wide streets and narrow minds."

And I thought, how sad. I wonder if we have moved away from that, but, as I'm out and about and hear certain comments, I feel that's still the notion of some people. Sometimes there are certain people that are recognized, but not everyone as a whole.

And, if I may elaborate, generally speaking, the Mexican culture, we tend to be very humble. We don't go and tell people what we are doing because we don't want to be seen as presumidos *(presumptuous), as if we are just trying to make a name for ourselves. So, we are behind the scenes. We do things for others, but we are not out there publicizing it. Maybe people don't truly see all the wonderful things people are doing and we're not recognized (Wendirad, 2023).*

(Romero) Horning pointed out the work that many *Latinas* and *Latinos* are doing. She said they are beginning to receive some recognition.

I think it has become more prevalent that those who made contributions in the past are recognized. I think about people like Carlos Leal and Alice Leal. I think about people like Al Dominguez. I think about people like

*Billie Martinez. There are so many unnamed people that have contrib-
uted on a day-to-day basis, not only to build our community, actually
physically build our community, to enrich it through many avenues, but
then those who just do the work everyday ((Romero) Horning, 2023).*

Several historians look to the future and ways that *Latinas* and *Latinos* can
receive more recognition for their contributions. Martinez Rocha said:

*We need to be better about telling our stories and letting them know the
things that we have accomplished. For example, helping with the Boys
and Girls Club, helping with the Rodarte Center, things like that. We
need to boast more about that (Martinez Rocha, 2023).*

Perez said:

*We're still Latinos, and we need to take pride in the fact that we're all on
the same uphill struggle to be recognized for our contributions as Latinos.
For the contributions that our abuelitos (grandparents) have made to
this country through the hard labor of field laborers or other contributions
through the jobs that they do (Perez, 2023).*

Greeley's Future

Our historians constantly looked to the future and the hopes and dreams they
have for their community. Many discussed specific organizations supporting
greater equity for *Latinas* and *Latinos* in Greeley. Brittni Laura Hernandez said:

*Projects like this and a lot of the work that Hispanic Women of Weld
County and so many organizations are doing is shifting the way that we
see Mexican Americans in Greeley for the good and the better.*

Nickie Archibeque talked about strength in politics, organizations, and the
new generation. She added:

If we're all climbing up the ladder, we need to help each other climb up the ladder and not push anybody out of the way.

Gama said that she sees growth and improvement. She added that she hoped:

… our role will grow a lot more in positions of power and decision-making boards. From the school board to nonprofit boards, to other types of boards, and in the business community. I just hope that we'll see a lot more representation. I feel like the United Way of Weld County does a great job because I'm not the only Mexican American on the board. I think there are four of us actually (Gama, 2023).

Bustillos said that building more community centers would increase support for *Latinas* and *Latinos*. She said that the community centers:

… do a nice job of educating the community as to what resources are available to them, what programs they can become involved in, like voting.

Jacob and Josie Duran talked about more local businesses owned by *Latinas* and *Latinos*. They said this was a sign of greater equity. However, Josie added:

We need to get better.

Abraham Garcia offered his thoughts.

Education's going to have to be a big part of it for the Chicano *community, to get more involved like you guys are doing here. With different clubs, Boys Clubs, Girls Clubs, and I think that that's a big opportunity for the* Chicanos *to come up.*

Many historians spoke of the younger generation. They talked about the importance of engaging them in helping Greeley's growth. Stacy Suniga expressed the importance of equity, engaging, and empowering younger generations. She said that the torch should be passed to the youth that value their culture, that they should be helped with the tools, resources, and training (they need), particularly from Aims and UNC. She also mentioned the importance of working with other groups across Colorado through the *Latino* Action Council. Baca, a retired Colorado Representative and longtime activist, added:

And in the 1960s, because of the civil rights movement, a lot of that started to change. By the 1970s here in Greeley, even some of my cousins don't remember. The younger cousins don't remember the hard times because, by then, things had started to change. And Greeley, now, I'm proud of what's happening here! I really am! You know, we've got, I mean, my goodness, the work that you're doing and the work that the Latino Coalition of Weld County *are doing! And the different professors at the University of Northern Colorado, my goodness. I could not have imagined having Mexican and Mexican American women as college professors!*

I mean, my sister, my older sister, got her doctorate degree and was a professor at the University of Colorado at Denver. But it's so exciting for me to see young people achieve so much more than I could have ever imagined that any of us would be able to achieve! Quite honestly, I think there's still some bigotry in this town, but what I believe is, treat it as any bigotry that you have. Treat it as a gift to make you work harder, to overcome it, when you see discrimination, stand up to it and let it help to make you stronger! Because it's when you are discriminated against that you can then stand up, not only for your rights but the rights for any group that is being discriminated against!

That's why I became so involved in the civil rights movement, and I still am. I don't want to see any group being discriminated against the way I was as a child and having suffered the pain that I suffered as a child (Baca, 2023).

Montalvo repeated that this work still needed to be done.

I think we need to step up. I think we need to fight more, and I don't think we should lay back and just take hand-me-downs. I think we need to get out there and do it.

Gabriel Lopez said that he didn't see a lot of improvement happening.

… unless you have a lot of forceful people. I'm not one of them. I just do what I do, and I love what I'm doing, and Jody and I are just happy the way we are.

Perez stressed the importance of encouraging young people and others to express their concerns. He said they should stand up against abuse or inequality, whether based on race or education. He said that new immigrants, like those from African countries in Greeley, face similar issues to the ones previous generations experienced. He stresses the importance of treating people well and speaking up against wrongs.

The sense of unity and connections within the *Latina* and *Latino* community appeared in many narratives from our historians.

Mendoza shared her ideas.

We have great talent and great ideas because we have a special background; we're able to connect with the people that come from Mexico. And not just from Mexico but other immigrants. I think this is a country of immigrants and we all have something to share from our own experience. It helps others. They encourage the others to do great for the community, to come together and make sure that all the rights are respected, regardless of our background or our immigrant status (Mendoza, 2023).

Montoya leaves us with his pearls of wisdom from over thirty years of very active civic engagement. He has served on multiple boards, including the school board. Here are his thoughts and suggestions for more *Latina* and *Latino* engagement and representation in Greeley.

I look at what lessons are to be learned. First, we can elect Latinas/os with a cross section of support. Second, more than one voice made a difference in hiring leadership to increase achievement and graduation for our students. And third, having two Mexican board members and a Mexican superintendent (John Pacheco) did not equal success for our Mexican students.

The hard truth, in my opinion, is that we lost the momentum of increasing Latina and Latino staff, and achievement/graduation for our students, when the school board let go of Tim Waters, along with Dr. Ernie Andrade, whose focus was on achievement and graduation. That was over thirty years ago. Since then, our Mexican population has increased from three thousand students to over twelve thousand today, with nearly 70 percent on free and reduced lunch because of their low income.

We hit some real lows with poverty, gangs, single parents, and drugs, which is still a major problem in our community. However, we have much more hope and improvement with Diedre Pilch (District 6 Superintendent), past board member Rhonda Solis, and current member Dr. Brenda Campos-Spitze. Dr. Campos-Spitze is very focused on the achievement of our students. Lastly, we no longer have mostly Mexican American students, we have a variety of Latino students along with many other cultures in our district (Montoya, 2025).

Ben (Mitch) Gonzales is also hopeful that each generation will continue to do better than the previous generation.

Like I said, times change. I mean, as you get older, you realize that, you know … it gets a little bit easier as we go on. People change, attitudes change, and mentalities change, and … my grandkids have a lot more opportunities than we had growing up. And even my own kids. Like I said … change happens, and you see families that own beautiful homes. That wouldn't happen in the 1960s because we weren't allowed to live in those types of homes.

We were shown neighborhoods that were where the Mexicans were supposed to live. …Times have changed. My children are managers and leaders. My son has twenty men under him. My oldest son runs an entire nursing home. He's the head administrator. I have another son who has ten men under him in a water facility for oil and gas. Like I said, if we push ourselves, I think, I really think we can run this country in about twenty years (B.M. Gonzales, 2023)!

The history of Mexicans and Mexican Americans in Greeley has been one of struggle. The first Mexican and Mexican Americans in Greeley faced many challenges, just as *Latinas/os* do today. *Latinas/os* have always worked hard to survive and thrive, even when times were difficult.

The authors sincerely hope that this book and the history told within its pages depict a genuine and heartfelt picture of the legacy that *Latinos* of long ago and not so long ago have given to present-day *Latinos*. Today's *Latinos* stand on the shoulders of these 20th-century Mexicans and Mexican Americans, inheriting their grit, determination, toughness, and ganas. Their legacy continues to propel new generations of *Latinos* in pursuing not only a better life for themselves but for their community as well..

NARRATIVES FOR CHAPTER 6

Nickie Archibeque and Hernandez

What Brown and Indigenous people had already known is how to be in relationship with the land. It helped me to see the value in where I came from. —Hernandez

The Archibeque family celebrating their parents' Charles and Laura's sixtieth wedding anniversary.
Left to right: C.J. Archibeque (son), Karen Esquibel (daughter), Lori Trujillo (daughter), Charles and Laura Archibeque, Carla Esquibel (daughter), Lisa Archibeque (daughter), Julee Archibeque-Martinez (daughter), and Nickie Archibeque (daughter).
Photo courtesy of the Nickie Archibeque Collection.

Nickie Archibeque's parents and Hernandez's grandparents, Charles and Laura Archibeque, are known in Greeley for their selfless contributions to the community. As the second bilingual City of Greeley Councilman, Charles helped with the Rodarte Center expansion program. Their son CJ continued to grow the Rodarte expansion and its programs. Charles founded the *Plaza del Sol* and *Plaza del Milagro* Migrant Housing Project for Catholic Charities. Charles noticed East Greeley lacked affordable housing, so he facilitated building thirty-two units to create stable housing for families. The complex was called Lincoln Square Apartments.

On top of raising six strong, independent, and intelligent women and one son, Nickie Archibeque's mom, Laura, worked for the Weld County Sheriff's Department, North Range Behavioral Health, and the Migrant Education Program. Laura and Charles opened the Mirasol Mexican Restaurant, where Laura was the head chef and shared her culinary knowledge with her staff. In honor of Nickie Archibeque's parents, in 2017, the city renamed Sunrise Park as Charlie and Laura Archibeque Park.

Nickie Archibeque went from being a first-generation college student herself to supporting first-generation college students as the director of the Colorado Opportunity Scholarship Initiative at the University of Northern Colorado. She explained:

I get to help students of color. They get to see someone who looks like them through me.

Nickie Archibeque also sits on the Weld County Workforce Youth Advisory Board, which helps youth ages fifteen to twenty-four to find jobs, careers, and technical centers for support.

Hernandez's work within the community and at CU Boulder is guided by her passion to create a difference in the world. At CU Boulder, she supported the process of passing Colorado's Advancing Students for a Stronger Tomorrow (ASSET). Her and her colleagues also launched "A Queer Endeavor," which gives teachers resources necessary to support LGBTQIA+ students in the classroom. She helped found MiraSoul, a women-owned, family business that serves as Greeley's first community healing space.

Hernandez asked:

What might it look like to have spaces where we can be our full selves and we don't have to always assimilate?

Archibeque answered:

We need to… let others know we're here to stay… we need to help each other climb up the ladder and not push anybody out of the way.

Hernandez added:

We can look inward, confronting our assumptions and our biases. To me, that looks like conversations and community circles. I see us moving towards wellness and healing … and really prioritizing our mental, physical, and emotional well-being. Whether that means growing our community gardens or … growing the way we communicate with one another.

Nickie Archibeque and Hernandez see potential in our community's ability to connect, heal, and thrive.

—ADRIANA TRUJILLO

Susana (Susie) Taes Grimm

I've lived here my whole life, and it's always been, to me, it's always been a racist town. There's always been discrimination here. —Grimm

Originally from New Mexico, Susana (Susie) Taes Grimm's father moved to Greeley to work in the sugar beet factory. Her grandfather owned a pool hall and store in Greeley's Spanish Colony, where they lived. Her father also worked as a barber serving the men there.

When my family was growing up, they always had the Ku Klux Klan over in the Spanish Colony. When I was going to school, you could tell that they didn't like us.

Taes Grimm explained:

I remember we were a poor family.

Wedding photo.
Back row: Anastacio Taes, groom, Jennie Garcia, and Alvin Garcia.
Seated: Lillian Garcia Taes (bride).
Photo courtesy of the Susana Taes Grimm Collection.

In elementary school, the principal would take her and her sister to buy shoes at the start of every year. Taes Grimm recalls a time when she wanted a new dress for a party at school and how her parents worked tirelessly to pull together the money to buy her a brand-new dress.

Taes Grimm graduated from high school in 1967.

I wanted to become a nurse when I was in high school. I went to go see the counselor, Mr. Gardner, he said that I wasn't smart enough to go to school.

They told her family that she probably wouldn't make it to college and recommended secretarial or trade school.

So that's what I did. I went to secretarial school, and then later, I went to college.

After completing Parks Business School in Denver, she returned to Greeley to work at a law firm. She has had several jobs at the University of Northern Colorado, the most notable and influential being her work alongside Jose Córdova in bilingual education. He and Professor Felix Garcia were prominent role models for her family.

Taes Grimm attended several sit-ins and walks during the *Chicano* Movement alongside Corky Gonzales and Jose Calderon. She supports her niece, Stacy Suniga, a political activist and advocate for people of color.

I think some political party would like to see less of us and keep us quiet, but that's one thing that I think we have to try and change.

She feels Greeley can be more inclusive by:

Getting rid of some of the people who are in power right now.

And hopes:

To see more Hispanics involved in the city council, on the school board, and in all of the areas that would help our people.

—Beth Bullard

Brandi Lynn Nieto

We don't make money to have all these great things. We do it so we can help more people out.—Nieto

Brandi L. Nieto with her brothers.
Left to right: Robert Martinez, L. Nieto, and Epifañio Nieto, Jr.
Photo courtesy of the Brandi L. Nieto Collection.

Brandi Lynn Nieto, born and raised in La Junta, Colorado, was taught to work hard, do well in school, get a good job, and help support her family. Her mother's family downplayed their Mexican culture and traditions. However, Nieto feels it may have been an effort to fit in.

While in high school, a friend's mother asked what she wanted to do after graduation. Nieto told her of her desire to be a lawyer. The woman suggested she become a paralegal instead. She was hurt, confused, and felt unsupported and judged for being a poor Brown child. Nieto, fueled with the desire to prove her wrong, became an attorney!

In 2005, Nieto accepted a prosecutor position in Greeley and later went on to become the first *Latina* municipal court judge and executive team member. Working within a peer group of primarily older White men was an adjustment for her. Sometimes, she felt her opinions weren't respected based on her age, gender, or skin color. Regardless, she remained diligent in offering her ideas and perspectives.

There are times I feel other people are given the benefit of the doubt and I'm not.

Nieto recognizes that Greeley subscribes to diversity, equity, and inclusion but feels that action or practice is lacking. She hopes to see more diverse progressive leadership and initiatives. Another concern is the racial divide and discrimination she observes and has experienced. Feeling that far too often, Brown or poor children aren't given the benefit of the doubt afforded to White or connected children.

Nieto learned the importance of being seen and connected and feels *Latinos* need to be present, visible, and engaged in their communities. After her son was born, she became a guardian ad litem for the State of Colorado, representing the voices and interests of children. Her service to children and their families goes far beyond that role.

I have a tendency to say yes if it's for a good cause and then figure out how to do it. We try to give back as much as we can.

Being a natural redhead and light-skinned, Nieto has always felt she wasn't Brown enough and that the absence of her ethnicity in childhood was a disservice. It is wrong, but she's mindful of changing it for her son.

I want him to be proud to be Brown and to make a difference.

—BETH BULLARD

Deborah and Stacy Suniga

We need to have a voice; we need to have representation.

—Deborah Suniga

Benito and Tonita Gonzales, great-grandparents of Deborah Suniga.
Photo courtesy of the Deborah Suniga Collection.

Deborah and Stacy were introduced to political and social activism at an early age. Stacey's mother and Deborah's grandmother were activists alongside Baca, Cesar Chavez, and Corky Gonzales. Deborah and Stacy founded The *Latino* Coalition of Weld County with a commitment to ensuring cross-cultural inclusion and equal opportunity to participate in the direction of local laws and governmental issues. They want to empower *Latinos* to use their voice and their vote, believing representation on every committee, council, and commission is possible. These two are committed to not only edifying Weld County and Greeley but the entire 8th Congressional District.

Deborah explained:

If we can get the vote out, get our community educated and let them know that they do have a voice and their vote does matter, we can make a difference.

She feels there's more work to do to educate, celebrate, and honor *Latinos'* contributions to our community and throughout the state. She is a member of the *Latino* Action Council, the *Latino* Caucus in Denver, represents Weld County on the Supreme Court Nomination Committee, and is Colorado District 8's first commissioner on the Board of Authority for the State Fair.

When running for office, Stacy felt there was a deliberate effort to ensure Latina and Latino candidates didn't succeed, and while in office, she battled discrimination. She was the first *Latina* Democrat to sit on Greeley's city council and describes her term as frustrating, feeling it was more about aiding people of means and power than those who needed the help. Stacy reflected:

> *My life has been threatened while on city council ... and it's like, you don't understand, you threaten me, you just embolden me! I'm going to be even more dedicated to my cause.*

Regarding the status of equity and inclusion in Greeley, Stacy and Deborah were glad to see a Black city manager's appointment. They are excited about his commitment to equity but expressed concern over influential community members who may pull strings behind the scenes. They feel culture matters and Greeley needs a bigger table with a diverse guest list and bilingual invitations and menus. Stacy explained:

> *I think we put ourselves in a position that we're going to be a force to reckon with. To make sure that the status quo doesn't stay, that we're more inclusive, more respectful in this community towards people of color.*

Deborah, a self-proclaimed rabble-rouser, agrees and is committed to being a voice and bridge for their people.

—BETH BULLARD

Vicente Vega Ruiz

I honestly don't think Greeley would be anywhere close to where it is if it wasn't for our community. —Vega Ruiz

Vicente Vega Ruiz's family, originally from the mountain ranges in *Chihuahua*, Mexico, moved to Greeley in the early 1990s. His father hoped to find work and settle in a small community where his family could grow. Vega Ruiz's parents began working in the fields and afterward worked at Monfort and JBS (meat packing plant). His father received amnesty under the 1986 Immigration Reform and Control Act, and his family benefited from bilingual education programs.

Vega Ruiz feels blessed to have supportive parents who, seeking a better future, brought their family to the U.S. They were positive role models who were present in their children's lives and a constant reminder to do better. They instilled the values of hard work, responsibility, and integrity into Vega Ruiz and his siblings.

Seeing my parents do everything and anything they could to provide for us ... to having a roof over our head, to having food on the table. It was always doing as much as they could, the right way. There were never any shortcuts or ideas of shortcuts. It was always, we are here to work hard and get beyond.

Vega Ruiz attended Adams State College on a soccer scholarship, earning a degree in business administration. He currently works as a real estate professional. He serves on several community boards focusing on helping others, educating, and leading by example.

Unfortunately, Vega Ruiz has experienced discrimination. The police were called when he and his wife were walking in their West Greeley neighborhood to retrieve the mail.

I'm sure if we didn't look a certain way, it wouldn't have happened.

A downtown karaoke establishment they patronize strictly prohibits Latin music and refuses to recognize foreign passports as valid proof of identification.

Regarding the recognition and inclusivity of *Latinos* in Greeley, Vega Ruiz stated:

There is a lot of room for improvement.

He feels more needs to be done to recognize those who built and continue to support the city through their agriculture, industry, and construction work by reinvesting the community's income. He hopes to see more diverse leadership who are willing to invest time, listen, appreciate, and embrace the cultures living in our melting pot city.

There is no stopping us. We're just going to keep growing and helping those around us.

—BETH BULLARD

Author Biographies

Dr. Lorretta Chávez

Dr. Chávez is longtime educator who has taught in public schools and at the university level for thirty-seven years. She holds a B.A. in elementary education, a masters degree in linguistically diverse education, and a Ph.D. in culturally and linguistically diverse education. She is spending her retirement, or golden years, writing this book.

Dr. Juli Sarris

Dr. Juli Sarris is a contributing writer. She is affiliate faculty at CU-Boulder's School of Education, and has been teaching teachers for over fifteen years in six different countries, in addition to the U.S. She holds a Ph.D. in education/educational equity and cultural diversity from CU-Boulder. She and her family live in Boulder and enjoy hiking, camping, and snowboarding in Colorado's beautiful outdoors.

Dr. Gonzales Guerrero Jr.

Dr. Gonzales Guerrero, Jr. was born in *La Colonia del Alcarán* in Houston, Texas. He was married twice to two beautiful, strong, and intelligent women. He has four children and six grandchildren. He is a strong advocate for the poor and oppressed caused by capitalism. He has taught in Houston, Chicago, Saginaw, and Greeley. He also worked as a college recruiter for LULAC Service Centers. He has published several articles and two books: *A* Chicano *Theology* (1987) and *Freedom, Justice and Love* (2018). He currently has three books in process: *Pouring New Wine Into Old Wineskins, A Socio-Theology of Mexican American Imprisonment,* and *Stop The Madness.* He has a degree in philosophy and five graduate degrees in divinity/theology and Spanish from the University of St. Thomas, Harvard Divinity School, and the University of Northern Colorado.

Narrative Writers

Beth Bullard

Beth Bullard is the author of *Tragically Beautiful Essays of Love, Loss and Hope, Sandwiched Essays on Life From the In-between*, and is a contributing author to the *Chicken Soup for the Soul* series. She is a seasoned clinician, educator, healthcare leader, and executive. Beth lives on a small farm in Colorado with her children and a menagerie of animals.

Caleb Flores

Caleb Flores, a lifelong Greeley resident and proud Mexican American, has worked in public schools for nearly a decade, primarily as a teacher of multilingual learners at Greeley West High School. He now serves as the ML coordinator for Greeley-Evans School District 6. Flores is a two-time graduate from the University of Northern Colorado with a B.A. in English literature and an M.A. in educational leadership.

Yvette Flores

Yvette Flores, a proud Greeley native, daughter of Mexican immigrants, and first-generation college graduate, earned her degree in criminal justice and legal studies from the University of Northern Colorado in 2017. She is currently the director of operations at H&R Concrete Corp. in Greeley, CO. She also serves as a member of the Rodarte Community Center Advisory Board. Passionate about her Mexican heritage, Yvette actively seeks ways to empower her *Latino* community.

Adriana Trujillo

Adriana Trujillo, a second-generation immigrant, has defied stereotypes by graduating from the University of Northern Colorado as a McNair Scholar and receiving a master's degree in world heritage studies in Germany. Through her work, she conserves and brings awareness to marginalized groups and histories, such as working with the people of Taos Pueblo, New Mexico to learn about their conservation approaches. She was also involved in architectural conservation in Cairo, Egypt. As an archivist at UNC, she continues to dedicate her work to the representation of marginalized groups.

Spanish Language Translation and Editing

Dr. Madeline Milian and Narrative Writer

Dr. Madeline Milian, is a professor emerita at the University of Northern Colorado. Her academic preparation includes bilingual education, English as a second language, and special education. She earned degrees from Florida International University (B.S.), California State University, Los Angeles (M.A.) and Teachers College, Columbia University (Ed.D.). She has been a teacher and educator for forty years.

Nancy Wendirad

Nancy Wendirad completed her undergraduate and graduate work at UNC and *Universidad de Salamanca,* Spain. Her professional experience includes community health, migrant education advocacy public education, curriculum development, interpreting, and translating. Wendirad is an active volunteer and has served on various boards. She has also received several awards.

The Mexican American History Project Greeley Committee

Emma Peña-McCleave, Project Coordinator

Emma Peña-McCleave's lifelong commitment to community began with the Colorado Migrant Council. Her studies in education, sociology, *Chicano* studies, Spanish, and business administration support her dedication to serving the *Latino* Community. Her motto is: "If you are not at the decision-making table, you're just screaming at the door." She is from Ovid, Colorado, and currently lives in Greeley with her husband, Robert McCleave.

She is currently serving as coordinator of the Mexican American History Project of Greeley (founder and coordinator 2022–2025). She is the president of the Rodarte Community Center, Greeley, and a board member of the Greeley History Museum.

Emma served two terms as president of the CU *Latino* Alumni of CU at Boulder. She is a past board member of the Hispanic Women of Weld County and the Logan County Judicial Review Committee.

She has earned bachelor's degrees in Spanish and sociology from CU Boulder and a degree in business administration from Regis University. She studied master's work in education from CSU and attended the University of *Veracruz, Jalapa Veracruz*, Mexico, Spanish. She was inducted into the Colorado *Latino* Hall of Fame in 2000.

Dr. Maria Sanchez, Project Co-coordinator and Narrative Writer

Dr. Maria Sanchez is a retired registered nurse with forty-five-plus years of experience. She holds a bachelor's degree in nursing, a master's degree in public health from UNC, and a doctorate degree in education and human resource studies from CSU.

She has been actively involved in the community, having served as a board member the Greeley Chamber of Commerce, Room at the Inn, March of Dimes, American Cancer Society, City of Greeley Historic Preservation Commission, Island Grove Detox Center, Weld County Food Bank, and the Saint Peter's Catholic Church Restoration Project.

Juanita Martinez Rocha

Juanita Martinez Rocha earned her AA degree in liberal arts from Aims Community College, a bachelor's degree in social science with an emphasis in English as a second language ESL (CLD) from the University of Northern Colorado, and a master's degree in interdisciplinary education with an emphasis in bilingual education. Juanita Martinez Rocha is a Evans School District 6 retired elementary educator and served on numerous boards and commissions. She has been the recipient of local and state recognition for her community involvement. Currently, she is the treasurer for the Mexican American History Project Greeley, in addition to being on the oral history sub-committee for MAHPG.

Clarence Lopez

Clarence Lopez has been an active licensed realtor in the state of Colorado since 1985. He currently owns and operates his own real estate company, Property One of the Rockies. His primary focus in real estate has always been to serve Greeley's Spanish-speaking *Latino* community, with an emphasis on first time homebuyers. Clarence holds a B.A. in business and a B.A. in sociology from UNC. He has been a member of several city boards and committees, including vice chairing the Greeley Housing Authority 1986 thru 1990. He was one of the founding members of Northern Colorado Hispanic Chamber of Commerce and is a Greeley Area Realtors Association member.

Daniel Reyez

Daniel Reyez retired from the U.S. Postal Service after forty years of service. While there, he served as a union steward. He joined the U.S. Army in 1962 and was honorably discharged in 1964. He is active with the American Legion's baseball youth program. He is a member of the Greeley American Legion Post 18, and he serves on Rodarte Center's executive board and advisory board. He has served on several Greeley School District 6 committees: Citizens' Bond Oversight, Community Facility Master Planning, Mill Levy Override, and Citizens Oversight.

Katie Ross

Katie Ross, museum liaison, is the curator of collections of the City of Greeley Museums. She has been in this role since 2020 and has worked for the museums since 2012. Katie has a BA in anthropology from Kansas State University and a MS in anthropology from the University of Wisconsin-Milwaukee with an accompanied certificate in museum studies.

Jay Trask

Jay Trask has been head of archives and special collections at the University of Northern Colorado since March 2009. He worked in archival institutions throughout Colorado, including the National Wildlife Research Center, the Colorado State Archives, and Colorado State University-Pueblo. One of the most challenging positions held by Trask was head archivist for the Colorado Fuel and Iron Archives in Pueblo, Colorado. This grant-funded project consisted of organizing over twenty-thousand-cubic feet of papers, photographs, and other materials left abandoned in the industrial and administrative offices of a major western steel and mining company, including a colony of feral cats living in the basement. Trask assisted with the creation of the Colorado *Chicano* Archives at Colorado State University-Pueblo.

Statement by artist Armando Silva:

The mural portrays a Greeley student (Julian Villanueva) in wonder with his writing utensil. Like many young students in the area, their work is in their discipline and passion to show up for themselves and their *familia* in the classroom and beyond. He enjoys learning and doing the work to get the answer right. He dreams of a brighter future and pays off the sacrifices those before them have made.

"*El Poder Es Saber*" is to say that the power is in knowing you can. That you can go further than the mountains grow. The gloves hang behind him as an homage to the boxing culture and community that sprouted at The Rodarte Center. The Mayan ruin speaks to the deep roots and culture that are still with us today. While the red-winged blackbird symbolizes the boy's new home in Northern Colorado, the *gallo* lives within the young boy still with his bravery and canto. The *gallo's canto* speaks truths and beauty.

El Poder Es Saber!

—Dedicated to all Greeley students. Be proud of your community, and take care of it.

Community Participant Historians

Complete interviews available at the University of Northern Colorado Archives and Special Collections. The interviews are available on Digital UNC.

Nickie Archibeque

Polly Baca

Angelina Bustillos

Damion Córdova

Francisco Cortez

Jacob Duran

Josie Duran

Lori Gama

Abraham Garcia

Jenny Garcia

Fabian Garcia Martinez

Patricia Garcia-Nelson

Ben (Mitch) Gonzales

Penny Gonzales-Soto

Susana Taes Grimm

Andrés Gonzales Guerrero, Jr.

Brittni Laura Hernandez

Kathleen (Romero) Horning

Alicia Johnson

Clarence Lopez

Gabriel A. Lopez

Jody L. Lopez

Henry Lee Martinez

Juanita Martinez Rocha

Yolanda Mendoza

Pauline Montalvo

Pres Montoya

Brandi L. Nieto

Joe Perez

Teresa Rodriguez-McNeill

Ray Romero

Maria Sanchez

Tomasa (Cynthia) Silva

Rhonda Solis

Jessie Theresa Solis

Stacy Suniga

Deborah Suniga

Eddie Treviño

Adriana Trujillo

Ana Trujillo

Cleto Vázquez Robles

Vicente Vega Ruiz

Susie Velasquez

Vivian A. Watson

Nancy Wendirad

Key Contributors

Book Campaign Donors & Project Funders

We would like to express our gratitude for the financial contributions to the Mexican American History Project of Greeley Book Campaign for *Our History Our Voices*. We are grateful to all the outstanding members of our community who responded to our requests for donations to ensure a free copy of this book could be provided to the local schools, libraries, and community centers. These contributions totaled approximately fifteen thousand dollars. Your kindness and support truly meant the world to us and while we cannot name every community member individually, please know that your contributions are deeply appreciated. Major donors include Mr. Arlo Richardson and Family, Weld Community Foundation, Mineral Resources, Inc, Mr. Mark Watson, director of the Union Colony Company of Colorado, ALLO Fiber, ENT Credit Union 47th Ave & W. 25th Street Greeley, CO, and the Walmart Community Grants Team Facility #5051 on 47th Avenue in Greeley.

This project is made possible in part by a grant from the National Park Foundation.

Project Contributors

Mexican American History Project of Greeley Committee: This incredible group of volunteers set out to fill a gap in history and did so by documenting 44 oral histories, dividing the work up among committee members, bringing on project contributors, and writing this book. *www.mahpg.org*

Emma Pena-McCleave: Emma has served as the Project Coordinator casting a vision for the project, providing the seed funding, and seeing the project through to completion.

Weld Community Foundation: The Weld Community Foundation served as the Fiscal Sponsor for the Mexican American History Project of Greeley. *www.WeldCommunityFoundation.org*

Cache la Poudre River National Heritage Area (Cache NHA): Cache NHA secured significant project funding from the National Park Foundation and provided technical assistance in the development and publication of the book, the accompanying curriculum, and museum exhibits. They provided marketing support and produced a compilation video of oral histories. The Cache NHA will publish and promote this book in perpetuity to ensure these stories will continue to be told. *www.PoudreHeritage.org*

Greeley History Museum (GHM) and Friends of the Greeley History Museum: GMH hosted MAHPG's monthly meetings, co-curated two exhibits focused on Mexican American history.

Glossary

Ability to survive and thrive

Ability—the power or skill to do something. *Survive*—stay alive even when facing something very dangerous or life-threatening.

Abundant large in amount or number; more than enough.

Abuse actions that hurt or harm someone, whether physically, emotionally, or through neglect. That's never okay.

Academic progress succeeding in school, learning, and many times, getting good grades.

Accolades special awards or praise for doing something well.

Accomplishment something you've successfully done, especially after putting in some effort.

Accounting degree teaches you how to work with money, keep records, and understand financial information so you can get a job in accounting, finance, or a similar field.

Acculturation process learning about and taking on new customs and ideas from other cultures, while still keeping your own traditions.

Accumulation collecting things and bringing them together.

Achievable able to be reached or achieved.

Activist someone who campaigns to bring about political or social change.

Adapt to change or adjust something or yourself to get used to a new situation.

Adobe homes houses built with special sun-dried bricks of mud, small sticks, and native grass.

Adopt to accept a new thing or person as your own.

Adult someone who is fully grown up, like a mature person who can vote, drive, and make their own decisions.

Advisor an expert who guides other people.

Advocacy vigorously supporting and arguing for an idea or cause.

Advocacy group a team of people who care about a specific issue and work together to make sure everyone knows about it and supports it.

Advocate someone who speaks up or acts in support of something or someone they believe in.

Affected it has an impact on you (changes the way you feel, think, or act).

Affirming saying something positive or true.

Aggression unfriendly and violent action.

Altercation fight or disagreement.

Americanization when people who come to America from other countries learn about and assimilate into American culture and customs.

Ancestral something that is related to or comes from your family members who lived long ago.

Anglo-Saxon the original English people who came to the U.S. from places like Germany, England, and Denmark.

Animus strong dislike or hostility toward someone, often because of their race, ethnicity, or another personal trait.

Apparently used when something seems to be true or is the case, but you're not completely sure. It's like when you've heard it or it looks that way, but you haven't seen it for yourself.

Application a form to fill out in order to get a job.

Appointed someone or something has been officially chosen or assigned for a specific job or task.

Appreciate to understand and value the worth of something or to be grateful for it.

Appropriate right or suitable for a particular situation or purpose.

Approves applications a person or group who looks at an application and decides whether to say yes. For example, someone who approves your request to buy a house.

Approximately "about" or "close to" but not exactly.

Archives a place where important old photos, documents, and materials are safely stored so people can find and use them later.

Array of vendors a large number (array) of people (vendors) who sell unique goods.

As a result because of something or what happens after something else. A chain reaction where one thing leads to another.

Aspirations dreams and goals you want to achieve in the future.

Assets something owned by a person.

Assimilate becoming part of a group or culture, like when someone moves to a new country and learns the language and customs.

Assimilation when a group of people (like immigrants) adopt the customs, language, and values of a dominant culture.

Assistance help or support that someone gives.

Assistant someone who helps another person by doing tasks or providing support.

At this point in time right now or in this moment.

Attendance when you attend something, you are physically at that place or event.

Attendance clerk a school employee who keeps track of who is and isn't in class, making sure everyone is where they should be. They also answer phone calls and help parents if there are any questions about attendance.

Attitude your inner feeling or way of thinking about something and how it shows in your actions and words.

Automate and downgrade workforce *Automate*—to start using machines or technology to do work people used to do. *Downgrade*—to make something worse or lower in quality, value, or importance. Workforce—a team of people who work together.

Avocation a person's job.

Back-breaking work work that's so physically tough and tiring, like digging deep trenches or harvesting food. It feels like it's breaking your back.

Balcony a special porch that sticks out from the side of a building, usually on an upper floor with a low wall or railing around it, so people can sit outside and enjoy the view.

Barons people who own land.

Behave to act in a certain way, like being polite, following rules, or doing what's expected.

Beliefs a belief is an idea or thought that someone accepts as being true, real, or good, even if there's no proof or evidence.

Bench warmer a backup player who doesn't usually get to play much in games. They mostly sit on the bench waiting for their chance to play.

Beneficial something that is helpful, useful, or good for you or someone else.

Benefit something good that helps you or gives you an advantage.

Best interests the action or situation that will help someone the most.

Betterment improve something or improve a situation.

Beverage anything you can drink, like juice, milk, water, soda or beverages.

Bias believing someone is beneath another person because of their race, ethnicity, or other personal feature.

Biases the way we think things are or should be, even if it's not always true or accurate.

Big Leagues the highest level or most important league in a sport.

Bigotry believing someone is beneath you because of race, ethnicity, or other personal feature.

Blatant obvious and clear.

Blending putting sounds together, like mixing ingredients in a smoothie, to make a new word.

Bonds a feeling or shared interest that brings people together.

Breadwinner a person whose wages provide support for his or her family.

Bridal shower a fun party thrown for a woman who's about to get married, where her friends and family give her gifts to help her start her new life with her husband.

Brilliantly it's done in a super impressive and smart way.

Broader context of the culture includes lifestyles, value systems, traditions, and beliefs in addition to creative works.

Brood of offspring a group of young animals, especially birds, that were born or hatched at the same time from the same parent.

Built ourselves up to make ourselves stronger, more confident, or better at something.

Bully a person who purposely hurts others physically and/or verbally.

Butcher someone who kills or cuts up meat to make it ready for sale.

Canvas heavy, strong cloth made of cotton, linen, or hemp.

Capacity the greatest possible amount or number. When something is filled or used as much as it can be.

Caravans of immigrants a group of immigrants (people from another country) walking or traveling together, often in hopes of making a better life in the country they are traveling to.

Casual something that's relaxed, not planned, and maybe even a little bit offhand.

Catalyst a person or action that makes something else start happening or happen faster without being used up in the process.

Catering supporting other people.

Catholic Sacraments a religious act that is a sign or symbol of a spiritual existence. The Catholic Sacraments are Baptism, Confirmation, Eucharist or Communion, Reconciliation or Confession, Anointing the Sick, Holy Orders, and marriage.

Caught up on utilities not late on payments for gas, water, or electricity.

Celebrations a special time when people get together to have fun and be happy.

Center aisles a main path that runs down the middle of a space, like a church or movie theater.

Certificate a document that proves something is true.

Challenge an interesting or difficult problem or task.

Charges for room and board the amount of money you have to pay to stay in a hotel room.

Charter school a public school that is free to attend but can choose its own unique approach to learning.

Cheap something that costs very little money, like a bargain.

Chicana a girl or woman who lives in the U.S. and whose family originally came from Mexico.

Child caretaker people who look after and take care of children, like parents, babysitters, or teachers at daycare.

Child protection social worker a person who looks into situations where children might be hurt or not taken care of and steps in to help keep them safe and healthy.

Child-rearing the process of taking care of and raising children.

Christian faith the belief held by Christians that Jesus Christ is the Son of God and the practice of following his teachings and the teachings of the Christian churches that developed after his death.

Circumvent finding a clever or sneaky way to get around something, like a rule or a problem, instead of dealing with it directly.

Civic about a city or its citizens.

Civics the study of how our community and government work, and what rights and responsibilities we have as citizens. It helps us understand how to take part in making our community and country better.

Civil rights protections that make sure everyone, no matter who they are, is treated fairly and has the same opportunities.

Close-knit community a group of friends or family who really look out for each other and stick together, kind of like a tight hug.

Closeness having a strong, loving, and friendly connection with someone, like a really good friend or family member. You feel comfortable and happy being around them.

Clout having influence or power.

Collaboration working together as a group.

Collect to gather or get things together.

Collection a group of things you like or find interesting that you put together.

Collective people acting together for a common cause.

Collectivist view thinking that a group or community is more important than any one person. Everyone works together to help each other and achieve common goals.

College material having the knowledge and skills to succeed in college.

Colonized settlers from another place move in and take over an area.

Comfortable feels good and makes you relaxed.

Commissioner a leader or official in charge of something important, like a government department, a political office, a sports league, or a group that does a specific job.

Commitment promising to do something and then actually doing it, showing that you're responsible and reliable.

Committed connected strongly to a person or a cause.

Common it's usual, happens often, or is shared by many people.

Common strategy a plan or a way of doing things to help you reach a goal, such as deciding what moves to make in a game to win.

Community constitution a set of rules or guidelines that everyone in a community agrees to follow to make sure things are fair and everyone can live together peacefully.

Compete trying hard to win or be better than others who are trying for the same goal, like in games, races, or contests.

Competitor someone who tries to win or do better than others.

Complacent not worried about a poor situation.

Complained when someone says that something was wrong, not good enough, or made them unhappy.

Compounding combining things into something new.

Compulsory something that you have to do, like a rule you can't break or something a law requires.

Comrades your close friends or buddies.

Concentrate something that is stronger or more focused, like when you're really paying attention to something.

Concession stand a place where snacks and drinks are sold.

Condition describing how something or someone is doing or looking. For example, a car is in good condition isn't broken or damaged.

Conditions the state or situation something or someone is in.

Conflict a disagreement or a problem that happens when two or more people want different things or have different ideas.

Connected when things are joined or linked together.

Consent asking someone if it's okay to do something and respecting their answer, whether it's yes or no. It's about respecting personal space and boundaries and making sure everyone feels safe and comfortable.

Consulting firm a firm of experts providing professional advice to an organization for a fee.

Contest disagreed with.

Contesting saying something is not true or accurate.

Continuity remaining for a long period of time.

Contributed gave or donated something to someone.

Convert making a change that alters its form, appearance, or how it's used.

Convinced someone believes something is true, and they don't question it.

Coordinated different parts that work together smoothly and well.

Courtesy being polite, respectful, and kind to others.

Courtyard a special open yard or area inside a building or surrounded by walls, perfect for playing or having fun outside.

Credited give praise to.

Creditors people who loan money.

Crowded too many people in a small amount of space.

Curfews a rule that says you have to be home by a certain time, usually in the evening.

Cycle when things happen in the same order over and over again, like the seasons or the steps in a plant's life.

Date to spend time with someone in a romantic way.

Deceased someone who is no longer alive.

Decolonization when a place that was controlled by another country or group gains its freedom and becomes independent.

Dedicated loyal to a cause or purpose.

Defend to protect someone or something from harm or danger, like standing up for a friend who is being teased.

Defiantly resilient describes someone who stays strong and recovers from hard times while boldly standing up for what they believe in, even when it's unpopular.

Delegates giving someone a task or responsibility to do for you.

Delved carefully searched or explored it to find out more information or to dig around for something.

Demand how much people want something.

Demolish to completely tear something down or destroy something.

Deploy it's been moved or put into place so it's ready to be used or to do its job, like soldiers being sent to a new location to fight.

Derogatory a mean or unkind comment that tries to make someone or something seem bad or unimportant, like saying something that's meant to hurt someone's feelings.

Desegregate ending the practice of keeping people of different races separate, like in schools or other places, so everyone can be together.

Designate something or someone has been chosen or set aside for a specific purpose or job, like when you're assigned to be the team captain or a place is marked as a playground.

Desire a "really strong want." When you really, really want something, that's a desire.

Despite "even though" or "no matter that." It's like saying something happens even if something else is true or happening.

Determination having a strong will and not giving up.

Detriment a disadvantage or loss.

Devout someone who is very dedicated and loyal to their beliefs or religion.

Dialect a special version of a language spoken by people in a certain place or group, with its own unique words, pronunciations, and grammar.

Digital marketing agency a company that deals exclusively in marketing to consumers or businesses through digital channels.

Diligently to do something with a lot of effort and care.

Director a person who guides the affairs of a business or other organizations.

Disabled describes someone who has a physical, mental, or learning difference that makes it harder for them to do certain tasks or activities.

Disallowing saying no or not allowing something.

Discharged something or someone is released or let go from a place or the military.

Disciplinary methods teaching tools that help kids learn what's right and wrong, and how to behave well, using clear rules and consequences.

Discourage to make someone feel less excited or hopeful about something, or to try to stop them from doing it.

Discrepancies unfair difference or inequality.

Discrimination complaints when someone feels they've been treated unfairly or differently because of something like their race, religion, or gender and they are telling someone about it.

Discrimination/discriminatory unfair treatment against another person or group because of their race, ethnicity, or other personal feature.

Disparity unfair difference or inequality.

Disregard ignored, not seen as important.

Dissension disagreement or arguments, especially within a group or organization. Think of it as when people have different opinions and can't agree on something, leading to a bit of a squabble.

Dissenting disagreeing with someone.

Diversity many different kinds of people.

Diversity training learning to appreciate and respect that everyone is unique (whether in how they look, what they like, or where they come from) and understanding how to be kind and inclusive to all.

Document a written, drawn, spoken, or recorded way of showing an idea or thought, often as a story that is either made up (fictional) or real (non-fictional).

Domestic things related to a home, family, or country, like your house, your family members, or things made or done in your own country.

Domestic relations a type of law that deals with family or household matters, like marriage, divorce, and child custody.

Domestic servants domestic workers help families by doing things like cleaning, cooking, laundry, or watching kids.

Dominance one person or group having power over another.

Dominant being the most important, powerful, or noticeable compared to others.

Donations something you give to help others in need.

Drafted into the military the government requiring someone to join the army, navy, or other armed forces, instead of them choosing to join on their own.

Dramatic (of an event or circumstance) sudden, surprising, and striking.

Dropout a person who quits high school before graduation.

Drug and alcohol counselor a person who provides expert care and support to people who have substance use disorders.

Eager to be excited to do something.

Earn it to get something, like money or a reward, because you worked hard or did something good and deserve it.

Earnest a person who is focused and takes things seriously.

Echoed repeated.

Economic opportunity having chances to improve your financial situation.

Economic prosperity thriving in an economy, often characterized by high levels of income, employment, and overall wealth among a population.

Economics the study of how people make choices about using limited resources.

Elocution speaking clearly and beautifully, like practicing your voice and making sure you pronounce words correctly when you're talking, especially when you're speaking in front of others.

Embraces makes something important; celebrates it.

Emergency assistance getting help right away when something dangerous or urgent happens.

Emphasis to make something stand out or show that it's extra important.

Empower to give someone the ability and confidence to do something.

Empowering giving someone strength and confidence.

Enchiladas a tortilla rolled around a meat or cheese filling and covered with a chile sauce.

Encompasses includes.

Encouraged given the support, confidence, or motivation to do something.

Endure to keep going through a tough or difficult time, like when you have to wait for something or deal with something unpleasant.

Enforce something is required, like a rule or a law, and the people in charge make sure everyone obeys it.

Engaging participating in something.

Enhance to make something better or improve it.

Enroll signing up or registering for something.

Ensure to make sure or certain.

Entrepreneurship starting a business.

Enumerated counted.

Environment everything that surrounds us, including the air, water, land, plants, animals, people, and the places we live.

Environmental justice ensuring everyone, regardless of their background, has a fair and equal chance to live in a healthy environment and participate in decisions that affect it.

Equality treating everyone the same and giving everyone the same chances, no matter who they are or where they come from.

Equitable fair and just.

Equivalent two things are the same in value or amount.

Erasure making something disappear.

Ethnicity something resulting from where you or your family members were born.

Euro-American someone who is American and has European ancestors, like those whose families came from countries in Europe.

Evidenced something that is clearly shown or proven.

Exacerbating making something worse.

Excel to do something well or be highly skilled.

Exhaustion being so tired that you have no energy left.

Expanded it's been made bigger, wider, or longer.

Expectations a belief that something will happen or is likely to happen.

Expensive something is not cheap, and you need a lot of money to buy it.

Experience something you do or that happens to you, especially something important that you learn from or remember.

Exploitation treats other people poorly or unfairly.

Exposure putting someone in contact with someone/something else.

Extended family one's big family circle, including relatives beyond your immediate parents and siblings, like grandparents, aunts, uncles, and cousins, who you might not live with but still love and connect with.

Facility a special place or something that helps you do something, like a playground or a swimming pool.

Family ties special bonds and connections that make family members feel loved, cared for, and supported, like the strong glue that holds aa family together.

Family's generational DNA the genetic information inside the cells of the body that makes people who they are. It is carried to the next generation in a family.

Fast forward to skip ahead to a later time, like jumping forward in a video or story.

Favoritism giving special treatment or attention to one person or group but not to others who deserve the same treatment.

Fellow people who are working together.

Festivities activities and celebrations, like parties, games, and special events during holidays or other occasions.

Fierce strong.

Financial having to do with money, like how much you have, how you spend it, and how you save it.

Financial support when someone or an organization gives money or resources to help someone else, like a family or a school.

Financially stable being able to comfortably live every month without worrying about money.

Fine a sum of money that one is required to pay as a punishment for breaking a rule or law.

First-generation college student someone who goes to college, but their parents, grandparents, or great-grandparents did not.

Firsthand direct and actual.

Flailing someone or something is moving their arms or legs in a wild, uncontrolled way.

Flexed bent in a way to effect a situation.

Flunk failing to do well, not passing a test or class, or being unsuccessful at something.

Focus to pay really close attention to one thing and ignore everything else.

Forceful strong, confident.

Foregrounded making something most important.

Fortitude strength, courage.

Foul balls a ball in baseball that's hit but lands outside the lines on the field.

Foundation the base or support for something.

Fundraisers an event that raises money for a cause.

Gainful employment having a job that pays you enough money to buy the things you need and want, like food, clothes, and a place to live.

Gen X the group of people who were born between the early 1960s and 1980.

Gender roles how we're expected to act, speak, dress, groom, and conduct ourselves based on being a man or woman.

General something that applies to many things or people, not just one specific thing or person.

Generation a group of people born around the same time, like your classmates or your parents' friends, who are all around the same age.

Geopolitical world events.

Good spread a variety of food items, often arranged for a meal or event.

Grant money given that does not have to be paid back.

Grassroots involving ordinary people.

Great strides to maintain Great strides—making big improvements or progress. Maintain—keep something going or in good condition.

Grueling something is really hard, tiring, and exhausting.

Habitat for Humanity an organization that builds, renovates, and repairs housing for families in need.

Handiwork something you make or do with your hands, like drawing, making a craft, or a job you did.

Harsh something unkind, unpleasant, or rough.

Harsh working conditions a job that's really tough, unsafe, or makes someone feel bad or hurt, whether physically or emotionally.

Heritage the cool and interesting things, like traditions, stories, and customs, that your family or others who came before you have passed down.

Hide and seek fun game where some children hide and one child tries to find them.

High worker turnover many employees, more than expected, quit the organization over a certain period of time.

Highlighted it's been made to stand out or be noticed.

Hispanic someone who speaks Spanish or whose family comes from a Spanish-speaking country.

Hispano someone who has a connection to Spain or Spanish-speaking countries.

Hoeing tool to dig, weed, or loosen the soil around plants.

Homemakers someone who takes care of their home and family.

Hopscotch a children's game where players toss a stone onto a pattern of numbered squares drawn on the ground. The players then hop or jump from square to square.

Hostile environment a place or situation where people are unfriendly, mean, or aggressive.

Human resources coordinator someone who recommends, designs, develops, and implements creative training and development programs.

Humanitarian someone who cares about and helps people who are in need.

Humble not being proud or boastful. Being kind, respectful, and understanding of others' feelings, even when you're happy or successful.

Hygiene keeping yourself and your surroundings clean to stay healthy and prevent sickness.

Idealized aggression of one country against another.

Identity who you are: your likes, dislikes, interests, family, and how you see yourself in the world. It's about what makes you unique and how you connect with others.

Identity crisis when someone feels a bit lost or unsure about who they are and what they want to be. They're trying to figure out their place in the world.

Ignite set something on fire.

Immaculate something is super clean, spotless, and perfect.

Immersed to be completely wrapped up in something.

Impact when something has a strong effect or influence.

Impacted had an effect on.

Implement to put a plan, idea, or policy into action; to do something that was planned.

In awe to feel a mix of wonder, respect, and maybe even a little bit of amazement when you see or experience something really amazing or impressive.

In particular focusing on one specific thing or happening, rather than everything in general. It's like saying "especially" or "specifically."

Inability not being able to do something or having trouble doing it.

Incarcerated a person who is in jail.

Inclusion making everyone feel they are a part of the group.

Inclusive bringing everyone into a group.

Independence not ruled by another; ruling oneself.

Indigenous the original people or things that belong to a place, like the first people who lived there before others came.

Individual a single person or thing, separate from a group or a collection of things.

Individualistic view a way of thinking that focuses more on a person's own needs and goals than on the needs of the group.

Inequality different or unfair treatment against another person because of their race, ethnicity, or other personal feature.

Infest unwanted things taking over an area.

Influence to affect or change something or someone.

Influenced when something is affected or changed by something else.

Infuse to fill or add something.

Ingrained something is firmly stuck or deeply rooted, like a habit you can't easily get rid of.

Inherent something is a natural part of something else, like stripes are inherently part of a zebra. You can't have a zebra without stripes.

Initial at first.

Injustice when something isn't fair or right, like when someone is treated unfairly or someone's rights are taken away.

Ins and outs all the details, facts, and complexities of something.

Inspiration encouraging another person to action.

Inspire something or someone has made you feel excited and motivated to do something amazing or try something new.

Instill teach someone about values and emotions.

Instrumental something that is very important.

Intangible something that is vague and hard to see or touch.

Integrate school a school where kids from different backgrounds, like different races, cultures, or abilities, learn together in the same classrooms and school environment. It fosters understanding and friendship.

Integration combining people into one group.

Integrity being honest and doing what's right, even when no one is watching, like always telling the truth and being true to your word.

Interact to talk or do things with other people, like sharing experiences. It's about communicating and reacting to each other.

Interact to talk, play, or do things with other people.

Internship a practice session or a trial run in a real-world workplace, where you get to learn and experience what it's like to work in a particular field.

Interpreter a person who helps people who speak different languages understand each other by translating what one person says into the language of the other.

Interstate highway system special highways (like freeways) that crisscross the U.S., connecting many cities and states.

Intertwined twisted together or closely connected so as to be difficult to separate.

Intervene get involved to stop a bad situation from continuing.

Interview conversation where someone asks you questions to learn more about you, your ideas, or experiences.

Interwoven connected together.

Invent to think of, come up with, or create something new.

Investigated someone is trying to find out the truth about something.

Involve to include someone or something in an activity or situation.

Job referral a person who speaks in support of another for a position or job.

Johnny on the spot someone who's always ready and available to help or do something when needed.

Joke a short story or saying, usually with a funny ending, that is meant to make people laugh.

Journalism like being a news reporter, gathering and sharing important information, like what's happening in the world, through newspapers, TV, radio, or online.

Journeyman electrician a skilled electrician who has finished their training (an apprenticeship) and can now work alone on projects, like fixing or installing lights and outlets.

Juris Doctorate a special degree you get after studying law.

Juvenile delinquency when children do illegal things before they reach the statutory age of eighteen.

Juvenile probation officer someone who works with children who have been arrested.

Labor the work people do, like building, cooking, or cleaning. The effort and skills they use to make things or provide services.

Labor movement workers banding together to make their jobs better.

Lack something is missing, or there's not enough of something.

Latin country countries in the Americas where people mainly speak Spanish, like Mexico, Honduras, and Argentina.

Latina a girl or woman who comes from, or whose family comes from, a Latin American country.

Lead investigator the person in charge of an investigation. They make the key decisions and guide the process to find answers or solve a problem.

Legal clinics a legal aid or law-school program that provides services to various clients and often hands-on legal experience to law students.

Legal secretary someone who works in a law office and helps lawyers with their work. They process important legal documents and letters, keep track of files and records, and do other tasks to support the law practice.

Less than equal a phrase used to describe something that is not equal or fair (an inequality).

Limbo a situation where something is waiting to happen or someone is waiting for something to be decided.

Linguist a language detective who studies how people communicate using words, sounds, and even body language. To understand how language works and changes over time.

Literacy program a plan or set of activities that helps people learn to read, write, speak, and understand information effectively, so they can communicate and learn better.

Living conditions refers to how people live and what their surroundings are like.

Living quarters rooms or a place where someone lives.

Long, storied employment record many years of out-of-the-ordinary, high-performance things done in one's job.

Made fun of to laugh at or tease someone in a way that isn't kind or helpful. It's like making someone feel silly or bad about themselves.

Mainstream American culture the most common or popular way of doing things. The beliefs and the habits that most people in America share.

Maintaining repairs keeping up with things that need to be fixed.

Make ends meet to have just enough money to pay for things like rent and food.

Maltreatment cruel or violent treatment of a person or animal.

Managed it's been taken care of, controlled, or handled well.

Manipulation treating someone poorly to gain an advantage over them.

Manual laborer someone who does jobs that involve using their hands and body to do work, such as building something, moving heavy objects, or fixing things.

Marginalized to be treated as if you're not important or left out of opportunities and things that others get to do. It's like being pushed to the edge of a group or society.

***Mariachi* music** traditional Mexican music played on instruments like violins, trumpets, guitars, and a guitarrón (a special bass guitar).

Massive fines very large or serious money penalties given to someone for breaking a rule or law.

Maternal grandparents maternal grandparents are the parents of one's mother: your mom's mom (maternal grandmother) and your mom's dad (maternal grandfather).

Meals when you eat food, usually at a regular time like breakfast, lunch, or dinner.

Mean not nice.

Measurable able to be counted.

Meet the standard someone or something has reached a goal or done something to a level that's considered good or acceptable.

Micro-aggression small actions against another person because of their race, ethnicity, or other personal feature.

Microcosm a small part of a bigger thing.

Minimize the barriers to make something as small, insignificant, or unimportant as possible to overcome things that get in the way of success, obstacles, and impediments.

Modeled to show a certain behavior so that others can learn from it and do the same.

Monitoring paying attention to something.

Monumental very large.

Multicultural leadership the ability to work positively and in harmony with people of many different cultures.

Multiple more than one.

Municipal judge a person who is chosen (appointed) or elected to handle legal cases in a court that serves a city.

National Baseball Hall of Fame a special museum in Cooperstown, New York, that honors the greatest baseball players, managers, and other important people in the sport with plaques and recognition for their amazing accomplishments.

Natural resources things found in nature we use or need, such as water, trees, and the sun.

Necessities the basic things people need to live, like food, water, shelter, and clothing.

Neglect to pay too little or no attention to something or someone.

Negligence when someone doesn't pay enough attention or isn't careful enough, leading to something bad happening.

Negotiations talking with other people to find a solution.

Neither not either of two things.

Nerd someone who is really interested in something specific.

Networking meeting people in the same business.

Neuroticism being anxious, nervous, and stressed.

Non-denominational not connected to one specific religion or religious group. A non-denominational church doesn't follow the rules or leadership of just one organized religion.

Non-traditional student a student who did not go to college after high school. They waited and went later in their life.

Nonprofit a charitable organization.

Note to point out or bring attention to something.

Nurture take care of, supported.

Objects things you can see and touch.

Offering legal advice when a lawyer (someone who went to school for law) explains what someone should or shouldn't do in a legal situation, helping them understand their rights and choices.

On-site support help or assistance given directly at the place where something is happening or where people are working, instead of from far away.

Operational ready to work or is currently working.

Opinions a belief or attitude about something that isn't necessarily based on facts.

Opportunities chances or situations that allow you to do something you want to do or learn something new.

Opportunity a chance for a better situation.

Opposed someone or something is against it or disagrees with it.

Oppression dominating or keeping someone down.

Organize bringing people together and helping them work together.

Organize media coverage planning and managing how your message or event is shared in the news and other media, making sure it reaches people clearly and effectively.

Organize the farm workers to plan or orchestrate how people who pick our food can get better pay and working conditions.

Orientation a direction or focus.

Outreach trying to connect with other people.

Overlook leave out or ignore.

Overpriced something that costs more than it is worth.

Oversaw watched over something or someone and made sure things were done right.

Oversee public relations to manage how a company or school communicates with the public to create a good image and help people understand what it does.

Parade to walk or march together in a group, often to celebrate something or to show something off in a way that gets attention.

Paramedic a first responder who helps people who are sick or hurt, especially in emergencies, by doing things like CPR, giving medicine, and helping them get to the hospital. (They are not doctors or nurses.)

Participate to join in and be a part of something fun, like a game or an activity with your friends or family.

Pass stories down sharing stories from one generation to the next, like family traditions or tales, so younger ones can learn and remember them.

Passage of legislation when a bill suggested by the government is officially approved and becomes a law.

Passing on a gentle way to say that someone died.

Passive not being active or doing things. Letting things happen to you or watching instead of participating.

Patronize purchasing things from a business.

Pecking order a social structure where certain individuals or groups are considered more important or have more power than others.

Percentage a part or proportion of something. Shown as a fraction of one hundred.

Persevere kept going even when things were difficult.

Pew a long bench with a back where people sit during services.

Phenomenal very large.

Physical punishment when someone uses their hands or an object to hurt someone to change their behavior.

Pioneer a person who is one of the first to explore a new place, idea, or area of study.

Planted the seed to give an idea that may be carried out later.

Platform a raised, level surface used as a place to work, perform, or to speak to an audience.

Plumbing the pipes that bring water into a home.

Poignantly in an emotional way.

Political campaigns an organized effort to try to influence decisions made by a group, like in politics, business, or social causes.

Political system the way a country or community decides things, from electing leaders to making laws. It tries to help everyone gets along.

Politics relating to government and public affairs.

Potential a chance of something happening.

Powerful something that is really strong, like a superhero lifting a car, or someone who has a lot of influence, like a king who makes important decisions.

Practice as an attorney work as a lawyer to help people with legal problems and represent them in court.

Preferential giving someone or something a special advantage or treatment over others.

Prevalent common and widespread.

Previously something happened before now or a certain time.

Prioritize to decide what's most important and deal with those things first.

Processing stage when your brain takes in information (like what you see and hear) and figures out what it means, like a computer sorts and organizes data.

Professor a teacher with a high rank at a college or university.

Profound very extreme and deep.

Progress keeping something going or something in existence.

Progressive moving forward.

Prohibit not allowed or forbidden by a rule or law.

Prohibition act or practice of saying no or forbidding something.

Promote to help something grow or encourage someone to move up to a higher level, like a grade or a position.

Promoting to support the growth of or help move something forward.

Proper shelter a safe place to live, like a house or building, that protects people from weather and danger instead of being temporary or unsafe.

Prosecutor's office government or city lawyers who work to make sure people who break the law are held accountable.

Protestant a type of Christian who doesn't follow the Catholic Church and believes in the Bible as the main guide for their faith.

Public defender's office a government-funded legal office that provides free representation to people who are accused of crimes but can't afford a lawyer.

Pump a machine that uses power to move things like water, air, or gasoline from one place to another.

Punished given a consequence or penalty because they did something wrong or broke a rule, like losing a privilege or having to do something extra.

Pursue to attain, to get, to come by, to earn.

Quality how good something is. The degree of excellence it has. For example, a car made of strong metal is high quality, while a car that breaks apart is low quality.

Quintessential a perfect example of something.

Racial inferiority the belief or feeling that someone is less valuable or able to do things because of their race. It's often based on unfair ideas from history.

Racially having to do with someone's skin color.

Racism treating people badly because of the color of their skin.

Racist the harmful belief that one race or skin color is better than another. Racism can cause people to treat others unfairly or unkindly because of their race.

Racist discourse a conversation where someone or a group of people say racist things.

Realtor someone whose job involves helping people buy or sell a home.

Reauthorization giving something permission to continue or to happen again.

Rebellious someone who doesn't always listen or follow the rules.

Rebuild making something new or fixing something that's been broken or damaged.

Reception a place in a hotel or office where people go when they first arrive.

Recreation an activity that is relaxing and fun.

Recruiting workers the process of actively finding and hiring people for a specific job or position.

Recruitment asking people to join a group or support a cause.

Reevaluate look at something again and changing your opinion about it.

Refrigerated train car a train car designed to carry various food and non-food items, such as medications, while maintaining a cool, consistent temperature throughout the journey.

Registered nurse a healthcare worker who has finished a nursing program, passed a state test, and is allowed to take care of patients, like checking their needs, giving treatments, and helping patients and families understand how to stay healthy.

Regret to feel sad or sorry about something you did or didn't do, or something that happened, and wish you could change it.

Reimburse paying back the money someone spent.

Reinstate restoring something that had been taken away.

Relegated assign something to someone.

Religion a way of thinking about the world and life's meaning, often including a belief in a higher power or something greater than ourselves. It can involve special stories, rituals, and ideas about how people should live.

Religious believing in and following a set of ideas or practices about a higher power or a way of life, like a special way of thinking or behaving that many people share.

Remedial classes or activities that help students who are having a hard time with a particular subject.

Remunerated being paid for work.

Repetitive work work that involves performing the same operation over and over.

Represent to be a symbol of some-thing, like how a flag represents a coun-try or a picture represents a scene.

Representative someone who speaks or acts for a group of people.

Reprimand to scold someone for doing something wrong.

Research a way to find out more about a topic that interests you or that you need to know about. It can be done by reading books, searching the internet for information, watching YouTube, or asking questions.

Resent to feel angry or annoyed, like when someone does something you don't like or when you feel you've been treated unfairly.

Resilience ability to recover or rebound.

Resource something we use or need to help us do things, such as computers, money, the internet, skills, and talents.

Respectability being seen as someone who acts and behaves in a way that is considered good and acceptable by others, like being respectful, polite, and following rules.

Respectful treating others the way you want to be treated. Using kind words, and showing people that you care about their feelings and needs.

Retired no longer working, usually because someone has reached the age when people stop having a job.

Reveal to make something known or show something that was hidden.

Richly a high amount.

Ridicule to be made fun of in an un-kind way, like when someone laughs at you or tries to make you look silly.

Ridiculous violations *Ridiculous—* something is really silly, funny, or doesn't make any sense, like a funny hat or a silly story. *Violation—*breaking a rule, law, or promise, like when some-one runs a stop sign or doesn't keep their word.

Roast cooking food with dry heat.

Romanticized think something is more emotionally better than it actually is.

Routinely doing something often and in a regular way, like a usual habit or normal part of a day.

Rural an area that's far away from big cities with lots of open space, farms, and nature. There are fewer people and buildings than a city or town.

Sales and marketing activities for selling and advertising products by understanding what customers want, how much they'll pay, and how to get them to buy.

Scientist someone who explores, does research, and learns about the world by asking questions, doing experiments, and discovering new things.

Scold they are talking to you in a serious, almost angry way because they think you did something wrong.

Seeking to try to find or get something.

Segregated school a school where kids are kept separate from each other because of their race. Having different schools for kids who are White and kids who are not White.

Segregation separating people into different groups and keeping them separate.

Self-reliance being able to do things on your own, without needing someone else to do them for you. Trusting your own abilities and making your own decisions.

Set our sights to choose a goal and focus on reaching it by working hard and staying determined.

Sewer a giant, underground plumbing system that carries dirty water and waste away.

Sewer system a network of pipes that moves dirty water and waste from homes, businesses, and other places to a facility where it can be cleaned and treated.

Sheepskin leather plant a processing plant that makes leather from the skin of a sheep with the wool still on it. The leather and wool are used for things like coats and rugs.

Shock very surprised but not in a good way.

Shortcuts a quicker or easier path to get somewhere or do something, instead of taking the usual, longer route.

Significant something or someone that is important.

Situation what is happening around you or to you at a certain time.

Slang words people use in casual talk, not usually in formal writing.

Slaughter to kill animals, especially for food, or to kill a lot of people in a bad way.

Slaughterhouses a place where animals like cows and pigs are killed for the meat people eat.

Slew a lot of.

Slur a very insulting or disparaging remark said to someone to hurt them.

Smack to hit noisily with an open hand; slap.

Smithsonian Institute a research organization and collection of museums in Washington, DC.

Snide an unkind or mean comment said in a sneaky or indirect way, like a sly jab instead of an open insult.

Snorkeling swimming with your face down in the water, but you breathe through a special tube called a snorkel that's above the water.

Social work a job where people help others with problems and support their well-being, focusing on individuals, families, and communities. They also work for fairness and positive change.

Spanned to extend or reach across something, whether it is a distance, a period of time, or an area.

296

Special collections within an archive a group of documents or records connected to where they came from or what they're about.

Specialize to focus on and become skilled in one specific thing, like a certain job, subject, or activity.

Specific something that is detailed and exact.

Spirituality connection to a religion.

Sporadically it doesn't happen all the time, only sometimes or occasionally.

Spouse the person someone is married to.

Sprinkle to gently scatter or drop small pieces or drops of something, like water or sprinkles, over something else.

State-funded the money comes from the state government, like the money that Colorado uses to pay for schools or roads.

State-funded grant program money given for a specific purpose, like helping someone pay for college or fund a community project. The person or project doesn't have to pay it back.

Statewide throughout an entire state.

Stereotype an assumption about a group of people based on their characteristics, such as their age, gender, or race.

Storage a place or a way to keep things safe and tidy.

Strategy a process that helps someone **achieve** their goals.

Strengthening to make or grow strong or stronger.

Stress the body's alarm bell going off when you feel worried, scared, or faced with a challenge, helping you get ready to handle it. Stress can make your heart beat faster or make you feel a little tense.

Stressed to say or show that something is important.

Strict someone or something that follows rules very closely.

Strict limits having very clear and firm boundaries or rules that everyone must follow, with no wiggle room or exceptions.

Strictly something is done with a lot of rules and no wiggle room, like when a rule is followed exactly or something is very controlled.

Stringy and lean very thin.

Studious someone who really likes to learn and study.

Subjugates defeats and crushes other people.

Sue to take a person, group, or organization to court because you believe they did something wrong or caused harm. You want the court to make them fix it or pay for it.

Supervisor an authority figure who watches over people and activities to make sure everything is done correctly and safely.

Supper the meal you eat in the evening, after lunch, and before bed.

Supportive helpful.

Supposedly something is said or believed to be true, but it might not actually be true.

Surpassing going far beyond other things.

Survival staying alive and safe.

Sustenance supporting with food or emotional care.

Symbol a secret code or a picture that stands for something else.

Sympathetic understanding and caring for someone who is sad or having a tough time.

Tacos a Mexican dish consisting of a folded tortilla with a filling, such as beans or meat.

Tamales cornmeal dough rolled with ground meat or beans that's usually seasoned with chile. They're wrapped in corn husks and steamed.

Temporary work visas a U.S. visa that lets someone from another country enter and stay for a short time to work

Tended to care for or look after something or someone, like taking care of a garden watching over someone who is sick.

Tenet a widely held belief, especially one held in common by members of a group or profession.

Tenure the time when a job is held.

Tepidly being unenthusiastic or unexcited.

Thinning sugar beets removing excess (too many) seedlings (small young seeds) from a single row of plants so the remaining plants have enough space to grow properly.

Thrive to do well or be successful.

Thriving very lively and flourishing.

Tires blew out the tires on a car or truck go flat and don't move.

Toiled to work hard and for a long time.

Tortillas a thin, round, and soft flat-bread that's used to hold fillings like meat, cheese, or beans, especially in Mexican food.

Traditional something that follows old customs or ways of doing things that have been passed down through families or communities for a long time, like special foods or celebrations.

Transmit to send something from one place or person to another, like passing a message or a ball.

Trophy something given to recognize a win or other accomplishment.

Truancy staying away from school without a good reason.

Tuition assistance help or money that someone (like your school, your employer, or the government) gives you to help pay for school, so you don't have to pay as much yourself.

Typical something that is common, usual, or expected.

Ultimately in the end, or after everything else is said and done.

Uncle Sam called a way of saying that young men got a paper or notice telling them they had to join the military.

Undergirded supports or holds up.

Underrepresented group a group of people who don't have enough of a voice, presence, or visibility in certain places, like schools, jobs, or government.

Underserved students students who often don't have the same chances or resources as others, usually because of things like low income, race, or being the first in their family to go to college.

Unequivocally clearly and in agreement with other people.

Unique goods special things that are one of a kind or different from what you usually buy.

Unusual something that's not common or what you'd normally expect.

Upholding the importance supporting something important, meaningful, significant, or essential.

Uplift to lift something up, raise it, or improve it, whether physically, emotionally, or socially.

Usher someone who helps people find their seats, like at a movie theater, a wedding, or a church. They guide them to where they need to go.

Valid it's true, correct, or legally acceptable; it's based on facts or good reasons and can be accepted as such.

Values special things that are important to you, guiding you to make good choices and be your best self, like being kind, honest, or respectful.

Varied many different kinds or types.

Various many different kinds of things, people, or items.

Vegetation all of the plants, trees, and bushes in a place.

Vice chair someone who serves as an assistant or deputy chairman.

Vocation a hobby or interest.

Vulnerable something that is easily hurt.

Wag to move something back and forth, like a dog's tail when it's happy, or to shake something like a finger when you're a little bit grumpy.

Waves of immigration large groups of people moving to a new place at the same time, often to find a better life or to escape problems in their home country.

Wealthier having more money or possessions than someone else.

Web designer a person who makes the pages of an internet site appealing, user-friendly, and updated by using the latest technology.

Whim something you suddenly want to do or have. It's not something you planned or thought about beforehand.

White supremacy a belief that people with light skin are better than people with darker skin.

Widely celebrated known, celebrated, and esteemed by many people.

Widow a married person whose spouse has died.

Work contract a paper a worker and their employer sign that shows they agree about the job, pay, and other important details they've agreed on.

Work ethic being responsible, working hard, and doing one's best, whether it's at school, work, or anywhere else.

Workforce the group of workers available to work for a company.

Resources for Chapter 1

Cache la Poudre River National Heritage Area 2024. (August 23). *Spanish Colony: The story of a Hispanic neighborhood*. Retrieved from https://poudreheritage.org/spanish-colony-the-story-of-a-Hispanic-neighborhood/

Calavita, K. (2010). *Inside the state: The Bracero program, immigration, and the INS*. Quid Pro Books.

Cooper, M. (2007). Lockdown in Greeley. *The Nation,* February 26, para. 23.

Donato, R. (2007). *Mexicans and Hispanos in Colorado schools and communities, 1920–1960: 1920–1960*. SUNY Press.

Guerrero, A. G. (1987). *A Chicano Theology*. Orbis Books, Eugene, Oregon.

History Colorado (n.d.). Greeley. *Colorado Encyclopedia*. Retrieved from https://coloradoencyclopedia.org/article/greeley

History Colorado (2020, December 4). *Immigration to Colorado: Myth and reality*. Retrieved from https://www.historycolorado.org/story/2020/12/04/immigration-colorado-myth-and-reality

History Colorado (2021, September 21). *Immigration to Colorado: Myth and reality Part Two*. Retrieved from https://www.historycolorado.org/story/2021/09/27/immigration-colorado-myth-and-reality-part-two

Lopez, J. L., Lopez, G.A., and Ford, P.A. (2007). *White gold laborers: The story of Greeley's Spanish Colony*. AuthorHouse.

Marsh, R. N. (2016). Displaced but not without place: Refugee and immigrant integration experiences in Greeley, Colorado (master's thesis, University of Denver).

Steinhouser, J. (2015). The history of Mexican immigration to the U.S. in the early 20th century. U.S. Library of Congress Blogs. Retrieved from https://blogs.loc.gov/kluge/2015/03/the-history-of-Mexican-immigration-to-the-u-s-in-the-early-20th-century/

U.S. National Archives (2023, September 27). *The Bracero Program: Prelude to Cesar Chavez and the Farm Worker Movement*. Retrieved from https://prologue.blogs.archives.gov/2023/09/27/the-bracero-program-prelude-to-cesar-chavez-and-the-farm-worker-movement/

References for Chapter 2

Albaladejo, A. (2024, October 14). From farmworkers to athletes: Colorado's history of Hispanic baseball teams. Denver 7 ABC. Retrieved from https://www.denver7. com/news/local-news/from-farmworkers-to-athletes-colorados-history-of-Hispanic-baseball-teams

Alvin Vigil Garcia (2008, September 20). Alvin Vigil Garcia obituary. Retrieved from https://www.afterall.com/obituaries/AlvinGarcia).

Bilotte, M. (2020). Becoming native: Family labor and belonging in the sugar beet fields of Northern Colorado, 1900–1969 (Doctoral dissertation, University of Wisconsin-Madison).

Brooks, Sara L. (2013) Greeley, Colorado history for kids. Retrieved from https://greeleyhistory.org/pages/history.html

Downtown Greeley (n.d.). *Greeley Cinco de Mayo 2024*. Retrieved from https://www.facebook.com/events/downtown-greeley/cinco-de-mayo-downtown-greeley-2024/276557612162138/

Echevarria, M. (2005). Laying the foundation (ceramic tile). *Greeley History Museum*, Greeley, CO, USA.

Flórez, S. (2024). *A brief history of Latino baseball*. Retrieved from https://theLatinonewsletter.org/p/a-brief-history-of-Latino-baseball

Front Range League (n.d.) *About the Greeley Grays*. Retrieved from https://frontrangeleague.com/greeley-grays

Garcia, N. (2018, November 8). *The history of the Greeley Grays*, Channel 9 News. Retrieved from https://www.9news.com/article/news/the-history-of-the-greeley-grays/73-612699991

Gonzalez, J. (2016, October 11a). *Smithsonian recognizes Colorado's Latino baseball history in special exhibit*. Channel 9 News. Retrieved from https://www.9news. com/article/news/local/Hispanic-heritage-month/smithsonian-recognizes-colorados-Latino-baseball-history-in-special-exhibit/73-333934950#: ~:text= The%20baseball%20team%2C%20formed%20in%201925%2C%20was%20 initially,Grays%2C%20inspired%20by%20the%20Negro%20League%27s%20 Homestead%20Grays.

Gonzalez, J. (2016, October 12b). *Hispanic heritage month: Remembering the impact of the Greeley Grays*. Channel 9 News. Retrieved from https://www.9news.com/article/news/local/Hispanic-heritage-month/Hispanic-heritage-month-remembering-the-impact-of-the-greeley-grays/73-328713645

Greeley Creative District (n.d.) *Día de los Muertos*. Retrieved from https://greeley creativedistrict.org/dia-de-los-muertos

Greeley Daily Tribune (1929, September 17). Retrieved from https://www. newspapers.com/image/27257214

Greeley Grays Baseball (n.d.). Retrieved from https://www.greeleygrays.com/

Guadalupe Community Center - Guadalupe Shelter - 1442 North Avenue (n.d.) Retrieved from https://www.homelessshelterdirectory.org/shelter/co_ guadalupe-community-center-guadalupe-shelter

Knapp, J., Muller, B., and Quiros, A., (2009). Women, Men, and the Changing Role of Gender in Immigration. *Institute for Latino Studies University of Notre Dame.* 3(3). Retrieved from chrome-extension://efaidnbmnnnibpcajpcglclefindmkaj/ https://*Latino*studies.nd.edu/assets/95245/original/3.3_gender_migration.pdf

Lam, C. B., McHale, S. M., & Updegraff, K. A. (2012). Gender dynamics in Mexican American families: Connecting mothers', fathers', and youths' experiences. *Sex Roles, 67,* 17–28.

Lopez, J. and Lopez, G. (2009). *From sugar to diamonds: Spanish/*Mexican *baseball 1925–1969.* Author House.

Lopez, J., Lopez, G., and Ford, P. (2007). *White gold laborers: The story of Greeley's Spanish Colony.* AuthorHouse.

National Museum of American History (NMAH) (n.d. a). *De la Fuente sugar beet knife.* Retrieved from https://www.si.edu/object/3d/de-la-fuente-sugar-beet-knife:4dafe5d9-12fa-4aef-9805-653970f57b8d

National Museum of American History (NMAH) (n.d. b). *Azteca's baseball jersey.* Retrieved from https://3d.si.edu/object/3d/aztecas-baseball-jersey:5f8624f8-f738-4df3-968a-78144d49b19c

Our Lady of Peace (n.d.). *Our history.* https://ourladyofpeacegreeley.org/our-history/

Patrick's Irish Pub (2024, September 13). *Final Friday fest:* Mexican *independence day.* Retrieved from https://www.patricksgreeley.com/events/final-friday-fest-Mexican-independence-day

Smithsonian Institution (2021, January 21). *New traveling exhibition explores the history of Latinos and baseball.* Retrieved from https://www.si.edu/newsdesk/ releases/new-traveling-exhibition-explores-history-Latinos-and-baseball

Smithsonian Institution Scholarly Press (SISP) (n.d.). *¡Pleibol! In the barrios and the big leagues En los barrios y las grandes ligas*. Retrieved from https://scholarlypress. si.edu/store/all/peibol-barrios-and-big-leagues-en-los-barrios-y-la/

St. Peter's Catholic Church - 915 12th St (n.d.). Retrieved from https://apps.greeley-gov.com/HistoricPreservation/InventoriedProperties/default.aspx?id=5WL2578 #toTopLink

Su, D., Richardson, C., & Wang, G. Z. (2010). Assessing cultural assimilation of Mexican Americans: How rapidly do their gender-role attitudes converge to the US mainstream? *Social Science Quarterly, 91*(3), 762–776.

Vasconcelos, J. (1997). *The Cosmic Race / La raza cosmica*. JHU Press

References for Chapter 3

Cache la Poudre River National Heritage Area (2024, August 23). Spanish Colony: The story of a Hispanic neighborhood. Retrieved from https://poudreheritage. org/spanish-colony-the-story-of-a-Hispanic-neighborhood/.

City of Fort Collins (n.d.). *The history of the civil rights movement in Fort Collins, Colorado: Racial desegregation in public education in Fort Collins (1867–1975)*. Retrieved from https://www.fcgov.com/historicpreservation/files/fc-3-public-education.pdf.

Chávez, L. (2007). We are who we study/somos los que estudiamos: An exploratory study of *Chicana*/o educators' identities and agency (Doctoral dissertation, University of Colorado). search.proquest.com

Colorado Department of Education (CDE) (2024). *Greeley Central High School*. Retrieved from https://www.cde.state.co.us/schoolview/explore/graduation/ 3120/3610.

Colorado Department of Higher Education (CDHE) (2024). *Search data*. Retrieved from https://highered.colorado.gov/Data/Search.aspx.

Darling, M. R. (1932). *Americanization of the foreign-born in Greeley, Colorado* (Doctoral dissertation, Colorado State Teachers College, Department of Education).

Donato, R. (2003). Sugar beets, segregation, and schools: Mexican Americans in a northern Colorado community, 1920–1960. *Journal of Latinos and Education, 2*(2), 69–88.

Donato, R. (2007). Mexicans *and Hispanos in Colorado schools and communities, 1920–1960: 1920–1960*. SUNY Press.

Greeley Daily Tribune (1934, January 4). *16 new students at Gipson*. Retrieved from https://www.newspapers.com/article/greeley-daily-tribune-spanish-colony-gre/139341539/

Lopez, J., Lopez, G., and Ford, P. (2007). *White gold laborers: The story of Greeley's Spanish Colony*. AuthorHouse.

The League of United Latin American Citizens (LULAC) (2024). *LULAC education issues*. Retrieved from https://lulac.org/advocacy/issues/education/

Maddux, H. C. (1932). *Some conditions which influence the Mexican children in Greeley, Colorado, and its vicinity* (Doctoral dissertation, Colorado State Teachers College, Department of Home Economics).

Meltzer, E. (2020). Mexican Americans in southern Colorado fought one of the nation's early school desegregation battles. *Chalkbeat*. Retrieved from https://www.chalkbeat.org/colorado/2020/2/24/21178646/Mexican-americans-in-southern-colorado-fought-one-of-the-nation-s-early-school-desegregation-battles/

Robles, Y. (2022). Driving a decade of progress, *Hispanic* students made huge gains in high school graduation. *Chalkbeat*. Retrieved from https://www.chalkbeat.org/colorado/2022/6/2/23143015/Hispanic-students-high-school-graduation-rates-colorado-success-chasing-progress/.

Ruiz, V. L. (2001). South by southwest: Mexican Americans and segregated schooling, 1900–1950. *OAH Magazine of History, 15*(2), 23–27.

University of Northern Colorado (2024). *University of Northern Colorado Achieves Federal Designation as Hispanic Serving Institution*. Retrieved from https://www.unco.edu/news/articles/Hispanic-serving-institution-designation-2024.aspx.

References for Chapter 4

Aguilera, E. and Whaley, M. (2005; updated 2016). Greeley's great divide. *The Denver Post*. Retrieved from https://www.denverpost.com/2005/06/25/greeleys-great-divide/

Al Frente de Lucha Community Center (n.d.). Retrieved from https://www.facebook.com/alfrentedelucha/.Carmichael, S., & Hamilton, CV (1967). Black power: The politics of liberation in America. Vintage Books. Chicago.

Chicano History and Culture (n.d.). *West High School Blowout 1969*. Retrieved from https://*Chicano*historyandculture.com/west-highschool-blowout-1969/

Cumming, A. (2020, May 13). Weld's untold story. *Greeley Tribune*. Retrieved from https://www.greeleytribune.com/2002/11/13/welds-untold-story/?clearUser State=true 12/10/2024.

Deutsch, S. (1992). Landscape of enclaves: Race relations in the West, 1865–1990. *Under an Open Sky: Rethinking America's Western Past*, 110–31.

Esquibel, A. (2015). El Movimiento *Chicano* de Colorado, 1960–1980. In *Colorado heritage, The magazine of history Colorado*. March/April, 2015, p. 16–21. Retrieved from https://www.historycolorado.org/sites/default/files/media/document/2018/Heritage%20MarApr15-web_0.pdf

Greeley Daily Tribune (1934a). Retrieved from https://access-newspaperarchive-com.hpld.idm.oclc.org/us/colorado/greeley/greeley-daily-tribune/1934/01-25/page-4

Greeley Daily Tribune (1934b). Retrieved from https://access-newspaperarchive-com.hpld.idm.oclc.org/us/colorado/greeley/greeley-daily-tribune/1934/01-30/page-4

The Greeley Dream Team (n.d.). Retrieved from https://www.thegreeleydreamteam.org/about-us/.

History Colorado (n.d.). *Colorado Hispanic / Latino historical overview*. Retrieved from https://www.historycolorado.org/colorado-*Hispanic-Latino*-historical-overview.

Holdman, R. (2023, October) *"The border crossed us" becomes a rallying cry for Coloradans active in the Denver Chicano movement*. Retrieved from https://www.cbsnews.com/colorado/news/*Chicano*-movement-denver-colorado-border-crossed-us-michelle-griego/12/10/2024.

Hubbard. J. (2023). *Navy Vet Honored for Getting Colorado Highway Named for War Heroes*. Retrieved from https://kdvr.com/news/problem-solvers/serving-those-who-serve/joe-p-martinez-memorial-highway-col-stan-cass/.

Joe P. Martinez. (2024). *Wikipedia*. Retrieved from https://military-history.fandom.com/wiki/Joe_P._Martínez.

Lopez, J., Lopez, G. and Ford, P. (2007). *White gold laborers: The story of Greeley's Spanish Colony*. AuthorHouse.

Mautner, B.H. and Abbott, W.L. (1929) *Child labor in agriculture and farm life in the Arkansas Valley of Colorado.* Colorado College Publication, General Series Number 164. Retrieved from https://babel.hathitrust.org/cgi/pt?id=osu.32435062234430&seq=116

Mills, C.K., Battisto, J., Lieberman, S., Orozco, M., Perez, I., & Lee, N.S. (2018). *Latino*-owned businesses: Shining a light on National Trends. *Federal Reserve Bank of New York.* Retrieved from https://www.newyorkfed.org/medialibrary/media/smallbusiness/2017/Report-on-*Latino*-Owned-Small-Businesses.pdf

NoCo (Northern Colorado) Latinx Businesses/Services (n.d.). Retrieved from https://elcentro.colostate.edu/noco-latinx-businesses-services/)

Northern Colorado Chamber of Commerce (n.d.). Retrieved from https://nocolcc.com/

Sánchez-Esquivel, G. (2024). In tribute to El Soldado de Colorado. *The Freedom Archives.* Retrieved from https://freedomarchives.org/in-tribute-to-el-soldado-de-colorado/

Vargas, Z. (2013). *Labor rights are civil rights: Mexican American workers in twentieth-century America.* Princeton University Press.

References for Chapter 5

Angelou, M. (1978). *And still I rise. New York, Random House.*

Bilotte, M. (2020). *Becoming native: Family labor and belonging in the sugar beet fields of Northern Colorado, 1900–1969* (Doctoral dissertation, University of Wisconsin-Madison).

Blakemore, E. (2024). What is colonialism? *National Geographic.* Retrieved from https://www.nationalgeographic.com/culture/article/colonialism?

Falcón, P. (2022). *Mexican foreign policy 1934–1992.* Vanishing Horizons, Pueblo, CO.

Donato, R. (2007). *Mexicans and Hispanos in Colorado schools and communities, 1920–1960.* SUNY Press.

Gonzales, P. M., Blanton, H., & Williams, K. J. (2002). The effects of stereotype threat and double-minority status on the test performance of *Latino* women. *Personality and social psychology bulletin, 28*(5), 659–670.

Mapes, K. (2010). *Sweet tyranny: Migrant labor, industrial agriculture, and imperial politics*. University of Illinois Press.

Morris, A. (2019) What is settler-colonialism? *Learning for Justice*. Retrieved from https://www.learningforjustice.org/magazine/what-is-settlercolonialism.

Office of the Historian, Foreign Service Institute, U.S. Department of State (n.d.) *Roosevelt Corollary to the Monroe Doctrine, 1904*. Retrieved from https://history.state.gov/milestones/1899–1913/roosevelt-and-monroe-doctrine.

Pichardo, C. M., Molina, K. M., Rosas, C. E., Uriostegui, M., & Sanchez-Johnsen, L. (2021). Racial discrimination and depressive symptoms among *Latino* college students: The role of racism-related vigilance and sleep. *Race and social problems, 13*, 86–101.

Stahl, D. (2021). Confronting US imperialism with international law. Central America and the arms trade of the inter-war period. *Journal of Modern European History, 19*(4), 489–509.

Steele, C. M., & Aronson, J. (1995). Stereotype threat and the intellectual test performance of African Americans. *Journal of Personality and Social Psychology. 96*(5), 797–811.

Totonchi, D. A., Perez, T., Lee, Y. K., Robinson, K. A., & Linnenbrink-Garcia, L. (2021). The role of stereotype threat in ethnically minoritized student's science motivation: A four-year longitudinal study of achievement and persistence in STEM. *Contemporary educational psychology, 67*, 102015.

Turochy, E., Ballesteros, Linnel, Marie S., Nelson, Toby nii tairo, Perez, M., Estes, K., Poleacovschi, C., … & Yuen, T. I. M. O. T. H. Y. (2023). Stereotypes and stereotype threats experienced by Latinx engineering undergraduates. *International Journal of Engineering Education, 39*(5), 1181–1195.

United Nations (2006). Social justice in an open world: The role of the United Nations. *Department Of Economic And Social Affairs, Division For Social Policy And Development*. Retrieved from https://www.un.org/esa/socdev/documents/ifsd/SocialJustice.pdf.

U.S. Census Bureau (2024). *How Is population shifting in your state?* Retrieved from https://www.census.gov/library/visualizations/interactive/population-shifting-in-cities-or-towns-2023.html.

Williams, D. R., & Etkins, O. S. (2021). Racism and mental health. *World Psychiatry, 20*(2), 194.

References for Chapter 6

UnidosUS (2024). *Latino inclusion landscape, March 2024. Retrieved from https://unidosus.org/wp-content/uploads/2024/07/unidosus_Latinoinclusionlandscape.pdf*